T0196514

Becoming One

The Journey Toward God

Written by Janae King, 1995
Rewritten by Janae Thorne-Bird, 2010

iUniverse, Inc.
New York   Bloomington

Becoming One
The Journey Toward God

iUniverse books may be ordered through booksellers or by contacting:

iUniverse
1663 Liberty Drive
Bloomington, IN 47403
www.iuniverse.com
1-800-Authors (1-800-288-4677)

ISBN: 978-1-4502-1269-4 (pbk)
ISBN: 978-1-4502-1270-0 (ebk)

Library of Congress Control Number: 2010912017

Printed in the United States of America

iUniverse rev. date: 9/10/2010

"I say unto you, be one:
and if ye are not one
ye are not mine."
(D&C 38:27)

Foreword

We are all one! When that simple truth was revealed to me, it was like a bolt of lightning had illuminated my soul. Another truth followed: *Anything that brings us closer to oneness is reality. Anything that draws us farther away from oneness is illusion.*

These truths seemed extremely simplistic at the time, but as I've pondered and applied these principles to numerous and varied situations, I've come to realize the profundity of these simple truths. Consequently, the revelations and experiential information that have come from the application of these principles have inspired me (compelled me, really) to write this book.

But let's first clarify something—this book was not written by me alone. In fact, it's a compilation of universal truths contained in that extraordinary connection that we are all part of—the oneness. And the oneness is known by many names—universal mind, cosmic consciousness, the-spirit-that-moves-in-all-things, the Divine Matrix, the Holy Spirit—perhaps as many names as there are for each varying religion and philosophy.

I suppose the most common term to which most of us can relate is "God." But to claim that this book was written by God may be a bit presumptuous, and the truth of that inference will have to stand on its own. I have no doubt, however, that this book has been inspired by a higher source. But there are other spiritual and human energies that have been involved in this work, and I would be ungrateful not to give them the acknowledgement they deserve. It is through their efforts, written or otherwise, that the formulation of this book was made possible. I appreciate their willingness to share the knowledge they've received from God so that the complete picture of who we are and why we are here can begin to manifest itself at this very significant point in time. The eternal *now*.

Although the following is an incomplete list of contributors, these are the ones I am directly aware of. To those whose information I have used directly or indirectly, I hope (and pray) you will allow me the liberty to use your thoughts and words. I feel this information is timely and want to get it out to as many hands and hearts as will receive it. I also feel that *all* truth can be accessed by everyone and is *for* everyone, and to say that we are originators or owners of any particular truth is an illusion. It is your willingness to be facilitators of that truth that I am acknowledging. *Only God holds the corner on truth, right?* And we are all part of God or that vast oneness we call God. For if we are part of the Divine Matrix called "love" then we are all part of God. For *God is Love!*

So let us begin that extraordinary journey *back* to that original and most glorious time when we were all one…heaven. Then let us journey *forward* to God.

Acknowledgments

To my husband, lover, partner and friend, Kurt, whose undying love and support have helped to produce this book. (That is still true—now and forever—even though we've since divorced.)

To my sister-wife, Christy, who has devoted hours of her precious time to edit this book and has "taken over" many of my domestic duties so I could fulfill my writing passion.

To my children: Aubrey Jeanne, Jared Kurt, Deserae Janis, Ariel Janae, Destiny Rose, Jordan Michael, Jonathan Heart, Kelsey May and Jenny Pearl—for their patience in doing without "Mom" while she writes "her" book. And also to Christy's children: Brendan Jacob and Jesse Alma, who taught me to love someone else's children as my own.

To Speaking Wind for his spiritual guidance and support.

To Wendy, my sister in spirit and in flesh.

To my sister-wife, Sandy, who helped me to realize how difficult love can be.

To Lorraine for getting me "un-stuck."

To Jody and Ranelle for their teachings and friendship.

To Jadon David King, whose spiritual guidance has pulled me through those "tight places." To you and others who are on the other side of the veil—preparing to be reunited.

To any and all who are still on this side of the veil and whose effort and work have made this book possible—Thanks!

And special thanks to Jim Catano for his stylistic edits.

And also, since the rewriting of this book, to Brad Bird, my current husband and lover.

To Andrew, my eleventh child, who had to grow up without Mom as she followed her spiritual path.

(Note: I went through a divorce from Kurt King in 1998 and have since married Brad Bird in 1999. Sometimes the illusion of separation is necessary on the journey to oneness.)

Books and Authors

Bible—King James Version
Published by the Church of Jesus Christ of Latter-day Saints; 1979
Salt Lake City, UT

Bhagavad-Gita As It Is by His Divine Grace A. C. Bhaktivedanta Swami Prabhupada; The Bhaktivedanta Book Trust; 1968, 1972

Tao Te Ching by Lao Tsu

Book of Mormon—Another Testament of Jesus Christ
Published by the Church of Jesus Christ of Latter-day Saints; 1982
Salt Lake City, UT

Doctrine and Covenants of the Church of Jesus Christ of Latter-day Saints
Published by the Church of Jesus Christ of Latter-day Saints; 1982
Salt Lake City, UT

Pearl of Great Price
Published by the Church of Jesus Christ of Latter-day Saints; 1982
Salt Lake City, UT

Kabbalah—Tradition of Hidden Knowledge by Z'ev ben Shimon Halevi
Published in the United States in 1980 by Thames and Hudson Inc.; 1992
500 Fifth Avenue, New York, NY 10110

Sefer Yetzirah—The Book of Creation in Theory and Practice by Aryeh Kaplan
Published by Samuel Weiser, Inc.; 1990
York Beach, MN

On the Kabbalah and Its Symbolism by Gershom Scholem
Translated by Ralph Manheim
Published by Shocken Books, Inc.; 1965
New York, NY

Written by the Finger of God by Joe Sampson
Published by Wellspring Publishing and Distributing; 1993
P.O. Box 1113, Sandy, UT 84091

A Blessing Hitherto Unknown—Looking Beyond the Mark by Max B. Skousen
Published and distributed by Skousen Publishing and Distributing Co.; 1994
2681 Cameron Park Dr., Unit 122 Cameron Park, CA 95682

Great Cosmic Mother by Monica Sjor and Barbara Mor
Published by Harper & Row; 1987
10 East 53rd St., New York, NY 10022

When Spirits Touch the Red Path by Patrick Edward Quirk
Published by Northwest Publishing, Inc.; 1994
5949 South 350 West, Salt Lake City, UT 84121-8466

The Message by Patrick Edward Quirk
Published by Woodland Press, Inc; 1994
P.O. Box 211466, Salt Lake City, UT 84121-8466

The Gospel of the Great Spirit by Joshua Moses Bennett
Published by Morning Star; Publishing Company, Inc.; 1990
Zion, UT

Wheels of Light by Rosalyn L. Bruyere
Published by Simon & Schuster; Fireside, Rockefeller Center; 1994
1230 Avenue of the Americas, New York, NY 10020

Feelings Buried Alive Never Die by Karol Kuhn Truman
Copyright by Olympus Distributing Corp.; 1991
P.O. Box 97693, Las Vegas, NV 89193-7693

Dianetics by L. Ron Hubbard
Published by Bridge Publications, Inc; 1986
4751 Fountain Avenue, Los Angeles, CA 90029

The Magic of Conflict by Thomas F. Crum
Published by Touchstone; 1979
Simon and Schuster Building, Rockefeller Center,
1230 Avenue of the Americas, New York, NY 10020

Journey to Center by Thomas F. Crum
Published by Simon & Schuster; 1997
FIRESIDE, Rockefeller Center,
1230 Avenue of the Americas, New York, NY 10020

Love is Letting Go of Fear by Gerald G. Jampolsky, M.D.
Published by Bantam Books, Inc.; 1979
666 Fifth Avenue, New York, NY 10103

Living, Loving and Learning by Leo Buscaglia, P.H.D.
Published by Ballantine Books, Random House Inc.; 1982
New York, NY

Shared Heart by Barry and Joyce Vissell
Copyright by Ramira Publishing; 1984
P.O. Box 1707, Aptos, CA 95001

Teachings of the Prophet Joseph Smith by Joseph Fielding Smith
Published by The Deseret News Press; 1938

Beginnings by Carol Lynn Pearson
A Trilogy Arts Publication; 1969
Box 843, Provo, UT 84601

Books by Tom Brown Jr.:
The Tracker
The Search
The Vision
The Quest
Grandfather
Published by the Berkley Publishing Group
200 Madison Avenue, New York, NY 10016

Books by Frank E. Peretti:
The Present Darkness
Piercing the Darkness
The Prophet
Published by Crossway Books;
Westchester, Illinois 60154; 1989

Books by Dan Brown:
Angels and Demons
The Da Vinci Code
The Lost Symbol
Published by Doubleday
Randomhouse, Inc. New York, N.Y. 10022

Mother Earth Spirituality, by Ed McGaa, Eagle Man
HarperCollins Publishers; 1990
10 East 53rd Street, New York, NY 10022

Liberalism, Conservatism and Mormonism by Hyrum L. Andrus

The Screwtape Letters by C.S. Lewis;
Published by Whitaker House; 1984

The Coming of the Cosmic Christ by Matthew Fox
Published by Harper San Francisco; 1988

The Secret of the Flower of Life by Drunvalo Melchizedek
Published by Clear Light Trust; 1998

The Middle Pillar by Israel Regardie
Published by Llewellyn Publications, St. Paul, Minnesota; 1985

Dedication

It's been said that music is the prayer of Spirit.

All of us have experienced the song of the heart that can reach out and touch heaven. Some songwriters are able to mark a path into eternity with an ability to cut through the illusion of our separations and into the reality of our oneness. One such gifted musical poet, John Denver, has been able to do this for me.

It was said about John Denver's music in an interview in a 1981 East/ West Journal: "Looking back over your music during the last fifteen years, one of the things that I see is that your lyrics are becoming increasingly prophetic."

Whether his music is prophetic remains to be seen, but if the purpose of a prophet is to testify of love, truth and God—then John Denver certainly qualifies.

So this book is dedicated to you, my dearest John, and to your dedication in following the path of Spirit which has helped me to follow my own. Thank you for being my Spirit Guide—on Earth and in Heaven.

And lo, thou art unto them as a very lovely song of one that hath a pleasant voice, and can play well on an instrument: for they hear thy words, but they do them not. And when this cometh to pass, (lo, it will come,) then shall they know that a prophet hath been among them. (Ezekiel 33:32, 33)

Introduction

Singer and songwriter, John Denver, once wrote: "It's about time we start to see it—we're all in this together; It's about time we recognize it—it's all of us or none." And it's true. *We are all in this together!* Whether we admit it or not, we are all involved in this planetary experiment we call "life." If it weren't so, you wouldn't be reading this book, and I wouldn't have written it.

That's the reality.

The illusion is that we are all walking separate paths. This has been the misconception of the past, but the reality of the present, *the here and now,* is that those separate paths are *all coming together.* The truth this book will demonstrate is that even though we've all been walking separate paths, they will all bring us to the same reality—that *we are all one.* The more we struggle in our desire to keep our illusion alive—that we are all separate—the longer it will take us to get to that great realization that *we are all one.*

Consider the example of the group of mountain climbers who start off at different points at the base of a mountain to begin their noble assent to the top. In their own limited perspective, each is alone in the climb to the top. Each rocky crevice or steep incline encountered is a personal and individual challenge. Each confronts personal challenges and sets a private pace according to his or her ability. Then each reaches the top and discovers the exhilarating feeling of completing a quest. The world class climber might be alone for a short time enjoying the inspiring view in solitude. But it won't be long before other climbers scramble to the summit and join in to bask in the breathtaking view.

Then, not only can they enjoy the vast expanse when viewing the world from "Higher Ground" and a higher perspective, but they can also look down and see the path that each climber took or is still taking. Comparing this to our own spiritual climb, perhaps from a higher viewpoint we can then call down to assist and direct other "climbers" to alternate paths that might be easier and more effective. But better yet, when we all get to the top, we can share in the celebration and discussion of our adventures and the discoveries we made along the way even though each will be different.

Each of us at birth begins a personal climb up "the mountain of infinite perspective," and our journey is an individual path in the search for spiritual truth. Some have easier paths than others. Some are born into established religions or spiritual traditions that have been traveled by many who have achieved enlightenment or have already reached the top of the mountain. Those who follow them are the climbers whose paths are well marked. But even so, their journey is always an individual one. Each will have a story to tell of individual discoveries and enlightenments along the way.

As for me, I was born into the Mormon tradition and have traveled the path of Latter-day Saint Christianity for a better part of my life. At this present moment, I can honestly say I belong to no particular religious sect or group. The best I can do is to say that I'm a "Gnostic Christian" or a "Christian Mystic," as I attempt to discover and follow the teachings of Jesus Christ as embraced by the "Primitive Church." I believe that most of these teachings have been lost through the manipulations of mankind. I do believe Mormonism is the closest "religion" to the Primitive Church which Christ established when he was here on earth, although he never did establish his own "church." The closest organization resembling a church was a gathering of followers who shared all things common. Or what I've chosen to call "a family of friends."

In this book, I do use Mormon references and theological principles as they formed the beginning of my individual path to enlightenment. But, as I've gained a broader perspective, I've included a wider range of references from many other religions for the benefit of those who may not be familiar with Mormon doctrine. These religious doctrines also support the fact that "we are all one and each of us holds a piece of the puzzle."

I admit that my background in comparative world religions is limited, but this is really not a book about religion…it's about spirit, and spirit is unlimited. Through spirit I have been able to access and understand the foundational principles of many religions some of which, unfortunately, keep us apart. And ultimately, this book at its core is about relationships as that's what life is all about—*our relationships with each other and our relationship with God.*

One of the simple but profound truths I discovered is that *all relationships are eternal.* All of them are happening in the past, present, and future, and the idea that there are short-term or transient relationships is a *big illusion* we become trapped into believing. It's one we tend to use as an excuse to not handle *all* relationships with the greatest degree of TLC (tender loving care). And when we fail to do that, we remain in the illusion that we are separate and alone.

So you might call this book a manual on how to create and maintain loving *eternal* relationships. As I've personally witnessed relationship after relationship (including some of my own) deteriorate and disintegrate right before my eyes, I realize (real eyes) that there's a great need for information on how to maintain loving, sustainable, *eternal* relationships.

Having been married for nearly twenty years to the same man, having had ten children with him and having helped raise others children, my life experiences have taught me a bit about relationships. I experienced the "illusion of divorce" and married another man eight years ago as I write this. I'm not an expert in psychology or sociology. What information and enlightenment I've received and processed have not been though formal education but include "hands-on" experience, personal revelation, and insights from various books, conversations with other people and literally "conversations with God." (By the way, I was going to name this book "Conversations with God" until I discovered Neale Donald Walsch's wonderful books.)

Finally, whatever truth you can glean from this book will be your own and not mine or anyone else's. In the end, we are all facilitators…terminals if you will hooked up to a vast computer we call God. Some may be faster at processing information than others, but that's not important. The fun part is the processing. So…let's begin our journey forward to God.

Contents

Chapter One 1
  In the Beginning

Chapter Two 17
  Agreements and Contracts

Chapter Three 28
  The Tree of Life

Chapter Four 45
  A Walk in the Garden

Chapter Five 59
  Dancing with the Serpent

Chapter Six 78
  Balancing Male and Female

Chapter Seven 97
  The River of Religion

Chapter Eight 109
  Facing Our Fears

Chapter Nine 118
  Surrendering to Love

Chapter Ten 134
  Clearing the Channels

Chapter Eleven 146
  Journey to Center

Chapter Twelve 155
  Returning to Oneness

Chapter Thirteen 176
  The Merkabah

Chapter Fourteen 181
  Returning to Oneness: Vision of Rainbow Light Centers

Chapter One

IN THE BEGINNING

In the beginning we were all one. That's right, all of us were together—you and me, Grandpa and Grandma, Uncle Arthur and Aunt Hazel, your neighbor Burt, the guy down the street whose name you can never remember, and the bum on the corner who asked you for a hand-out yesterday.

We were all there together in one vast exquisite oneness we call heaven or "God." (Yes, even God was there, whatever you conceive Him/Her to be.) And Mary, Jesus, Buddha, Mohammad, Adam, Eve, Noah, Abraham, Sarah, Enoch, George Washington, Abraham Lincoln, Albert Einstein, Thomas Edison, Chief Joseph, Martin Luther King, Gandhi, Mother Theresa etc.—all the big league heavy-hitters who helped to make the Earth what it is today. We were all together in the beginning like pieces in one vast gigantic jigsaw puzzle. The only thing different is that we were all put together in the right places (integrated, so to speak) so that the picture was perfect and we all knew who we were and where we belonged. And we called this place "Heaven."

But as it is with all jigsaw puzzles, we were taken apart, piece by piece, and sent down to this planet we call "Earth" to try and figure out just how that perfect picture of Heaven looked like and just how our piece of the puzzle fits in.

You see, we lost our remembrance of the big picture and how we fit into it to make it whole and complete. Now it's our task to remember how we do fit in so that we can find our way back to the oneness of God. That's why it's called "re-membering."

Sometimes we meet people who seem familiar to us and to whom we feel drawn to. We want to "connect" with them. Perhaps they are pieces of the puzzle with whom we were closely integrated in the beginning, and now we're trying to figure out how we fit together with them in the big picture. Those are the people we can "relate" to and want to form "relationships" with. We feel compelled to find them so we can reassemble that vast, exquisite picture of heaven or the "integrity of God." But what exactly is "integrity?"

A few years ago I was in Kansas City, Missouri watching my children play in a swimming pool while reflecting upon the deeper meanings of "integrity." We were traveling with my husband, Kurt, who was lecturing at a National Health Federation convention, and we had decided to also tour some of the historical Mormon Church sites in Missouri.

As I meditated upon the word "integrity," a flood of information started flowing into me like when you plug in a key word into a computer. As the Holy Spirit began to flood my mind with profound enlightenment, I grabbed a pencil and notepad to write it all down. (It's always good to keep those handy for times of spontaneous revelation.) What follows is a revised summary of that revelation.

The word "integrity" can mean a lot of things to a lot of people. It brings to mind the character or nature of a person as being honest, upright, someone who follows through, and one whose word is as good as his name when one has the reputation of having integrity.

In my research into integrity, one dictionary defines "integrity" as: "The state of being entire or complete; entireness; a genuine or unimpaired state; honesty; uprightness in mutual dealing." Such a definition brings to mind the qualities of God who exists in a complete, whole and unimpaired state. He is omniscient (all-knowing), omnipotent (all-powerful), and omnipresent (in all places at the same time). This is the condition we were all part of in the beginning when we were spiritually connected as spirit offspring of our Father in Heaven. You might say we are all part of the Holy Spirit God.

But in our progression towards our own personal integrity or "Godhood," our spirit cried out for a denser, physical existence—a chance to see if our own integrity would hold. And so we were placed in a state of mortality to see if the powers of corruption would break down our spiritual integrity. In physics, the integrity in the molecular sphere is based on the relationship of refined molecules integrated anywhere from a highly adamant (inflexible, unyielding) substance such as a diamond to a highly corruptible (subject to breaking down) or combustible substance such as coal. The integrity of all molecular relationships in the material or mortal sphere is continually being challenged by the process of dis-solution (being "out of solution") or dis-integration (not together; separate) resulting in matter returning to its pre-integrated or primary state. This is the law of mortality referred to in Genesis 3:19 … "for dust thou art, and unto dust shalt thou return."

We, as mortal beings, are subject to the law of dissolution (death) and disintegration (separation) and have been since the time of the fall of Adam when the separation of man from God began. We became corruptible beings at the beginning of mankind and would have been in a hopeless state of dissolution (death) and disintegration (separation) had it not been for the advent of Jesus Christ into the world.

When Jesus Christ entered this mortal existence in the meridian of time, he "transcended" (climbed above) the law of mortality by making an atonement or an "at-one-ment" between body and spirit. He was able to integrate his entire molecular structure so it became incorruptible or "celestial" and was no longer subject to the mortal laws of dissolution and disintegration. He did this by subjecting himself from the beginning to celestial laws based on unconditional truth or "correct principle"—those principles of truth which are incorruptible and never changing.

You might say that Christ gained "celestial integrity" or "oneness with God" by having his spiritual and mortal bodies "unified upon correct principle." His example opened the gateway for all of us to gain celestial integrity. In other words, he showed us the way into the kingdom of God.

So how can we, as mortals, learn from what Christ did and thus gain the promises of eternal life for ourselves? I've developed a basic mathematical equation: integrity = unity upon correct principle…an example of the "kiss" method (keep it simple, sweetheart). First, let's examine the two elements of integrity—*unity* and *correct principle*—so we can understand what is required by each.

Unity is the process of joining together in oneness…the first essential element of integrity. As the political statement goes: "United we stand, divided we fall." But is unity all there is to integrity or oneness with God? There are those who would believe that unity is all that counts. We form coalitions like the United Nations, United Way, Unity Church, United Negro College, one world governments, United Order, communism, etc., thinking that as long as we're united or "unified" *that's all that matters.* That somehow by uniting ourselves, whether by choice or by force, it will bring us closer to world peace and to God.

But unity isn't all there is to integrity. Otherwise the devils themselves would have integrity as their unity in purpose (to destroy mankind) is what gives them strength and power. This is an obvious misconception when we realize that *celestial integrity* is based on both *unity* and *correct principle.*

An example of unity based upon incorrect principle (corruption) is seen in the children's story "The Emperor's New Clothes." Just because nearly everyone in the empire was unified in believing that the Emperor was wearing clothes, did it make it so? Of course not! Did they, as a community, gain integrity because they were united in a lie? Again, of course not. The only one who possessed *real* integrity was the little boy who pointed his finger at the Emperor and cried, "He has no clothes!" Perhaps in his pure and innocent state he could detect the illusion of incorrect principle (a lie) and recognize the reality of correct principle (the truth). Jesus said, "Ye shall know the truth…and the truth shall make you free" and "… except ye be converted, and become as little children, ye shall not enter into the kingdom of God." (John 8:32; Matt. 18:3)

So how do we, as individuals, recognize the reality of correct principle or the "truth?" This has probably been the paramount question of truth seekers throughout the ages. How do we recognize what is truth from what is error? How do we, ourselves, "gain a corner on truth" or, in other words, come to realize truth?

I'm not sure anyone has the answer to that, but for most of my life I have used the following formula (with much success I can say) for recognizing and applying truth. I call it my "three witnesses to truth" formula. As I stated earlier, correct principles are those which are celestial or eternal in nature and never change. These are the correct principles or laws which Christ lived by wherein He gained celestial integrity. These correct principles are continually made manifest to us in three ways or by three witnesses.

> For there are three that bear record in heaven, the Father, the Word, and the Holy Ghost: and these three are one. (1 John 5:7) … and in the mouth of two or three witnesses shall every word be established. (D&C 6:28)

The first witness to truth is God, the Father, who manifests correct principle through nature or natural laws. God is our creator and the creator of this planet, and natural laws are visibly observed when we attune ourselves to nature and understand the laws of nature that are manifest. This is God's purest and simplest way of teaching us what is truth or reality. Those who attune to nature have recognized and lived correct principle and have been greatly blessed with knowledge of God's ways (the Anasazi Indians, for example, and other indigenous peoples).

Also, the first century Christians—the Essenes—took their laws from nature as the Dead Sea Scrolls have recently revealed. I quote from *The Essene Gospel of Peace, Book Three*, translated by Edmond Bordeaux Szekely from a Dead Sea Scroll:

> Seek not the law in thy scriptures, for the law is Life, whereas the

scriptures are only words. I tell thee truly, Moses received not his laws from God in writing, but through the living word. The law is living word of living God to living prophets for living men. In everything that is life is the law written. It is found in the grass, in the trees, in the river, in the mountains, in the birds of heaven, in the forest creatures and the fishes of the sea; but it is found chiefly in thyselves. All living things are nearer to God than the scriptures which are without life. God so made life and all living things that they might be the everliving word. Teach the laws of the Heavenly Father and the Earthly Mother to the sons of men.

One would do well to live in a natural environment close to Mother Earth and free from the corruption (break down) of mankind where we can discern clearly the laws of God. Since most of us don't have that opportunity (because we have chosen not to), we can learn from others who have. (Tom Brown's series of books is an excellent teaching resource.) Or we can take time to vacation or "Vision Quest" in a natural setting where we can receive the enlightenment only nature can provide. These were the spiritual practices of our indigenous forebears—the Native Americans.

It would also be beneficial to include the study of pure sciences in our personal curriculum or, if we have chosen to home-school our children, their curriculum. These studies may include physics, chemistry, biology, holistic health, anatomy, physiology, mathematics, astronomy, etc. When we apply the "principle approach" to education, then real learning takes place as we can conceive and understand correct principle for what it is (truth), and then learn to apply (integrate) it into our daily lives. This is the ideal form of education, and I would love to see a public school curriculum take this approach of not just *learning* pure science but actually *applying* it.

The second witness to truth in my three witnesses to truth formula is "the Word." So what or who exactly is "the Word?" The Gospel of John, of course, teaches that "the Word" is Jesus Christ.

> In the beginning was the Word, and the Word was with God, and the Word was God. The same was in the beginning with God. And the Word was made flesh, and dwelt among us, (and we beheld his glory, the glory as of the only begotten of the Father) full of grace and truth. (St. John 1:1, 2, 14)

If Jesus Christ is the second witness to truth, how can we, as individuals, learn from him since he is no longer available for observation? The answer is to study his life as recorded in the scriptures. The Gospels of Jesus Christ are filled with light and truth to help us form our own firm foundation for truth. But don't believe everything written in the Bible. Much has been corrupted by the designing concepts of men, especially during the time of the Council of Nicene when a group of men determined which scriptures would be included in the "canonized" Bible. The recent discoveries and translations of the Dead Sea Scrolls and the Nag Hammadi Library also contain valuable records of Christ and his lifestyle. Many have found these to be even more accurate than the Bible since they have had fewer hands to pass through which corrupted them.

Other divine revelations and scriptures have also been revealed to prophets and sages down through the ages and are valuable resources for "the Word." I believe that "the Word" is *all* scripture which has been revealed by God. Studying other religious works such as the Bhagavad-Gita, the Zohar, the Vedas, the Tao, the Koran, the Kabbalah, etc. can give us insights and perspectives regarding other spiritual paths besides Christianity. They can all be considered "the Word" to the extent that they are a pure source from God and have not been corrupted by human mistranslations and misinterpretations. But I feel, as a Christian, that the purest "Word of God" can be found in the Gnostic Gospels as Gnostic means "to know for oneself." And also in the first four books of the New Testament—Matthew, Mark, Luke and John—as they were Christ's contemporaries and/or apostles and can best speak for Christ. That's why they are called, "The Gospels of Jesus Christ."

The study of the life of Jesus Christ through daily scripture study has been a routine in my life since I was a little girl and what propelled me on my own spiritual path and continues to enlighten and inspire me daily. It also gives solace to my soul.

Growing up in the LDS or Mormon Church and having staunch Mormon ancestors four generations back on all four sides, writings such as the *Book of Mormon, Doctrine and Covenants* and *Pearl of Great Price* became part of my existence. I honor this religious heritage, although much was based on a fraudulent historical premise and false doctrinal evidence. Whatever truth there is in Mormonism must be carefully sifted through as with any other organized religion. That's why I don't hold up any single source as the sole standard of truth.

My own scriptural study has not been limited to Mormon theology. I've been a "truth gleaner" for most of my life and have never failed to find truth wherever I've looked. As long as it lines up with my "three witnesses," I will acknowledge something as truth. If not, I either discard it or put it on a shelf to look at later when I've discovered other evidence to support it. Basically, however, I use the life and words of Jesus Christ as a witness to truth as found in the Essene Gospels, the Gnostic Gospels, and the New Testament as I feel these books have been less corrupted.

The third witness to truth is the Holy Ghost (as I was taught in Mormonism) or the Holy Spirit...our own personal confirmation of truth. This witness is given to us in varying degrees according to our awareness and willingness to follow its guidance and direction. When I've followed the path of the Holy Spirit, I've been greatly blessed. When I've gone against it, I've regretted it. It's part of an individual "attunement" process, and there are times in my life when I've been more or less in-tune with the whisperings of the Spirit. It's a daily habit we grow proficient at—like a muscle that you exercise in order for it to develop strength. "Following the path of the Spirit" is indeed the mystery and ecstasy of life and is what it's all about in *my* book.

Only by following the path of Spirit can we gain a knowledge of who we are and what our special piece of the puzzle looks like and discover its purpose. It also helps us to "realize" (real eyes) truth, as it is our own personal confirmation to truth. It is the true "mystic" or "sourcer/sorcerer" that lies within us that longs to have a direct connection with God. And this is as it should be as "becoming one with God" is the very purpose of life.

The following is the three witnesses to truth illustration—God, Jesus Christ (the Word), and the Holy Spirit which forms an equilateral triangle.

Three Witnesses to Truth Illustration:

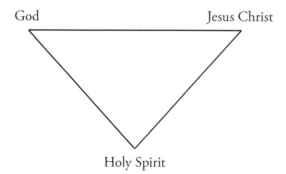

These witnesses to truth are the "three that bear record in heaven." They are the physical, mental and spiritual manifestations of correct principle. But how can we as individuals incorporate (embody) truth or unify ourselves on correct principles once we've discovered them and thus gain celestial integrity? *Simply by living them!* But if *living* correct principle was as simple as *discovering*

correct principle, then we would never have the struggles of overcoming the flesh because that's exactly what living correct principle means—"making every word of God flesh." Or in other words, unifying our bodies and spirits on correct principle or "becoming one."

Yet *becoming one* is one of the greatest challenges we face as humans. It's not impossible. Christ did it. The City of Enoch did it. The Anasazi Indians did it (or so many believe). And once we as individuals *become one*, we can extend that oneness to our personal, intimate relationships, and then to our communities and eventually to the world. But it all starts with our own personal integrity. So how then do we *live correct principle* so that we can gain personal integrity? Again, I've discovered a "three witnesses to truth" formula for incorporating or embodying truth in the flesh in 1John 5:8:

> And there are three that bear witness in earth, the Spirit, and the water, and the blood, and these three agree in one.

For practical purposes, we will describe these three witnesses as the three parts or "bodies" of the human soul—spiritual, intellectual and physical. The three together constitute the whole of our being. When all three bodies are functioning as one, they are whole (or "holy" which means sacred). To gain celestial integrity, we must unify all three of our bodies with the correct principles we've discovered through the three witnesses to truth. Let's examine how to do this by looking at how we incorporate (into embodiment) truth into each of our three bodies.

We incorporate truth in the spiritual body by becoming as a little child. This means we become *totally* open to *all* truth no matter what the source.

Have you ever watched small children approach a new discovery? Their senses (all of them) are wide open to the wonder that each new discovery brings. Whether experiencing the soft purr of a furry kitten or the icy thrill of a snowflake—a child plunges in completely—seeing it, hearing it, feeling it, smelling it, and even tasting it to gain the greatest amount of information about each new object.

This is what I call a oneness relationship with life. Can we as adults remember the magical wonder we felt as a child—unafraid of the adventure life offered us each new day? Being open to learn from both the bad and the good, spills as well as thrills, disappointments as well as triumphs— each experience leading us to more knowledge of what we find desirable in the world. Each took us one step further in the direction of becoming—of *becoming one* with our true selves and who we really are. This is the spiritual embodiment of truth—of total *acceptance* of *what is real* in life. This, in essence, is the spiritual "gathering of what is real." We gather into ourselves what we discover to be true.

The second witness in which we incorporate truth is our intellectual body, which involves both the logical and emotional sides of our brain. (We will get more into this later.)

We process all truth through what we may call our intellect or our minds. This procedure of "processing truth" happens differently for each individual depending on how integrated our minds are and how passionate we are about seeking truth. The more open we are to it (becoming as a little child), the more information we have available for us to process. Our minds have an enormous capacity to process information, and the more we seek it, the greater our capacity to process and gain an understanding of truth.

My Grandfather Callister, who I greatly admired, wrote a book entitled, *Man's Powers of Reasoning are Only as Great as His Experiences*. The title, in my opinion, says it all concerning becoming open or one with the experiences of life. Because if we isolate ourselves from the experiences life has to offer, we do not develop the ability to reason (or determine that which is desirable from that which is undesirable). Just as a small child learns quickly from that first encounter with a hot stove or a prickly thistle what is its appropriate use; we can *rationalize* (use our rational mind) with each new experience we encounter to determine which is appropriate and desirable. This is where our intellectual capacities for incorporating truth come into play. This is where we begin to *understand* truth.

> For behold, thus saith the Lord God: I will give unto the children of men line upon line, precept upon precept, here a little and there a little; and blessed are those who hearken unto my precepts, and lend an ear unto my counsel, for they shall learn wisdom; for unto him that receiveth I will give more; and from them that shall say, we have enough, from them shall be taken away even that which they have. (2 Nephi 28:30)

But the mind is an interesting thing. Sometimes we "rationalize" ourselves right out of some incredible experiences just because they resemble other similar but painful experiences from our past. That's why it's important to "clear out all the old programs" before we judge incorrectly whether something is desirable or undesirable. (More on that later.)

The third and final body that acts as a witness for truth is our physical body. This is where we become a living example of the truth which we have accepted to *be* truth. This is where we "walk our talk," so to speak, and become a living witness for truth.

What good is it for us to learn and understand truth if we never intend on incorporating (embodying) it into our lives? This may perhaps be the most difficult step for us to take, but it's an *absolute* necessary one to gain celestial integrity. If not, we simply become hypocrites and ultimately lose the truth that we've been given. It's not enough just to *receive and understand truth*. We must learn to *live* truth in all aspects of our daily existence. It must *become a part of us* as we learn to become walking examples of it in our daily lives. We must *be* truth! This is the third witness to truth…the *application* of truth.

If we were to diagram these three witnesses to incorporating truth or correct principle, it again would be like an equilateral triangle with all three sides being equal.

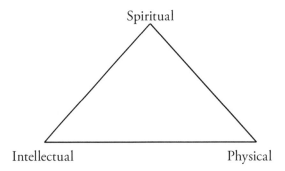

This is the diagram for the incorporation of truth on all three bodies or levels of existence. When all of these "three witnesses to truth" are combined, a powerful symbol results—the Judaic Star of David or Solomon's Seal—which is one of the most sacred geometric symbols available to mankind. It is the foundational blueprint for Solomon's Temple and the Rosslyn Temple and also the blueprint for my own Heartsong Living Centers. (See Chapter Fourteen)

Just as there needs be an *acceptance, understanding* and *application* of correct principle in order to obtain integrity, there must also needs be unity. But what exactly is unity? Unity has been interpreted and defined in many ways depending upon the circumstances. One dictionary defines it as "the property of being one; oneness; concord; agreement; oneness of sentiment, affection and the like." My own definition of unity is "the coming together in the bonds of unconditional love without the confines of restraint, coercion or prejudgment."

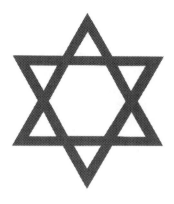

Unity is *love* in the highest sense of the word. It is the redeeming quality in mankind and the cohesive quality in all matter from the basic unit of energy, the atom, to the relationships of planets in all star systems. It is this quality of unity or "love" which predisposes all matter, organized or unorganized, to come together and work together for the highest good of all. It is not a self-serving, self-actualizing quality, as it calls upon the ultimate in self-sacrifice—that of the laying down of one's life for the benefit of the whole. This was one of the greatest challenges Christ faced in testing his love and unity for us in the Garden of Gethsemane and when he hung upon the cross. It may also be ours and facing it is the ultimate requirement in obtaining celestial integrity. This "unity of heart" is the cohesive quality which binds relationships together beyond death and into eternity.

Therefore, *unity* is just as important as *correct principle* in obtaining celestial integrity. It is impossible to have one without the other as the following examples illustrate:

In the Bible, the Pharisees and Sadducees preached and lived by the "letter of the law" or correct principle as far as they were able to interpret it. Yet Jesus renounced their example by comparing them to "whited sepulchers with nothing but dead men's bones inside." But why were Jesus' critics so severely chastised when, as far as they were concerned, they were "living correct principle?" Only when one can combine the *letter* of the law with the *spirit* of the law, (which is the spirit of *love* and *unity*) can we understand the concept Christ was attempting to convey when he said, "A new commandment I give unto you, That ye love one another; as I have loved you, that ye also love one another." (St. John 13:34)

When we can begin to comprehend the love Jesus Christ had for us, we will understand that *all* truth is given to bring us ultimately into a state of complete unity and love...*the at-one-ment*. Then we will understand how interconnected the two principles of *unity* and *correct principle* are in realizing our goal of celestial integrity. *We cannot have one without the other.*

Another example of an imbalanced relationship of having correct principle without unity is that of the husband or wife who will not make allowances for their spouse's imperfections and thus will not unify themselves in the true sense of a marriage relationship. We, as mortals, all have weaknesses that inhibit us from living all the principles we know to be correct. But when we allow those imperfections in ourselves and others to block our progress towards unity we become like the Pharisees and judge unrighteously.

Yes, it's easier to be unified upon correct principle, just as it's easier to love righteousness more than unrighteousness. Righteous simply means "the right use of"—it is not a means by which we can judge others. The more we ourselves gain integrity, the less we are critical and judgmental of the righteousness of others. We come to understand that we are all progressing at different rates; and those who are fast learners can only benefit when they assist those who are somewhat resistant to truth. This is part of the compassionate, self-sacrificing quality of love and unity, which can make a mortal marriage relationship into a celestial one.

"We can't get to heaven by ourselves," is definitely a true statement. Just as we require those ahead of us to lead and illuminate the way; we also get to lead and illuminate the way for those behind us. We are all interconnected whether we acknowledge it or not, and those who feel they can redeem themselves in isolation are as misguided and deceived as those who attempt to create a Zion community based upon incorrect principles. When we become frustrated because of the seemingly slow progress of others and withdraw ourselves into independent isolation, thinking we're saving ourselves, we lose the opportunity for unity and true brotherly love. Only when we "lose ourselves in the service of others" can we truly find ourselves in the truest sense of the word.

When we strive to become unified with our brothers and sisters, whoever they may be, by loving them unconditionally and accepting their weaknesses as well as their strengths, we then realize they are on the same path to integrity as we are. Only then can we obtain the redeeming power of love which consecrates our hearts in celestial integrity.

In considering the two aspects of integrity, one might ask: "Which is more important, unity or correct principle?" As I've stated earlier, you cannot have one without the other in order to obtain integrity. They are both of equal importance as are the ones in the equation: $1+1=2$.

But then the question arises: "But what if they are in direct conflict with each another such as in a situation where one must choose between correct principle *or* being unified with a partner or brother on an incorrect principle?

The whole concept of unity is not based on forced compliance as unity is a free-flowing desire for brotherly love and oneness. Any person or system that interferes with the free agency of an individual in the pursuit of celestial integrity has already violated the first and foremost law of heaven...*free will.*

There is no other law or correct principle as essential as free will or free agency (as I learned to call it), for no one can obtain either unity or live correct principle without it. No one can be forced or obliged to love another for the sake of unity. *It is literally impossible!* Nor can individuals be forced to comply with correct principle even if it is intended for their own benefit or it is also a violation of their free will.

We, as children of God, are *free agents* unto ourselves, and that inheritance can never be extinguished either by systems of government or by the unrighteous dominion of one person over another. If and/or when a corrupt system of power exists, it must ultimately be destroyed or a way must be opened that an individual can escape it. This is our inalienable rights as God's children and citizens of the United States of American. We have the rights to life, liberty and the pursuit of happiness given to us by God and constitutional governments. But we, as individuals, must stand up for those rights or they will be taken away from us. It is on these principles of freedom and liberty that we will build intentional communities based on integrity.

When individuals chose to unify themselves on correct principle, then they can obtain the community integrity which Enoch and other translated communities obtained. This is prophesied to occur before the New Age is ushered in by Jesus Christ. "For all truth will be circumscribed into one great whole" was a prophecy made by Joseph Smith concerning the thousand years of peace promised us by prophets of old and the latter-day prophets. It's up to us as to make way for this great stage of our existence by first individually becoming unified on correct principle and then collectively doing the same. When we do this, another beautiful image emerges—that of a faceted diamond.

The diamond has always represented Celestial Integrity as it is the hardest material known to man. It cuts through the illusions of what is not real and shines light on what is real. It is also the three-dimensional design for the Merkabah—our own chariot of light—or Zion—the literal gathering of Israel (is real).

Note to reader: In *Becoming One* I have included scriptural references at the end of each chapter. This is for the benefit of those who wish to incorporate "the Word" part of correct principle into their intellectual body. These serve as a scriptural foundation to the chapter. I have also incorporated a great deal of symbolism and diagrams as the spiritual or "wisdom" part of our brain responds better to symbols and images. This will help incorporate the spiritual part of correct principle into the intellectual body. I've also included a section at the end of each chapter entitled "Walk your Talk Therapies." These are exercises to help incorporate the written word into the physical body.

Scriptural References: St. John 1:1-5,12-14, 17:21-26; 1Corinthians 6:17; 1John 5:7; 2Nephi 11:3, 31:21; Alma 11:43-44; 3Nephi 11:35-36; Ether 5:4; D&C 20:12-19,26-28, 93:23-40

Walk Your Talk Therapies: Chapter One

Therapy one: *Remembering*

To "remember" means to "bring back to mind again." But in this therapy, my definition of "remember" means to bring back to mind those *members* or individuals whom you had relationships with and experienced a *fall-out* or separation with.

With pencil and paper in hand, find a quiet place where you can be "alone" (all one). Begin by writing down the name of each and every person you can remember who has caused you pain as you have fallen out of relationship because of separation on some level. Go clear back to the time when you were born (even before that time if you have any impressions) and simply *remember*. Perhaps you can visualize your birth—being pulled from the womb, slapped on the butt, and carried off to cold hospital scales by a nurse to be weighed. If you know or can find out the doctor's and nurse's names—write them down. These medical personnel may have caused you pain at the moment of your birth which began the separation of spirit and body.

You'll probably need to include your mom's and dad's names for choosing that particular place of birth in the first place. And also any older siblings who may have terrorized you as a child either physically or emotionally. (Personally, I had two older brothers who teased me relentlessly whom I needed to include.) And, moving on, remember all those classmates you had grade school crushes on or high school romances that broke your heart—don't forget them. Again, if family members—parents, brothers, sisters, cousins, etc. teased, abused or belittled you—include them in your list of "remembering." And, of course, write down your spouse and children (if you have them), remembering the times they caused you pain. And don't forget your church and civic leaders who deceived you or "led you astray." This caused you pain and frustration so be sure to remember their names if you can. Write them all down as they come to mind until you can't think of anyone else who ever caused you pain.

Now look at each name, one by one, and try the best you can to see them in your "mind's eye." As you're able to "remember them" in your mind's eye, reach out and give them a great, big hug and say, "I forgive you for the pain you caused me. I realize (real eyes) it was because you didn't realize (real eyes) what you were doing to me at the time and understand it was hurting me." Try to feel as much love as you can for each person written on the list—as difficult as it may be. When you've done this with each name, cross it off.

After you've done your best to forgive each person, then write your *own* name down at the bottom of the list. This time you may want to look into a mirror and say to yourself (or out loud is even better), "I forgive *me* for all the pain *I* have caused *me* in my life. I didn't realize or understand myself at the time." Then give yourself a great big hug and say, *"I love me."*

The final step of this *remembering* and *forgiving* exercise is to take the piece of paper with all of the crossed out names (including your own) and *burn it*. You can either burn it in an ashtray or have a Christian or Indian "burnt offering" ceremony outside along with a ceremonial burial of the ashes.

When this process is complete, you should feel like a heavy burden has been lifted from your shoulders. You should feel cleansed and healed from the negative emotions of pain and resentment you've been carrying around for years. If negative emotions start to build up again inside you, repeat the process.

Therapy Two: *Spiritlinking*

This is a game I've played practically all my life but never knew what to call it. I got the name *Spiritlinking* from Donna Markham who spoke at the 1995 Windstar Symposium. (Thank you, Donna) You can play this game by yourself or with friends.

To begin this game (or therapy), choose a crowded public place like a shopping mall or a park—somewhere where there is sure to be *lots* of people.

Then, walk through the crowd and try to "spiritlink" with as many people as possible. Try to maintain direct eye contact with individuals as they walk by you. (The eyes are the windows to the soul or spirit.) Once you've done this, give them a great, big, smile. Make it sincere—not like you're trying to laugh at them or make fun—but one of those sincere smiles that say, "I love you!" You might try saying those words to yourself if you're having a hard time being sincere.

Then, if you get a smile in return, you win a point for your team! If you're able to get someone to strike up a conversation with you—add another five points to your score. If you don't get any response—smile or otherwise, then the "other team" gets a point.

Try to get as many points as you can for your team in the time you've allotted yourself to play the game.

The purpose of this game is to demonstrate that *we are all connected* and that acknowledging the spiritual connection we have with others can be fun and challenging. And you never know—you might meet someone you can develop a future, more intimate relationship with! Now that's *becoming one!*

Chapter Two

AGREEMENTS AND CONTRACTS

Every day we continually make contracts or agreements with each other. They could be as simple as an agreement between two parties to meet for lunch at a certain time and place or as complicated as a marriage contract or promise between two parties lasting a lifetime or perhaps into eternity.

In either case, whether in a simple agreement or a complex marriage contract, there are two parts of the contract—the *terms of the agreement* and the *signature or consent to the agreement.*

It's important that these two parts of the contract be understood and accepted by all parties involved, so that there's no miscommunication that may lead to misunderstanding and ultimately to the default or breaking of a contract. Any time this happens, it causes us to lose personal integrity; or the principle which makes us *one* with each other and *one* with God, begins to disintegrate or break down. When we begin to lose personal integrity, it causes our own wholesomeness (holiness) to become adulterated (separated from that which is whole or wholesome). This is because we are not "unified on correct principle" which is basically what creating and fulfilling contracts is about on an individual and collective level. When we lose individual integrity—it affects the entire global community (common unity).

Going back to our first equation of integrity=unity based on correct principle, the *terms of agreement* are the "correct principle" part of a contract which include all the desired "items" both parties decide to mutually agree upon. These could be as simple as when each person takes a turn driving in a car pool; to a complex agreement of conceiving, bearing and raising a child to the age of adulthood. These are all determined in the correct principle stage and are the terms of agreement. The important part to remember in this stage of contract making is that *all* the terms of the agreement must be understood completely and clearly by *all* parties. If there is *any* misunderstanding of the terms, it could cause problems later on and ultimately to the breaching or defaulting (neglecting to fulfill an obligation) of the contract and the disintegration of relationships.

The second part of the agreement or contract is the commitment or *signature of the agreement;* or in the integrity model—the "unity" principle of the commitment of both parties coming into unity or agreement. This happens after *all the terms of the agreement* have been completely discussed and understood; then the parties may *consent to the agreement* or, in other words, "sign the contract" for it to be valid. This can happen in several ways, but the first is perhaps the best. This is when all parties verbally state in their own words the *terms of the agreement* so that each clearly understands what is being agreed upon. After that they can either express verbally their commitment to the agreement, if it is a simple agreement; or in a more complex contract, a written signature or a verbal agreement in front of one or more witnesses makes it legal and binding.

This may seem painstaking and arduous to some, but there are so many times we knowingly or unknowingly break contracts or agreements which causes dis-agreements, mis-understandings, and dis-integrity in our relationships. This can eventually cause the break-up of the relationship and ultimately causes "fall-out"—that nasty, destructive energy we all hope to avoid. So if we take the extra few minutes to get clear on our contracts we make with each other, we can avoid future fall-out. Another thing which causes fall-out and disintegrity in relationships is when we default on an agreement or don't follow through on our end. Here are a few ways in which we can avoid default in our agreement and contract-making.

First off, there are what we call "assumptions." These happen when we're not exactly sure what we're agreeing to and are not willing to take the steps to make it clear. But as the popular saying goes, to "assume" anything, especially in making agreements or contracts, makes an "ass" out of "u" and "me." *Never assume anything!* Always make it perfectly clear what you're getting yourself into before you get into it...especially in your relationships if you want to avoid default and fall-out.

Secondly, there is what is called "acquiescing" or "silently agreeing to something without implying consent or agreement" which can really get us into trouble. It's important when negotiating an agreement that our silence in *not* agreeing to certain terms isn't understood as our *acquiescence* or a "silent agreement." It's better to say things twice or more to make sure things are crystal clear, even at the risk of being redundant, rather than to have any misunderstandings. Unfortunately, most relationships (business, personal or otherwise) usually start to break down because of too many disagreements or misunderstandings. That's why it's so important that all parties involved in agreement-making are crystal clear in what they're agreeing to and that the agreement is signed or consented to either in writing or verbally so there are no misunderstandings.

A third breach of contract we are often guilty of is "dis-appointments." That's when we make an appointment with someone to meet or talk to them at a certain time or place and we either don't show up or are disappointingly late. All of us know what this feels like in a relationship when someone is always disappointing us with their late and/or missed appointments. If we can't make an appointment or we know we are going to be late, at least have the courtesy to communicate that to all parties involved. This will avoid a lot of the disappointment and fall-out in the future.

Misunderstandings and disappointments, more often than not, cause what I've termed "fall-out" which means "to separate from." Of course, fall-out is also the deadly radioactive particles from a nuclear explosion. Fall-out comes more from *fission*—when the unity of the particles of an atom is split apart; than from *fusion*—when particles are merged together (especially in cold-fusion). Each process creates great amounts of energy; so much so, that bombs have been created that could be used to destroy the entire planet. (But that is definitely another subject.) But from a nuclear physics point of view, we can learn a lot about relationships from this process of *fission* and *fusion* so that we can create the least amount of *fall-out* or negative energy. God teaches us correct principles in the laws of nature. These are physical laws or laws of physics which, if understood, we can learn from in our own personal relationships.

So let's talk about *personal relationship contracts*. First off, I've come to realize that there are contracts each of us made in the spiritual realm before we came to Earth. These contracts may include: agreements we made with God concerning our life's work; covenants or promises we made with other spirits to provide physical tabernacles for (our children); contracts we made with other spirits to develop and experience relationship with in order to assist them with their life's work. These are "partnership contracts" we have made with others.

Aside from the contracts we made with others, first and foremost is the contract we made with ourselves. We each come to Earth equipped with a "prime directive," so to speak, or a spiritual program of our life's work or mission. Whenever we go against our *prime directive*, it causes spiritual and physical separation or disintegration in our soul which creates distress and discomfort. This leads to "dis-ease" (not in peace) in ourselves which usually manifests itself in physical or emotional forms of illness or disease. (This subject is covered thoroughly in the book *Feelings Buried Alive Never Die* by Carol S. Truman. Also Ron L. Hubbard has done an excellent work in his book *Dianetics*, which deals more in the emotional or mental realm than in the spiritual. Also the chapter in this book on "Clearing the Channels" covers ways of clearing up the spiritual and emotional *fall-out* caused by the breaking of contracts—spiritual and otherwise.) But for now, let's talk about contracts we make in the "here and now" when we come into relationship with others.

"There are those in this life who are friends from our heavenly home," is a prophetic line from a popular John Denver song. It's true that some people whom we come into contact with seem familiar even though we've never met them before. And some people we are spiritually attracted to cause us to want to pursue a relationship with them. They either have something to teach us about love—or about ourselves.

Some people act as mirrors for us—reflecting back the things we may not like about ourselves and may want to change. They create a sort of "irritation" that brings to the surface or "to the light" things that are eluding or hiding from us. This can be illuminating and enlightening for us. Such people can be our *true* friends. They act as "rear view mirrors," so to speak, to show us what's hiding in our "blind spots." Sometimes our best friends are those we resist at first because of their blatant honesty. In the end, however, they help us uncover our authentic selves much better than those who flatter us with compliments.

Honesty in *all relationships* is valuable—but don't make your honesty so blatant that it blinds others. Mirrors also tend to blind people if too much light is drawn into them all at once. The following is a poem I wrote describing this metaphor:

Mirrors

We're perfect mirrors for one another,
Exposing all elusive sin.
What we see so clear in others,
Is in us hidden deep within.

With loving care, we're rear-view mirrors,
Reflecting blind-spots unaware.
But in the light of criticism,
Our mirror reflects a blinding glare.

So when you look into my mirror,
Don't judge it by the flaws you see.
Instead look deep your own reflection,
And see the beauty you can be.

Another type of relationship is a "covenant" relationship made in the spiritual realm with those individuals with whom we have a work to do here on Earth. It may involve just a friendly business relationship or it could be an intimate marriage relationship. For some reason we feel drawn to certain people to connect with; or there is a certain synchronicity for them coming into our lives just at the right time.

When we begin to sense a certain spiritual connection or synchronicity, it's important that we don't jump immediately into the "marriage bed" or in other words *sign the contract* until we understand the *terms of the agreement.* Some of those terms may have been arbitrated spiritually before we came to Earth and it's important to remember *precisely* what they were before we get into a physically intimate relationship. Once this happens—that is to say we have sex with a person—two things occur. (Actually there are infinite consequences, but we'll only discuss two that relate to contracts.)

First, there's the possibility that a child could be conceived by this procreative act which would involve "signing a contract" to a "partnership agreement" to raise the child to adulthood. This is one of the underlying, yet often unexpressed, *terms of agreement* when two people come together in sexual intimacy. That is why it is *so* important that these *terms of agreement* are expressed and understood *before* having sex which in actuality is the *signing of the contract.* However, some people suffer the illusion that as long as they use some type of contraceptive, that it's fine to have "casual but intimate physical relationships" (there's an oxymoron for you) without any subsequent consequences.

But let's discuss the second consequence of physical intimacy or *the marriage contract.* The coming together of two (or more) beings in sexual intimacy causes great amounts of spiritual energy to be released just as in the fusion of hydrogen atoms can cause a nuclear explosion. This is usually felt and expressed as "positive energy" or *love* and can help to clear channels and "energize" the parties involved. What actually happens, which I've come to realize, is this:

Two things happen when people have sexual communion or "make love." First, they "access the assets" of the other person's spiritual, emotional, and physical being allowing them to utilize the knowledge and talents of the other persons faculties. In other words, they're able to "facilitate their faculties" more or less to the degree that they're able to become unified. That is the positive effect of "becoming one" with a person in the spiritual, emotional and physical sense of the phrase.

But there's also an opposite side to the coin or the negative effect. (You can't have one without the other.) In accessing the person's assets they also take upon themselves in this dynamic union the other person's liabilities or "karmic debt" which the person has incurred in this or past lifetimes. This is the "down-side" of sexual communion or the marriage contract. They then contract to help their marriage partner "work through" or "clear-up" this *karmic debt.* In other words, they are "liable for their liabilities" as marriage partners agree to share in each other's karma.

Now there may be those who deny that these consequences actually occur—but believe me they do. And since in reality *all* relationships are eternal, we eternally contract to help those persons with whom we have intimate relationships with to work out their karmic debt or liabilities.

That's what Jesus Christ did for us when He made the ultimate, infinite "at-one-ment" for all mankind. Through spiritual intimacy, Christ "accessed all of our assets" and became as God, knowing all things; and yet at the same time, became "liable for our liabilities" or sins which caused him to bleed from every pore and "shrink from partaking of the cup." Because He was a clear and perfect vessel of God and had overcome all of His own karmic debt, the process of taking upon Himself *all* of our karmic debt or "sins" did not affect His ability to remain as God and fulfill all of the contracts and agreements He agreed to do before He came to Earth. Because He was God, He fulfilled all things He contracted to do.

At this time of the *atonement,* God *covenanted* with us that if we would repent and return to Him and obey His commandments, we would be saved in the Kingdom of Heaven. This is how we can become a "covenant people," if we will fulfill our part of the *agreement* or *covenant.* Bible readers understand what blessings are in store for *God's covenant people.* He has already fulfilled His part of the covenant—all that remains is the fulfillment of our part. We are the children of "Israel" (is-real) and the covenant people of God. All we need to do is "realize" (real-eyes) who we really are.

It's important when we enter into intimate contracts with each other that we do it for righteous (right use) reasons and with complete understanding of what the *terms of agreement* are—spoken and unspoken. If we enter into sexual relationships just to satisfy the lusts of our flesh, we will ultimately be destroyed because of the liabilities or *karmic debt* we take upon ourselves that we're unable to deal with as we haven't cleared our own karma. We also incur more karmic debt each time we break contracts whether in relationships with others or with ourselves, so it's important that we enter into contracts wisely.

It's not the *making* of relationship contracts that gets us into trouble as this, as in *fusion,* causes a positive energy release of *love, caring,* and *sharing.* It's when we *break* those contracted relationships that cause the negative *fall-out,* as in *fission* because separation always releases *anger, bitterness,* and *resentment.* In other words, the making of intimate contracts brings us closer to that unity of spirit—that *oneness* that we all desire and long for. And when contracts are made based upon correct principle, that's to say that they're directed by the Holy Spirit, greater integrity is obtained.

On the other hand, when we make intimate contracts based upon the lusts and desires of the flesh, there's a greater possibility of breaking those contracts and causing separation and a state of "adultery," so to speak, which brings about greater *disintegration* of the body, mind, and spirit and ultimately the entire human family. That's why marriage and divorce should be considered *very carefully* and seriously because separation doesn't just cause *fall-out* affecting the parties involved—it has a negative effect on the entire human family. As I stated earlier and will reemphasize now—*we are all connected!*

So how do we avoid breaking our contracts with one another and avoid causing negative fall-out? First, consider Galatians 5:16, 17:

> This I say then, Walk in the Spirit, and ye shall not fulfill the lust of the flesh.
> For the flesh lusteth against the Spirit, and the Spirit against the flesh: and these are contrary the one to the other: so that ye cannot do the things that ye would.

The only way we can learn to "walk in the spirit" is when we are "in-tune" with it and can hear its directing influence. This can happen only when our "channel" with the Holy Spirit is cleared of all the static and distractions and when all the "desires of the flesh" are overcome or removed. (This will be covered in Chapter 10.) Otherwise we may be "misdirected" into a sexual relationship based on carnal lusts and desires which has a good potential of defaulting into fall-out with the accompanied heartache for everyone involved.

Another way to avoid breaking contracts is to understand the "buyer beware" clause in the contract. Anyone who has ever purchased a home or a car is familiar with clauses that state that it's the responsibility of the seller to disclose any of the "known" liabilities to the buyer. But it's the buyer's responsibility to search out any of the "unknown" liabilities which the buyer may or may not be disclosing. In other words—it's the obligation of both parties involved to be up-front and honest in their transactions with each other.

And so it is (or *should be*) when we enter into intimate "marriage" contracts. We *should be* as honest and open in our relationships as we can and spend lots of quality time—working together, playing together, talking together and planning together—so we can get to *know* the other person *before* the contract is signed in the marriage bed. Many religions and spiritual disciplines recommend at least one year of courtship before marriage. I believe that's a great rule of thumb since *marriage is the most important decision of our lives!* Many, if not most, marriage contracts wouldn't be broken by "default" if this one rule were followed. Most people reveal their "true colors" within a year, and we're able to drop our "rose-colored glasses" to see the reality of what we are getting ourselves into. (Excuse the clichés but they seem to work here.)

This process is important in a relationship as we all start out "putting our best foot forward," but it's also important that we learn to dance with both feet without stepping on anyone's toes. That's what the courtship dance is all about.

Another way we can avoid defaulting on a contract is to *not* get into more than one partnership agreement at a time without the explicit, uncoerced consent of the other partner or partners involved. This means we *don't ever* sign a marriage contract (go to bed with) another person *unless* the other partners have their *full consent and approval.* If your marriage is based on a "limited partnership agreement" (monogamy), then don't get into an "unlimited partnership agreement" (polyamory) until you've discussed *in detail* all of the *terms of agreement* involved and have all *signed the contract* in agreement to the terms.

This is where many couples get into trouble—when they "betray" or *default* on one contract to get into another one. In Biblical terms this is called "adultery," (the act of debasing or deteriorating by an admixture of foreign or baser materials) and is highly unfavorable in the eyes of the Lord if your relationship with Him and with each other is to have integrity.

On the other hand, there's an illusion that many of us get trapped into thinking. It is the belief that we have to "dis-engage" or separate ourselves from one marriage-relationship contract in order for us to get into another marriage-relationship contract.

This belief system which many of us hold—that marriage relationships are *always* "limited partnerships"—is a system that keeps us stuck, not allowing us to explore the path of Spirit which may lead us into other marriage partnerships. This can expand in us a greater capacity to love—perhaps to where we can love the way God loves—unconditionally.

One of the greatest potentials for growth in a marriage relationship is to consent to having other partners join with you in the love and intimacy which marriage provides. This can be the greatest opportunity for the expansion of your heart and soul. Perhaps this is the one and only way that opens up the opportunity for the ultimate connection of the *soul-mate* reunion.

When we get stuck in a monogamous relationship with partners other than our "soul-mates," there is frustration and a sense of emptiness and longing which can lead to *fornication* (strong or emotional desires to have sex with another person). When someone else comes along with whom we feel strong spiritual connections, this longing to be with them can ultimately lead to *adultery*. But when we become completely open to other partners whom the *Holy Spirit* directs into our lives and ultimately into our marriage relationship, we become free to explore those relationships and realize the growth and expansion they can offer without the negative effects of fornication and adultery.

This is what the old alchemical texts referred to as "The Bridal Chamber" or *sacred sexuality* which contain the secrets to personal, spiritual and sexual transformation. It's this idea that sexuality is the highest sacrament, bestowing not only joy but also oneness with the Divine and the universe. Sex is seen as the bridge between Heaven and Earth, bringing a release of enormous creative energy; besides revitalizing the lovers in a unique way—even down to the cellular level. Living the Celestial Laws of polygamy (or what I term polyamory) as outlined in the Bible and in modern-day scriptures offers the challenges of overcoming the negative qualities of the ego such as jealousy, possessiveness and control. But this "correct principle" is not only required of men but of women, also, as we are all on our own personal "alchemical" path to transformation.

Scriptural References: Exodus 19:5; Deuteronomy 4:13; Isaiah 55:11, 56:3-6; Amos 3:3; Matthew 18:18-20; Luke 24:44; Acts 3:25,26; Gal 3:15-29, 5:14;1 Nephi 14:14, 17:40; 2 Nephi 2:4-7; D&C 1:15,16,22, 54:6, 66:2, 98:4-15, 131:1-4, Sec.132

Walk Your Talk Therapies: Chapter Two

Therapy One: *Contracts and Agreements*

Since all agreements and contracts we get into are important and greatly affect our personal integrity when we make and break them—it's *vital* to remember to exercise caution whenever we make one. That could be as simple as promising the kids that you'll take them swimming on the weekend; to as serious as covenanting in a marriage vow before witnesses that you will stay with a person until "death do you part" or perhaps forever. These agreements and contracts we *fulfill* create greater *integrity* in our relationship with God and others. Those agreements and contracts we *break*, cause us *dis-integrity* in our relationship with God and others.

Guard your tongue and even your thoughts because the "seeds of thought" planted in the "soil of emotion" create the "tree of life" (celestial integrity) or the "tree of death" (separation) which resides within each of us. Monitor your "self-talk" and see when and if you start talking yourself out of agreements and contracts you have made so that the Seeds of separation will not grow into a "tree of death."

And then only verbally make agreements and contracts with others that you honestly plan to fulfill. Otherwise you will lose integrity in their eyes and in the eyes of God.

If there are any contracts or agreements you are aware of breaking, make a point to "clear the air" of the negative fall-out which occurred because of it. Apologize to the party or parties involved in the making and breaking of the contract and then make an agreement with them *never* to break another contract. Strive to fulfill all contracts you do make with everyone.

Therapy Two: *Clearing Contracts*

If you have made a contract or agreement that needs to be renegotiated—whether the *terms of agreement* or the *signature of the contract*—because either party has outgrown the contract, it's time to sit down with the other party and do some renegotiating.

For example, if you have contracted with or through the state in a *monogamous relationship contract,* and both or one of the parties has decided that you have outgrown monogamy and wish to enter into a polygamous or polyamorous relationship, it's time to sit down with your partner to renegotiate the contract. No state in the United States recognizes polygamy and so that contract with the state needs to be *terminated completely* before entering into a polygamous relationship.

All parties in a polygamous relationship must be considered equal in the eyes of the state and in the eyes of God. Otherwise, you will develop preferential or "legal" relationships that will dominate the relationship and cause others to feel inferior or "less than." For instance, if one wife is the "legal wife," what happens to the assets of the marriage if the husband dies? All parties should have equal access to them otherwise it is inequitable and unjust. Other contracts such as *wills* and *personalized wedding vows* can be drawn up and signed by all parties involved to assure that they become legal and binding. Otherwise the state becomes the executor of someone's estate after they die.

Other contracts and agreements, besides marriage contracts, can also be renegotiated if the parties have outgrown the parameters of the contract. Search within yourself and decide if there are contracts or agreements in your life which you have outgrown and wish to change. Then take a course of action to change them.

Chapter Three
The Tree of Life

In 1993 in Manti, Utah, I met a darling young couple who shared with me an inspiring concept called the "Tree of Life." Their teachings initiated me on a path of research into what is better known as the *Kabbalah*, a tradition of hidden knowledge that dates clear back to the time of Abraham.

The "tree of life tradition" is so basic that its structure is found in every life form—from the structure of the chromosome chain in every cell in every living organism, to how the body acts as a microcosm to the universe. The tree of life structure is so pervasive as to be the foundation for how God communicates to man—this is how *very* significant this concept of the "tree of life" is.

Although many religions have formed their own tree of life stories and traditions (Mormonism has a beautiful one in the Book of Mormon—see 1Nephi Chap. 8), Judaism has kept the Kabbalic tradition alive. *Kabbalah* is the inner and mystical aspect of Judaism handed down over the centuries by a discreet tradition that has periodically changed and corrupted it. Some of its corrupted forms have been found in the traditions of Free Masonry, and its structure was used to build Masonic temples and temple ceremonies. Any serious student of religion would do well to study the "tree of life" structure to grasp a deeper understanding of many of its hidden implications and meanings.

Basically, the *Kabbalah*, or the "tree of life" structure found in the Kabbalic tradition, is a representation of the principles or divine attributes of God and the *sefiroth* are parts of His perfect character. It's the Kabbalistic speculation of how God's creative power or divine emanations unfold through the *sefiroth*. Insofar as God reveals Himself, He does so through the creative power of the *sefiroth.* These principles or attributes of God are defined or counted by way of placement in a configuration called the Tree of Life. There are ten attributes known as *sefirot*, which complete the basic tree, and they are all derived from Old Testament scripture. (See chart below)

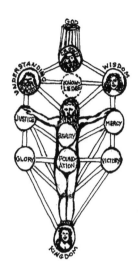

They speak of attributes and of spheres of light; but in the same context they also articulate divine names and the letters of which they are composed. From the very beginnings of Kabbalistic doctrine, these two manners of speaking appear side by side. The secret world of the godhead is a world of language, a world of divine names that unfold in accordance with their own laws. The elements of the divine language appear as the letters from the Holy Scriptures. These letters and names are not only conventional means of communication, but each one of them represents a concentration of energy. These concentric energy spheres express a wealth of meaning which cannot be translated, or at least not fully into human language.

In the book, *Kabbalah—Tradition of Hidden Knowledge* by Z'ev ben Shimon Halevi, we find the following:

> In recounting Bezaleel's qualifications, God says, "I have filled him with the *spirit of God,* in *wisdom,* and in *understanding,* and in *knowledge.*" (Exodus 31:3)
>
> This then forms the first four *Sefirot* or emanations of God referred to as:
>
> 1) The spirit of God or in the Hebrew language *Keter* (crown).

2) Wisdom or *Hokman* in Hebrew.
3) Understanding or *Binah*.
4) Knowledge or *Daat*.
These four *Sefirot* are also alluded to in Proverbs 3:19, 20:

"The Lord by *wisdom* hath founded the earth; by *understanding* hath established the heavens. By his *knowledge* the depths are broken up, and the clouds drop down dew."

It is also alluded to in Proverbs 24:3, 4:

"Through *wisdom* is an house builded; and by *understanding* it is established: And by *knowledge* shall the chambers be filled with all precious and pleasant riches."

The next seven Sefirot are named in the verse contained in 1 Chron. 29.11:

Thine, O Lord, is the *greatness,* and the *power* and the *glory*, and the *victory,* and the *majesty:* for all that is in the heaven and in the *earth* is thine; thine is the *kingdom*, O Lord, and thou art exalted as head above all.

These seven *Sefirot* or attributes of God would then comprise the rest of the Kabbalic tree of life to complete its ten-fold emanations. These in the Kabbalic tradition are:
5) Mercy or *Hesed* in Hebrew.
6) Judgment or *Gevurah*.
7) Beauty or *Tiferet*.
8) Eternity or *Nezah*.
9) Reverberation or *Hod*.
10) Foundation or *Yesed*.
11) Kingdom or *Malkhut*.

Okay, so you might be thinking that 4 plus 7 equals *11 not 10*. You're absolutely right, and I don't know where the Kabbalists come up with only 10 Sefirot rather than 11. (Actually what they do is to *not* count number 4 as an actual *Sefirot* but only as an "unmanifest" *Sefirot* or "*non-Sefirot ,*" but this is one of the mysteries of the Kabbalah I don't fully understand.) In my mind, I see the tree of life as a life-cycle whereas the 11th or last *Sefirot* becomes the beginning or 1st *Sefirot* of the next tree of life—which to me makes more sense. "On Earth as it is in Heaven" so to speak.

I definitely think that *Knowledge* is a manifest attribute of God when *Wisdom* and *Understanding* come into balance. (But we'll get into that later.) And basically this is what the "tree of life" is all about—balancing the polarities.

Although the following chart represents the "Tree of Life," it's actually a combination of the "Tree of Life" balanced with the "Tree of Knowledge of Good and Evil."

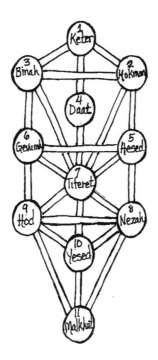

We see the outside poles as the expansive polarities of God or the outside walls of His Kingdom. This you might say is the "Tree of Knowledge of Good and Evil." Whereas the reconciliation of these poles or polarities represented by the central pole, you might say is the "Tree of Life." This reconciliation of opposites is the process of obtaining peace and a fullness of joy.

This is the "straight and narrow way" referred to in the scriptures. (See Matt. 3:3; Mark 1:3; Luke 3:4; John 1:23; D&C 33:10; 1 Nephi 8:20) It is by the eating of the fruits of this balanced tree that man comes to know the fullness of God's glory. The fruit of this tree referred to in 1Nephi 8:10-12, 11:22, 25 is the "pure love of God," and it can only be partaken of when and only when we have finished partaking of the fruit of the Tree of Knowledge of Good and Evil (the imbalances) and have moved into partaking of the Tree of Life (the balance).

But it is a necessary step in man's progress towards Godhood to become awake and fully aware of the opposites in life so we could find the balance in them. Thus were the words of the serpent to Mother Eve in the Garden wherein he counseled her saying:

> For God doth know that in the day ye eat thereof, then your eyes shall be opened, and ye shall be as the Gods, knowing good and evil. (Genesis 3:5)

There are many Christians and non-Christians alike who believe that Mother Eve made a "mis-take" (missed opportunity) when she partook of the fruit of the tree of knowledge of good and evil. Some even go so far as to cast blame on Eve and subsequently womankind for the perpetual separation and downfall of mankind.

But modern-day revelation helps us to *understand* that Eve could see the *wisdom* of partaking of the fruit of the tree of *knowledge* of good and evil in order to bring about the expansiveness necessary for mankind to undergo his probationary period—the period in which his spiritual integrity would be tested.

Therefore it was necessary for "sin" (separation within) to be brought into the world to test man's integrity—to see whether or not mankind (in general and each individual person) would choose good over evil. It gave man the perspective needed in order for him to make a "free-will" choice. That's why Earth is a perfect crucible for transformation—it holds the greatest opportunity for choice.

There is a beautiful passage in *The Book of Mormon* (I'm not actually sure who wrote this book, but it lends a lot of insight) that sheds light to this concept. According to the Mormon faith, Father Lehi (a character in *The Book of Mormon*) explained the fall of man to his son, Jacob this way:

> For it must needs be that there is an opposition in all things. If not so, my first-born in the wilderness, righteousness could not be brought to pass, neither wickedness, neither holiness nor misery, neither good nor bad. Wherefore, all things must needs be a compound in one; wherefore, if it should be one body it must needs remain as dead, having no life neither death, nor corruption nor incorruption, happiness nor misery, neither sense nor insensibility.
>
> It must needs be that there was an opposition to the tree of life; the one being sweet and the other bitter.
>
> And now, behold if Adam had not transgressed he would not have fallen, but he would have remained in the Garden of Eden. And all

things which were created must have remained in the same state in which they were created; and they must have remained forever, and had no end.

And they would have had no children; wherefore they would have remained in a state of innocence, having no joy, for they knew no misery; doing no good, for they knew no sin, But behold, all things have been done in the wisdom of him who knoweth all things.

Adam fell that men might be; and men are, that they might have joy. And the Messiah cometh in the fullness of time, that he may redeem the children of men from the fall. And because that they are redeemed from the fall they have become free forever, knowing good from evil; to act for themselves and not to be acted upon, save it be by the punishment of the law at the great and last day, according to the commandments which God hath given.

Wherefore, men are free according to the flesh; and all things are given them which are expedient unto man. And they are free to choose liberty and eternal life, through the great Mediator of all men, or to choose captivity and death, according to the captivity and power of the devil; for he seeketh that all men might be miserable like unto himself. (2Nephi 2:11, 15, 22-27)

And so we find, through this Mormon scripture, that the partaking of the forbidden fruit of the tree of knowledge of good and evil was a necessary step in mankind's evolution towards Godhood or Celestial Integrity.

On the one hand, it brought about expansiveness for spirit to manifest into flesh. On the other hand, it brought about separation which in reality is the spiritual and temporal "death" which was the consequence of partaking of the forbidden fruit. This duality of blessing and cursing is affixed to many of the difficult decisions Adam (and subsequently mankind) must make in his progression towards God.

But we'll get into all of that in the next chapter. For now, let's go back and really "get into" the Kabbalic Tree of Life and study the 10 different *Sefirot* or characteristics of God so that we can recognize and define the polarities and then discover the balance.

Before Adam (or Eve—depending upon who you want to blame) partook of the forbidden fruit, he became separated in that his God-self which was both male and female was separated into two distinguishable parts—Adam and Eve or male and female. "God created he him; male and female created he them." (Genesis 1:26-27, 21-25) According to the Kabbalic tradition, this was one of the first necessary steps for the physical manifestation of the *Keter* or crown (which is the first manifestation of God).

This is where the first branching off of the tree of knowledge of good and evil takes place wherein the spiritual man or God/man begins his descent into the physical plane or flesh. Thus begins the separation of his spiritual self or God/self from his physical self or oneself. Many religious traditions believe this is symbolized as the separation of the male and female—the male represented by the spirit/self or *Heaven* and the female represented by the physical/self or *Earth*.

In the early oriental tradition, this idea was formalized in the concept of yin/yang. Yin, or negative principle originally referred to as "the dark or shadow side of the mountain" and shared attributes with the Earth, moon and water. Yang, or positive principle, signifying "bright banners in the wind" or the light side of the mountain and was linked with the sky, sun and fire.

After several generations of Eastern philosophers, everything became classified under these two categories, including the sexes: yin was female, yang was male. But yin and yang were not seen as hostile and irreconcilable opposites, competing for control over the universe. Nor was one "good" and the other "evil." On the contrary, yin and yang constantly complement each other to maintain cosmic harmony. And they are not fixed static principles, but transform each other, in an ongoing process. Without the eternal movements and interchange of these forces, life wouldn't exist. Winter, which is yin, changes into summer which is yang. Both yin and yang can create; both can destroy. The life giving sun can also scorch and kill life. It gives way to the dark barren cold of the Earth in which new seeds of life can germinate. The symbol for yin/yang is illustrated below:

In the world of cosmology or the study of the cosmos, this process is symbolized by the spiral turning continuously on itself by conscious breath—waking from sleep and sinking back into sleep. In the book, *The Great Cosmic Mother* by Monica Sjoo and Barbara Mor we read:

The ascending spiral is matter transforming into spiritual/psychic energy. Simultaneously, from the descending spiral, the materialization of the spirit comes the differentiation of the whole manifest world. The spiral involution of energy into matter is the primary movement of the universe into created beings; the spiral evolution of matter into energy is the creative movement of these beings consciously evolving back to their source. Inhaling and exhaling breaths of living cosmos spirals the Universe into creation and dissolution Energy <-> Matter and World <-> Spirit. Radiant energy can be transformed into massive particles, and vice versa. The spiral is the symbolic key to immortality or eternal process.

This cosmic symbolism helps to redefine what actually took place in the Garden when Adam, as the first human being, was created from the elements of the Mother (Earth) and then the energy of the Father (the spirit of God) was breathed into him.

Thus began the initiation of the human race, but in order for the process of creation or (procreation) to continue on its own or independently from God, there had to be a process introduced whereby human beings could procreate on their own. Therefore in the next cyclical step towards materialization of the physical form but away from the spiritual realm it was necessary for the separation of Adam into two beings—male and female. Adam was put into a deep sleep and Eve was brought forth out of Adam as a separate living entity. (Perhaps by some process of genetic engineering—we're only now discovering new possibilities of creation.)

Therefore by this process of separating the male from the female, the possibilities of autonomous procreation became possible—and also the recognition and potential resolution of opposites. In this separation or branching off in the Kabbalic Tree of Life, we find the two first attributes of male and female being depicted in the *Sefirot* as *wisdom* and *understanding*.

A few years ago, I read a remarkable book called, *Written by the Finger of God*, by Joe Sampson. The following information is "gleaned" from that remarkable volume.

In the apocryphal structure, the Father, [Abba] (Adam) is given the attribute of Wisdom, but this is a reversal of the original concept wherein it is woman [Aima] who is wise. Hence, as an example in the Greek, we have Sophia as the type of feminine wisdom. Opposite the female, we have the male attribute of the Understanding of men.

Is there really a difference between the way the male and female minds work? The ancients understood these differences long before we knew of the dominance of the right and left brain. The war between the sexes has been going on from the beginning as each is both attracted to but confused by the other.

So what is it that makes a woman wise? Is it that quality of the heart we call intuition or just knowing by the way it feels? I believe that what women are feeling is a gift of the Sprit of God that works spirit to spirit and may not be at first noticed by the conscious mind.

Men, on the other hand, seem to delight in their ability to understand, to reason, to place concepts or things in a logical order, to think things through step by step, rather than by the leap of faith.

Both of these attributes we can recognize as being necessary for the divine. I believe this is one of the reasons why marriage was instituted by God for the benefit of mankind. It is not good for man to be alone because he is of himself incomplete until he acquires the attributes of the female and visa versa.

It is by experiencing the opposite then that we come to the reconciliation known as *Knowledge*. "Adam *knew* his wife, Eve, and she conceived," is a statement to be read on several levels. As a man and a woman live together, age together, sleep in the same bed, 40 years, procreate and provide together, they become as one flesh. Then woman begins to think and man begins to feel and they complete each other. Again, as we look at the tree as a rite of coronation, we recognize that both the male and female attributes are necessary to approach the Throne of God.

This marriage of male and female attributes should teach us something very important about the nature of the Godhead and that salvation for the individual is quite limited. We are exalted in pairs, and both male and female approaches are necessary for anyone to come to fulfillment or complete knowledge. In this context, we then begin to understand the words of Paul when he said: "Nevertheless, neither is the man without the woman, neither the woman without the man, in the Lord." (1Cor. 11:11)

The next section of the tree also contains two polarities and the balance in the center. In the Kabbalic Tree of Life, these polarities or opposites are named *Mercy* on the right and *Severity* on the left. But for clarity's sake, I'm going to substitute the word *Justice* for *Severity* as *Justice* is used more often in scripture and is more commonly understood as the opposite of *Mercy*.

So let's look at the meaning of these three attributes of God: *Mercy, Justice* and *Beauty,* which is the balance between the two polarities

In the *Zohar*, the principles of *Mercy* and *Justice* are referred to as the "Two arms of God." The one arm of *Mercy* gives life whereas the other arm of *Justice* gives death. In Hasidic prayer, the righteous Zadok can, by lifting both arms high towards heaven, call upon God to keep these principles in balance in his creation. The act of lifting the right arm higher becomes an appeal sign for *Mercy*; whereas when the left arm is raised higher, then this is an appeal sign for vengeance or *Justice* to be dispensed by the angels of heaven. When these principles are held in balance, the reconciliation is the principle of *Beauty*.

This Sefirot is located in chart number one over the breast and is considered the sum of all that is good. In this illustration, we also see that it is a depiction of Christ with his outstretched arms in the form of the crucifixion—the right arm holding out *mercy*, the left holding out *justice*. In the gospel of Luke, we find an interesting metaphor for *Mercy* and *Justice* played out in the description of the two men hanging on crosses on both sides or "arms" of Christ. Luke records:

> And when they were come to the place, which is called Calvary, there they crucified him, and the malefactors, one on the right hand, and the other on the left.
> And one of the malefactors which were hanged railed on him saying, If thou be Christ save thyself and us. (Luke 23:33, 39)

It is interesting to note that this man had not met any of the requirements for repentance. He shows no recognition or confession of his crime; no remorse; no willingness to pay restitution; no desire to repent or change; and definitely no resolution to never again return to his crimes. Because of this lack of a repentant heart (a broken heart and contrite spirit) the arm of *Justice* certainly awaits him. On the other hand, notice the attitude of the repentant man:

> But the other answering rebuked him saying, Dost not thou fear God, seeing thou art in the same condemnation?
> And we indeed justly; for we receive the due reward of our deeds: but this man hath done nothing amiss. And he said unto Jesus, Lord, remember me when thou comest into the kingdom.
>
> And Jesus said unto him, Verily I say unto thee, today shalt thou be with me in paradise. (Luke 23:40-43)

This man definitely shows signs of a repentant heart as he recognizes and confesses that he has committed a crime; is willing to pay the restitution; and cries out to the Lord for mercy as he recognizes in Him the power to save.

And what a *beautiful* resolution of *mercy* balancing *justice* when Jesus replies: "Today shalt thou be with me in paradise."

In Psalm 86, David implores God for *mercy*, and rightly so as the arm of *justice* requires this great King to spend time in the "lowest hell."

> For great is thy *mercy* toward me: and thou hast delivered my soul from the lowest hell. (Psalm 86:13)

Yet King David never discounts the necessity of God's *justice* being the other arm of *mercy* as he continues to describe the attributes of God in Psalm 89:

> Thou hast a mighty arm: strong is thy hand, and high is thy right hand.
> *Justice* and judgment are the habitation of thy throne: *mercy* and truth shall go before thy face. (Psalm 89: 13, 14)

The balance between the full extent of the *arm of justice* and the *arm of mercy* is found in the application of the redemptive power of Jesus Christ. *Beauty* is the central feature of the Tree of Life. The "tree of life" which the father Lehi saw in a dream and also his son Nephi witnessed in vision is Jesus Christ and all His attributes. The tree was described as truly *beautiful*.

> And behold this thing shall be given unto thee for a sign, that after thou hast beheld the tree which bore the fruit which thy father tasted, thou shalt also behold a man descending out of heaven and him shall ye witness and after ye have witnessed him ye shall bear record that it is the Son of God.
> And it came to pass that the Spirit said unto me: Look! And I looked and beheld a tree; and it was like unto the tree which my father had seen; and the *beauty* thereof was far beyond, yea, exceeding of all *beauty*; and the whiteness thereof did exceed the whiteness of the driven snow. (1Nephi 11:6-8)

The concept of being centered, balanced, organized and in proper order is considered *beautiful*. This concept is one that appears in the New World among the Native Americans. The Navajo word for balance is the same as for beauty.

The gospel of Jesus Christ is the most precious and beautiful gift we've been given. It is like the flower that we give to each other to say, "I love you."

One of my favorite Mormon scriptures speaks of the *beauty* of Zion in the last day:

> And blessed are they who shall seek to bring forth my Zion at that day for they shall have the gift and power of the Holy Ghost, and if they endure unto the end they shall be lifted up at the last day, and shall be saved in the everlasting kingdom of the Lamb; and whoso shall publish peace, yea tidings of great joy, how *beautiful* upon the mountains shall they be. (1Nephi 13:37)

The next section of the Kabbalic Tree of Life contains the three Sefirot or characteristics of God called *Victory, Glory,* and *Foundation.* It's curious to note that these three Sefirot are located in the groin or procreative area of the Christ figure signifying that this *Foundation* is the balance between *Victory* over the flesh and the *Glory* of the spirit. Christ is the foundation from where all life force or procreative powers flow. This sexual energy is in its perfect balance when it is directed by the Christ/self or Holy Spirit.

Sexual energy has always been a controversial subject among most if not all denominational and non-denominational religions alike. Most have attempted to impose strict regulations regarding the appropriate use or righteous (right use) of sexual energy. The extreme *victory* use of sexual energy is found within the Catholic Church wherein the highest service you can render to God is to become a celibate priest or nun. On the opposite hand is the *glory* use of sexual energy which is found in the Vedas and Kama Sutra where disciples are taught to awaken the *Kundalini* (serpent power) which is described as feminine energy or "opened" sexual energy. There are ancient Goddess rites and rituals which assist in activating and directing this sexual energy so one can experience the *glory* of *Nirvana* (heavenly bliss). Both arms (or legs in this case) are necessary to create dimension in this area of sexuality, so that we can gain the perspective of Divine Love which has been described as "the fountain of living waters."

Brother David Steindl-Rast portrays a beautiful picture of what he sees has occurred with the fountain of living waters:

> The image that I have is that this life-giving experience (spirituality) is like a fountain of living waters that gushed forth. But the environment in which we are living—and I don't mean the natural environment— but the kind of world that we have created is a very impersonal and cold environment, and so the living water freezes. And so what you've got there when you have dogmatism and moralism and ritualism is a frozen fountain. It still has a certain beauty, but it's frozen. So what

do you do to make it alive? With the warmth of your own heart you have to arm it.

It is a task to let this living water flow again and again—to make it flow by warming the frozen ice that hangs down there with the warmth of your own hearts. And that means living community—that means relationship.

"Wherever two or three are together in my name," Jesus says in the Gospels, "there I am in the midst of them." Wherever two or three of them are together in the spirit—in that life-giving aliveness—this divine life is in the midst of them. (Quoted by Bro. David Steindl-Rast in a presentation at the 1995 Windstar Symposium.)

Matthew Fox, another presenter at this same Windstar Symposium, describes the need for balance between the *victory* and the *glory sefirah* in the tree of life diagram in his book, *The Coming of the Cosmic Christ*. He calls it the "yes/no" dimension:

Just as the West has lost faith with the spiritual dimension to sexuality, so the East when translated to the West runs the risk of forgetting the justice dimension inherent in all relationships including sexual ones. Lifestyles must always keep justice as a test of authentic mysticism— just as mysticism is the authentic test for justice. Mysticism is the "yes" dimension, the "I am" dimension, the awareness that "my fruit is mine to give" dimension. Justice is the "no" dimension, the "fortified wall" dimension that the Song of Songs insists is a part of authentic love and real mystical sexuality. No one has carte blanche to bypass the justice dimension to sexuality, for the justice dimension is as much a part of the cosmic law as is ecstasy itself. Without the "no" or the "wall" dimension there is no true giving to a freely chosen partner—there is no commitment of mutuality. One cannot be legitimately welcomed by all—but only by one's freely chosen love.

Again the balance between the two poles—the "yes" and the "no" elements described here as "mysticism" and "justice" can be interpreted in the tree of life as the *victory* over the flesh and the *glory* of the spirit. These both comprise attributes of God and are found in Christianity and other religions. The balance between the two is the foundation or building block for the fullness of joy or in Kabblistic terms—the reunion of God and His *Shekhinah*.

In Gershom Sholem's book *On the Kabbalah and its Symbolism,* he talks about these last *sefirah* and the tenth being the *Shekhinah*.

The mythical nature of these conceptions is most clearly exemplified by the distinction between the masculine and feminine, begetting and receiving potencies in God. This mythical element recurs with rising intensity, in several pairs of *seforth,* and is expressed most forcefully in the symbolism of the last two. The ninth *sefirah, yesod,* is the male potency, described with clear phallic symbolism, the "foundation" of all life, which guarantees and consummates the *heiros gamos,* the holy union of male and female powers.

This notion of feminine potencies in God, which attain their fullest expression in the tenth and last *sefirah,* represents of course, a repristination of myth that seems utterly incongruous in Jewish thinking. Consequently it seems necessary to say a few words about this idea, that is, about the Kabblistic conception of *Shekhinah,* which is a radical departure from the old Rabbinical conception... the *Shekhinah*—literally in-dwelling, namely of God in the world—is taken to mean simply God himself in His omnipresence and activity in the world and especially in Israel...Here the *Shekhinah* becomes an aspect of God, a quasi-independent feminine element within Him.

The reunion of God and His *Shekhinah* constitutes the meaning of redemption. In this state again seen in purely mythical terms, the masculine and feminine are carried back to their original unity, and in this uninterrupted union of the two powers of generation will once again flow unimpeded through all the worlds. The Kabbalists held that every religious act should be accompanied by the formula: this is done "for the sake of the reunion of God and His *Shekhinah.*"

I was taught at an early age the concept of the "gathering of Israel" or the establishment of Zion—the pure in heart. I suppose I have always been a "Zionist" or one who seeks to bring forth Zion. "And blessed are they who shall seek to bring forth my Zion at that day for they shall have the gift and power of the Holy Ghost."

I read a fascinating book a few years ago by the brother of a dear friend, Cleon Skousen. The author of the book is Max Skousen and the name of the book is *A Blessing Hitherto Unknown."* (This book is one of those "must read" books.)

In his book, Max describes the people of modern-day so-called "Zion" as "looking beyond the mark." The "mark" is defined as being "the pure love of Jesus Christ." He's not just talking about his LDS audience missing the mark, but about how *all* religions go beyond the mark when they continue to partake of the fruit of the tree of good and evil.

Partaking of this forbidden fruit can only mean one thing to man and humanity—*death or separation from God!* That is why I've called "sin—separation within." Sin can also mean in archery terms "missing the mark." The only way to stop sinning is to *stop* partaking of the forbidden fruit which is all of the false judgments and belief systems which organized religion has incorporated to keep us in the tree of good and evil. And then we must *start* eating the fruit from the tree of life which is the pure love of Christ.

Then, and only then, can we begin to get back to that place where we all desire to exist which is Heaven on Earth or the *Kingdom of God.*

According to the Mormon prophet, Joseph Smith, in the *Doctrine and Covenants* section 65:2:

> The *keys* of the *kingdom of God* are committed unto man on the earth, and from thence shall the gospel roll forth unto the ends of the earth, as the stone which is cut out of the mountains without hands shall roll forth until it has filled the whole earth.

This means we can't look to anyone else to bring forth Zion in this, the latter days, because each one of us holds within ourselves the keys to the kingdom of God. These keys are the fruits of the tree of life or the pure love of Christ which is the gospel or "good news" which will roll forth until it has filled the entire planet! How exciting is that?!

Let us all seek to bring forth the kingdom of God in our lifetime!

Scriptural References: Genesis 2:9,17, 3:3,6; Exodus 31:3; 1Chronicles 29:11; Proverbs 3:13,18-20,4-7, 11:30,24:3,4; Jeremiah 17:7,8; St. John 13:34,35; 1Corinthians 13; Galatians 5:14,16-18; 1John 4:7,8; Revelations 22:1,2,14; 1Nephi 8:10-22,11:21-36,13:37,15:36; 2Nephi 2:11-30; Alma 5:14-62, 32:28-43; D&C Sec. 65,97:14-28,121:45,46

Walk Your Talk Therapies: Chapter Three

Therapy One: *Growing Your Own Tree of Life*

In the Book of Mormon there is a beautiful analogy of how to grow the Tree of Life within you beginning with planting the seed of faith (See Alma 32). It concludes in Alma 32:41-43:

> But if ye will nourish the word, yea, nourish the tree as it beginneth to grow. By your faith with great diligence, and with patience, looking forward to the fruit thereof, it shall take root; and behold it shall be a tree springing up unto everlasting life.
>
> And because of your diligence and your faith and your patience with

the word in nourishing it, that it may take root in you, behold, by and by ye shall pluck the fruit thereof, which is most precious, which is sweet above all that is sweet, and which is white above all that is white, yea, and pure above all that is pure; and ye shall feast upon this fruit even until ye are filled, that ye hunger not, neither shall ye thirst.

Then, my brethren, ye shall reap the rewards of your faith, and your diligence, and patience, and long-suffering, waiting for the tree to bring forth fruit unto you.

Design your own "tree of life" which resides deep within your soul. Mine is illustrated below:

- ENLIGHTENMENT
- KNOWLEDGE
- PRAISE
- JOY
- BEAUTY
- LOVE
- FAITH

Find a quiet place where there's no chance of being disturbed (in a locked bedroom, or on top of a mountain, preferably). Sit in that quiet, "sacred space" with your legs crossed in a comfortable position. Let your arms rest in a relaxed position in your lap.

Now close your eyes and concentrate on your breathing. Visualize each breath as a spiritual essence of light and energy that fills you, combining with your own spiritual essence, and then returning it to the universal Holy Spirit from which it was drawn. Do this until you sense a feeling of deep tranquility and peace—a sense of oneness with the universe.

Then, as the thoughts enter your mind, concentrate on one aspect of the "word of God" which you don't presently comprehend. Take this "word of God" (which could be a question or a concept), and breath it down deep within your soul until you can visualize it resting at the bottom of your very being.

Then, as you're able to do this, awaken the power of *faith* within you so you can *believe* that you will receive the answer to the question or concept. As you feel this *faith* begin to rise within yourself, feel the energy of this *faith* move up into the next aspect of *love*. Visualize *love* filling your being as you give gratitude to your Creator for answering your question in *faith*. Gratitude and appreciation are incredible emotions to open up the *love* channels to God. Let these feelings overcome you until they bring you into the next stage of *beauty*.

Beauty is the balance between justice and mercy, and as you embrace the *beauty* within you in balancing the right hand of *justice* and the left hand of *mercy,* you will feel the power of being centered between the two. If there are any sins (separations within) that need to be repented of, now is the time to take it up with the Lord. In His mercy He will forgive you of *all* sins. There are *no* sins that are *too great* for the Lord to forgive. Trust in Him to forgive you.

With this accomplished you will feel complete *joy* feel your heart as you realize that the Lord has heard and answered your prayers. This *joy* only comes from a pure heart that has been sanctified by the Lord. Embrace the *joy* within you as you impart generous *praise* towards the Lord for His infinite mercy. This will automatically bring you into the *praise* stage of your Tree of Life and so feel free to *praise* God for *all* things in your life. Give *praise* for the trials as well as the triumphs, for the pain as well as the joy realizing that they are all for your good. Give *praise* to God for *all* the lessons of life.

As you do this your consciousness will expand and you will gain the *knowledge* that you require and deserve from all learning experiences. God will flood you with this *knowledge* that there are really no "mis-takes" but simply missed opportunities for receiving the *knowledge* from each experience— whether good or bad. And then you will again realize (real eyes) that there are no "bad" experiences as they are all for the gaining of *knowledge*. And when you gain this knowledge you will be *enlightened with wisdom*. This enlightenment will surpass all *understanding* as it will be the balance between *understanding* and *wisdom*. As you become *enlightened* to the promise of who you really are—the son or daughter of God—you again will realize that there is nothing that you can't accomplish in this world—that God will give you *all* the necessary tools of *enlightenment* to fulfill your purpose in life—your final destiny—that you have been sent down to Earth to do. This is the real key to *enlightenment* and is the key to the Kingdom of Heaven on Earth. It is your heritage—so claim it!

Therapy Two: *Study the Kabbalah*

I recommend your own study of the Tree of Life or *Kabbalah* as an addition to your daily scripture study. There are many books available on the subject and you can refer to my own *Books and Authors* for recommendations.

Chapter Four
A Walk in the Garden

In the spring of 1979, I was privileged to participate in a sacred ceremony in the Salt Lake City Mormon Temple wherein Kurt and I became as Adam and Eve, respectively, and we walked through the Garden of Eden and subsequent "other worlds" as if we were Adam and Eve. These temple ceremonies, developed by Joseph Smith—a 33rd degree Mason—were taken from the original Masonic temple rites and introduced as part of the Mormon temple ceremonies, which included women (I'm all for that). These temple ceremonies originated from pieces and parts of the temple rites in King Solomon's temple based on the Judaic Kabbalic Tree of Life (discussed in Chapter Two).

So just for the fun of it, let's go for "a walk in the garden." I'll be your tour guide, interpreting in my own words how I personally relate to the Adam and Eve story. Starting with Genesis chapter 1:26-27, 5:2: (Italics are mine.)

> And God said, Let us make man in our image, after our image, after our likeness: and let them have dominion over the fish of the sea, and over the fowl of the air, and over the cattle and over all the earth, and over every creeping thing that creepeth upon the earth.
>
> So God created man in his own image in the image of God created he him; *male and female* created he *them*. (Genesis 1:26-27)
>
> *Male and female* created he *them*; and blessed *them*, and called *their* name *Adam*, in the day when *they* were created. (Genesis 5:2)

Let's get something straight right from the very beginning—when Adam first started out in life, he was *both male and female* joined together as *one*. At least that's what the Bible indicates, and I've chosen to italicize the relevant parts. So how does it happen that Adam came down to this earthly existence as both *male and female*? Well, my feelings are that Adam was an extension of God (as we all are) and in the beginning that extension was as *one unit* both *male and female*. Somewhat like a photon atom or an "Adam of light," as it has now been discovered by quantum physics that light acts both as a wave and a particle. If light is manifest as a particle, then perhaps it has one positive element—proton, and one negative element—electron; and this perhaps was the male/female relationship when Adam was first placed on the earth.

The oral tradition of *Kabbalah* states that the reason for existence is that "God wished to behold God." Thus there was a previous non-existence in which, as the written tradition of the Zohar states:

> Face did not gaze upon Face. In an act of total free will, God withdrew the Absolute All, *AYINSOF*, from one place to allow a void to appear in which the mirror of existence could be manifested. This act of *Zimzum*, contraction, lies behind the rabbinical saying, *"God's place is the world, but the world is not God's place."*

And so God in the beginning is understood here as a complete unit—or the unity of male and female combined as *one*. This, in essence, is what *God* is all about—the *integrity* of the relationship of *male* and *female*. And so why then did this separation of the first man (or Adam) from God occur and subsequently the separation of male and female?

There is much speculation regarding this subject, but here's my own personal opinion for what it's worth. I believe we were like elements of light (photons) emanating from the great source of light—God. "Like seeds within a bright and shining star." (John Denver lyric) We were called upon to be part of a great experiment (experience, actually) wherein the Universe, as we know it, would be created. In order for matter to be created, there had to be enough energy generated that a tremendous nuclear explosion was necessary (the "big bang" theory). In order for this nuclear explosion to take place, it was necessary to be split apart from our perspective selves—creating *soul-mates* or as some have suggested "split-aparts." This was the *negative* consequence of the experiment or the "sacrifice" factor. The *positive* side of the experiment was that the energy/matter that was generated by the explosion would be available to all of us so that we could create the earth on which we live. Our spirits would also be given physical tabernacles in which we could progress in our evolutionary path towards Godhood. Part of the glue or electricity that holds everything together is that intense desire and hope (faith, if you will) that someday we will be reconnected back to our "split-apart" or soul-mate.

And so here we are as Adam and Eve respectively, separated into the male and female aspects of ourselves. Perhaps it's for the purpose of recognizing the duality and polarities in each other in a more distinct way, so that we could learn the lessons necessary of unifying and harmonizing these two opposing poles.

And then, if that wasn't hard enough, God gives Adam and Eve two opposing commandments: "to multiply and replenish the earth" and "*not* to partake of the Tree of Knowledge of Good and Evil" which, in essence, is the only way possible to *know* just how they could multiply and replenish the earth.

Anyway, this is what I've been able to derive from the written material on the subject along with my own revelations. Perhaps there was another way out of this dilemma they were in, but it was obvious to me that Eve felt the responsibility of the first commandment weighing heavily upon her shoulders; whereas Adam felt the second commandment was more pressing.

Perhaps this "conflict of interests" escalated into their first marital dispute wherein Adam went sulking off to his part of the garden and Eve went to hers to be alone. Sometimes "aloneness" (all-one-ness) is necessary when we're unable to resolve conflict or disputes yet still want to maintain peace in a relationship. That first act of Garden of Eden separation, however, may have created the first polarity or politics in their relationship—that of *liberalism* versus *conservatism*—with Eve, the liberal, looking for a change in the status quo and *conservative* Adam completely satisfied in his garden paradise. (Sound familiar?)

Unfortunately, Eve went looking for an ally or "therapist" to help her solve her relationship problems, but Adam kept waiting for "further light and knowledge" from God.

Both were seeking for something outside of themselves (*externalism*) for answers rather than trying to seek the answers within (*internalism*) in order to heal their relationship issues with each other. (More on "isms" later.)

This created the perfect opportunity for Satan to make an appearance and set himself up as Eve's therapist (the-rapist) and establish the Earth's first "organized religion." He wanted from the very start to tell *man* what to do and, since *man* wasn't listening, he tried his strategies on *woman*. And since a woman when emotional (energy in motion) is in the female part of her brain (*intuition or wisdom*), she's open to almost anything. Whereas a man, when he's in the male side of the brain (*logic or understanding*), isn't open to anything...especially the whisperings of the Holy Spirit.

So Eve—trusting in her therapist's advice and without the mutual consent of her husband, Adam—went ahead with the suggested treatment program and partook of the *Tree of Knowledge of Good and Evil* so she could get on with God's program of "multiplying and replenishing the earth."

And so what did this do to their already strained and estranged relationship?

It compounded the problem! Now Adam was faced with making the hardest decision of his life: Whether or not to go along with his wife and partake of the forbidden fruit and thus bring about separation and death to himself and to all of creation or to "divorce" his soul-mate wife (impetuous as she may be) without bringing forth his promised posterity (us) into existence.

Fortunately for "us," he chose the later. But who knows—if it wasn't for Eve's impetuousness we might still be in the spirit-world looking down at Adam and Eve enjoying the fruits of the garden and wondering... *"When on Earth is it going to be our chance for existence?"* In the *Kabbalah* we read:

> Adam in *Beriah*, now existing as a separated entity on the level of the spirit, was still untried, and so the manifestation of God's image was brought forth into the third World of Formation, *Yezirah*, Eden. Here, the now divided but related aspects of male and female took up the active and passive roles (or, as some Kabbalists see it, the inner relationship of Adam the spirit to the soul of Eve.) With the intrusion of temptation into their idyllic world came the willful breaking of the one rule they had been given. With this came Knowledge of the World of Creation and the possibility of eating of the Tree of Life, that is *Azilut*; and so they were sent down into the lowest World of materiality and given coats of skins, that is, fleshly bodies. Here they were placed under the greatest number of laws, so that the universe was relatively safe from the results of their free will until they had matured into greater responsibility. In mythological form this is an account of how we arrived on the earth. Some Kabbalists see this event of the Fall as foreseen by God, as a parent lets a child make a mistake in order to learn. In this manner Adam experiences all the levels of existence, both on the way down and on the way up as he seeks to regain first Eden, then the Heaven of Creation and ultimately Union with the Divine.

Let's read from the Bible about what transpired next when God the Father came around to check up on His "children." (See Genesis 3:8-14)

> And they heard the voice of the Lord God walking in the garden in the cool of the day: and Adam and his wife hid themselves from the presence of the Lord God amongst the trees of the garden.
>
> And the Lord God called unto *Adam* and said unto *him*, Where art thou? And he said, I heard thy voice in the garden, and I was afraid, because I was *naked;* and I hid myself.
>
> And he said, Who told thee that thou wast *naked?* Hast thou eaten of the tree, whereof I commanded thee that thou shouldest not eat?

And the *man* said, The *woman* whom thou gavest *to be with me, she* gave me of the tree, and I did eat.

And the Lord God said unto the *woman*, what is this that thou hast done? And the *woman* said, The *serpent* beguiled me, and I did eat.

And the Lord God said unto the *serpent*, Because thou hast done this, thou art cursed above all cattle and above every beast of the field, upon thy belly shalt thou go, and dust shalt thou eat all the days of thy life.

First of all, let's make one thing clear for all the "naturists" of the world (myself included). God *never* accused Adam of being "naked." It was the so-called "serpent" or Satan that told Adam and Eve they were naked and to hide themselves from God. So, when God walked in on Adam and Eve hiding from Him, because they had been "naughty children" listening to Satan and playing around with the creative powers of the universe, He then asked Adam, "What the *hell* have you been up to, son? Do you *realize* (real eyes) what you've done?"

Then came the classic excuse scene played out with Adam initiating the earliest recorded "blame game." First, Adam points the finger at Eve for his unacceptable behavior. That got the spotlight off Adam while Eve is questioned about her part in the irresponsible act of disobedience. She then fingers the serpent and cries, "He made me do it!" And guess what? The serpent hasn't got a leg to stand on!

So what's a Father to do? He had no other choice then to punish His "naughty children" for misbehaving, and so he executed the proverbial punishments—which are mixed blessings in disguise when we examine them closely. Let's take a look at the curse or punishment given to Eve. (We'll cover the serpent's "crime and punishment" in the next chapter.) From the Bible we read in Genesis 3:16:

> Unto the woman he said, I will greatly *multiply thy sorrow and thy conception;* in sorrow thou *shalt bring forth children*; and thy desire shall be to thy husband, and he shall *rule* over thee. (Italics added for emphasis.)

When you examine the exact wording that God uses in the first part of Eve's punishment, you'll come to realize some interesting "hidden" meanings.

Most people who read the Bible (students and scholars alike) misinterpret this passage of scripture as reading: "I will greatly multiply thy sorrow *in* thy conception," rather than it saying, "I will multiply thy sorrow *and* thy conception."

There is a *big difference* in the meaning of these two passages. The first "incorrect" interpretation would mean that Eve had great sorrow in conception—or in the conceiving of a child. Well, any *normal* woman would agree that there isn't *any* sorrow in *conception*. That's the fun part—it's the birthing of the child that's the hard part. So *that* misquotation of the scripture doesn't make any sense.

But when we read it correctly as saying, "I will multiply thy sorrow *and* thy conception—it reveals a whole different meaning entirely. Obviously, God *did* multiply woman's sorrow (in childbirth and otherwise) as any mother will confirm—but how did he "multiply her conception?"

What exactly is this "conception" that the Lord multiplies? According to one dictionary it could mean one of two things—or perhaps both:

> Conception: the act of conceiving.
> Conceive: to become pregnant with, form in the womb, to form in the mind; to imagine or think: to understand.

If you take the first meaning of the word "conceive: to become pregnant," and plug it into the curse of Eve, then the curse would mean to "multiply Eve's pregnancies." But is this really a curse? Perhaps in modern times it would be when today's desired family size is 1.5 children. But back in the "good ol' days" it was a blessing to have a large family; and according to the Bible, to have a large posterity was woman's greatest "crown of glory." So this obviously isn't what God meant as Eve's (and womankind's) punishment.

If we take the second meaning of the word "conceive: to form in the mind: to imagine or think: to understand" and plug it into the curse, then it takes on a whole different meaning. Did God *multiply* Eve's abilities to *think* and *form concepts in the mind* as a "punishment" because of her listening to the serpent's misguided advice? One wouldn't think so! But if we add the other part to Eve's (and womankind's) punishment, then it makes more sense.

First, the sorrow part of the punishment is redefined or explained as: "in sorrow thou shalt bring forth children." But the second part of the punishment of "multiplying thy conception" becomes more interesting and enlightening when it is redefined by the addition of "and thy desire shall be to thy husband, and he shall *rule* over thee."

Now the *real* meaning behind the curse starts to become crystal clear. So here it is, from a woman's point of view, and you can take it for what it's worth. Here Eve, or woman, is given an abundance of brain power and *no one will listen to her!* She has nowhere to apply this useful information of how the planet should be run because she's stuck home taking care of kids and making sure that Adam's (her husband's) needs are met.

My God!—what a terrible curse He placed upon all womankind! No wonder women throughout the ages have felt so frustrated and repressed when here she's been given *all* the answers to *all* the world's problems and there's *no man on the planet who will listen to her!* (Except perhaps her husband, if he's not too busy watching the football game on television.)

This truly has become a curse, not only for womankind but for *all* humankind that may have benefited had we listened to the *wisdom* women have to offer.

Obviously, there was a "good" reason that God gave this unusual punishment to Eve (and womankind). Perhaps if Eve (or woman) hadn't been placed under her husband's "rule," the separation between male and female would be even greater than it is today. Nowadays, as women are discovering their greater capacities to think and reason, and they no longer accept the "curse" of being under a man's authority, we see increasing divorce or "split-ups" in marriage relationships and families. Women (and men) want to "do their own thing" and "think and act for themselves" without as much regard for the *integrity* of the marriage or family.

But seriously, who can blame women for wanting to "get out from under" the curse of a "patriarchal God" who is *male* anyway and never did understand the workings of the *female* mind?

In reality, *God is both male and female* and in His (their) infinite knowledge bestowed an extra portion of *wisdom* (the first manifestation of God in the Kabalistic tree of life) to the female segment of mankind. But in the process of this bestowal, He needed to place boundaries on that *wisdom* so the female potential wouldn't overrule the male potential (which occurred in the partaking of the forbidden fruit) and create even more separation between the two…and alienation from God. So *woman's wisdom* was placed under the rule of *man's understanding* and thus became *knowledge* which is a thing of *beauty*. "And Adam *knew* Eve his wife; and she *conceived*, and bare Cain, and said, "I have gotten a man from the Lord." (Well, perhaps Eve wasn't *too wise* when she made this proclamation concerning Cain; but therein lies another story.)

But let's get back to the curse or punishment God gave Adam (or mankind) when he listened to the misdirected advice of his wife, Eve:

> And unto Adam he said, Because thou hast hearkened unto the voice of *thy wife*, and hast eaten of the tree, of which I commanded thee saying, thou shalt *not* eat of it: *cursed is the ground* for thy sake; in *sorrow* shalt thou eat of it all the days of thy life…
>
> In the sweat of thy face shalt thou eat bread, till thou return unto the *ground*; for out of it wast thou taken: for dust thou art and unto dust shalt thou return. (Genesis 3:17, 19)

The hidden meanings behind this curse could fill volumes, but since this book is mainly concerned with relationships, let's discuss the hidden meanings behind Adam's (man's) relationship with the Earth (the feminine element).

We discussed earlier that part of Eve's punishment or curse was to be subject to the male influence of Adam. Subsequently, part of Adam's punishment or curse was to be subject to the female influence of Mother Earth.

Because of Adam's decision to partake of the forbidden fruit of the tree of knowledge of good and evil, he was given to understand that he had brought death or *separation from God* into the world of existence.

Before that happened, the Earth brought forth fruit spontaneously without much effort or assistance from mankind. But, after Adam partook of the forbidden fruit and caused death and disintegration, Mother Earth became subject to the same laws of disintegration and could no longer provide for Her children in the same spontaneous manner She did before.

This, indeed, was a "grave" curse not only for the family of man but for all creatures God had placed upon the earth. So when Adam was given the curse "in *sorrow* shalt thou eat of it," it was because it was necessary for him (and mankind) to *feel* and *understand* just how interconnected and responsible he was for the pain and suffering he ultimately caused Mother Earth and creatures that live and nourish themselves upon Her breast. He not only brought the curse of death or separation from God upon himself but also upon the Earth Mother and all of Her children. Adam (and man) must someday gain a *knowledge* of the reality of this fact, or he can never transcend the curse.

But enough of the "cussing out" part of the curse. As I said earlier, a curse contains two parts—the negative aspect (which we already discussed) and a positive part. In Eve's curse, we discussed some of the blessing…she was given a greater capacity to conceive—to receive wisdom and understanding. The part we didn't discuss was her ultimate pain and sorrow in childbirth.

As a mother of eleven children, I can personally attest to the great travail a woman goes through to bring forth children into this mortal world. There's so much apparent pain and suffering that many (if not most) women today choose to anesthetize themselves against it, so they won't be forced to comply to this part of the curse of Eve. Perhaps in some of their minds they believe that this is a way to "transcend" (climb over) this curse. But in reality they are doing themselves a terrible disservice.

I can speak from experience, because I have delivered children both ways—naturally and medicated. When I've chosen to have my children naturally—granted there is an increased amount of pain and suffering—yet this pain and suffering was only used as "a knife to carve away the chalice to contain more joy." With the children I've delivered naturally, particularly at home, there was an increase of euphoric feelings of joy experienced when the tiny babe was placed into my arms for the very first time. And it seems like the more pain I experienced in childbirth, the more joy I was able to experience in that first bonding of love.

Perhaps these "bonds of love" experienced between mother and child in that first passionate embrace are what help create the bonds necessary to survive adolescence. And perhaps this is part of what our society is missing when mothers leave their tiny babes in the hands of strangers so that they can go into the job market to "earn a living." Don't get me wrong. I'm not saying that there aren't times when it's necessary for a woman to leave her children in order to follow her "prime directive" or spiritual path, but ideally she needs to make sure there are adequate, loving caretakers (preferably her co-partner(s) in caring for their children) before she leaves. I believe in the age-old adage that it takes a village to raise one child. I'm all over that!

But on the other hand, I once heard on a Christian talk-radio show that an infant under the age of one year *should never* be separated from its mother overnight as it can cause "separation trauma." This "separation trauma" may even contribute to SIDS (Sudden Infant Death Syndrome) in infants under the age of 6 months when they are left alone in their cribs overnight. I've always preferred sleeping with my young babies until they're old enough to roll over and out of bed. Then I put them into a bassinet or crib right next to me.

It's important for *all* mothers to realize that they can't "transcend" (climb over) the curse of Eve by going around it. This means that they can't anesthetize themselves against the pain that childbirth *naturally* brings. Not only that, but there is strong evidence that the drugs they administer during childbirth, along with the trauma of circumcision (if you are a boy), and childhood immunizations, can set you up for a lifetime of health problems— both physical and mental.

As to the other part of the curse of "woman being subject to her husband," let's go back to Genesis 2:21-24 to see where Eve came from in the first place:

> And the Lord God caused a deep sleep to fall upon Adam, and he slept: and he took one of his ribs, and closed up the flesh instead thereof;
> And the rib, which the Lord God had taken from man, made he a woman, and brought her unto the man.

And Adam said, This is now bone of my bones, and flesh of my flesh: she shall be called Woman because she was taken out of Man. Therefore shall a man leave his father and his mother, and shall cleave unto his wife: and they shall be one flesh.

Whether we choose to take the story of Adam and Eve in Genesis literally or figuratively, the principle is still the same. Eve came out of the side or "rib" of Adam, which means she was meant to be his equal partner or "helpmeet" (mate). This doesn't mean she is *wiser* than Adam or that Adam *will never understand,* but that they were meant to be *partners* for each other and *helpmates* for each other, so that eventually they might return to that perfect *oneness* which is the "integrity of God."

When a man and woman *become one* on all three levels of their existence—spiritually, mentally and physically, they are on the path to returning to *oneness* which *is* the *integrity of God.* This is how they then can *transcend* the curse of Eve—by *becoming one flesh.*

So how then does mankind *transcend* the curse of Adam? Let's take another look in Genesis to find out where exactly man came from:

And the Lord God formed man of the *dust of the ground,* and breathed into his nostrils the breath of life; and man became a living soul. (Genesis 2:7)

So, according to the Bible, *man* was created out of the *dust of the ground,* or as mentioned in the curse "out of it (ground) wast thou taken." Man was, literally or figuratively speaking, taken out of the ground of our Earth Mother. And until he "returns unto the ground" he will surely be under *her* curse.

But does this mean that man will have to be under the curse until the day that he dies and the elements of his body become part of the elements of the Earth? I tend *not* to believe so as this would be a *grave* curse.

When a man (humankind) willingly chooses to "return to the Earth" to develop a *oneness* relationship with Her, he will in fact *transcend* the curse of Adam. There are many men, just as there are women, who believe in the illusion that they can somehow *transcend* (climb over) the curse of Adam by going around it. By this I mean they have chosen to "eat (get) bread" other than by the "sweat of their face" without having a oneness relationship with Mother Earth. When we separate ourselves from the "organic" or original roots from whence we came, we often become complacent and ungrateful for the "fruits of the earth" which our Mother Earth provides.

If you've ever done any organic farming or gardening, you've experienced the joy of eating the fruits of your own labors. There's nothing quite like the flavor of a fresh homegrown tomato or biting into a juicy strawberry grown from your own garden. It's a joy and delight that money just can't buy. All I can say is—try it, you'll like it!

I was privileged to have one of the most incredible experiences I've ever had while meditating. I was listening to the flute music of "Canyon Trilogy" a recording by a Native American musician named Carlos Nakai. During the meditative state I was in, I was able to connect spirit to spirit with Mother Earth. This *oneness experience* initiated me into crying uncontrollably for over two hours…and here's why.

As a mother, I could relate to Mother Earth's own desperate desire to nurture and care for *all* her hungry and crying children—without expecting anything in return. Of giving Her generous life-giving resources to all of "us children" without us returning a token word of appreciation or "thanks." I felt as She felt—always giving out *unconditionally*—loving and nurturing Her young, only thinking of *their* needs while *Her own needs* are neglected.

But what affected me to the point of unbearable pain, was realizing the instances She's been ravaged and pillaged by unconscionable men who steal Her resources without any regard for the irreparable damage they have caused Her. That's the worse violation of all, and *we* (yes, all of us) have *all* taken part in the suffering caused to our dearest Mother Earth. We have raped Her beauty to fulfill the lusts of our flesh and returned nothing to Her. Just look around at all the garbage and pollution we've created as Her children—it's an abomination that will not be easily forgiven—*and we are all guilty of it!*

I hope and pray that we *still can repent* (turn around) from this terrible atrocity we have caused our dear Mother Earth so She can forgive us and begin to heal from the wounds that we as humankind have inflicted upon Her. We *can* if we *will* turn our eyes to the Heavens and seek the guidance of His light; and then repent in the name of His/Her son, Jesus Christ, who has the power to redeem (heal) us and our most precious Mother Earth. And if our hands will reach down to our Earth Mother and seek Her goodness, we will find the loving oneness relationship with her that once was ours. Why not thank Her for all the gifts She gives to us daily. Then, and only then, can we gain back the integrity that was lost when Adam stretched forth his hand and partook of the forbidden fruit that brought about our separation and mortality into this earth plane.

Adam fell that men might be; and men are, that they might have joy. (2Nephi 2:25)

We can all experience a fullness of joy in *this* lifetime, wherein we, as Adam and Eve, can receive the same promises that were given to Adam in the *Pearl of Great Price* (LDS doctrine) wherein he could see God in the flesh. (Italics added for emphasis)

> And in that day Adam blessed God and was filled, and began to prophesy concerning all the families of the earth, saying: Blessed be the name of God, for because of my transgression *my eyes are opened,* and *in this life* I shall have joy, and again *in the flesh* I shall see God.
>
> And Eve, his wife, heard all these things and was glad, saying: *Were it not for our transgression we never should have known good and evil, and the joy of our redemption, and the eternal life which God giveth unto all the obedient.*
>
> And Adam and Eve *blessed* the name of God, and they made all things known unto their sons and their daughters. (Moses 5:10-12)

Although the transgression of partaking of the fruit of the Tree of Knowledge of Good and Evil was a necessary step in Adam and Eve's development, it's no longer necessary to partake of it today. As sons and daughters of Adam and Eve, we can *stop* partaking from the tree of good and evil which is *judgment.* In other words, *stop* judging our fellowman and then *start* partaking from the Tree of Life—which is *unconditional love*—to receive *eternal life* which is the greatest of all the gifts of God.

But there is one more element we need to discuss before readily partaking of the Tree of Life. If you recall, God placed "Cherubim, and a flaming sword which turned every way, to keep the way of the tree of life," that is to prevent Adam (man) from partaking of these marvelous fruits before his time.

There seems to be an ordered sequence, or evolution if you will, for man (and woman) to learn the lessons of personal integrity and relationship integrity before they partake of and can truly appreciate the fruits of the Tree of Life. Perhaps this evolution includes learning the lessons of the Tree of Good and Evil and discovering what is good (desirable) and evil (undesirable or the opposite of live). When we have learned how to exercise discretion, I believe God offers us the opportunity to partake from the Tree of Life. But only God knows—or God only knows—when that time has come. And it's both an individual and cooperative journey to "Become One" and move forward to God and God's love. For God is love.

Scriptural References: Genesis 1:26-28, 2:7, 8; 15-17, 21-25, Ch. 3, 4:1; 2Nephi 2:25; Moses 5:10-12.

Walk Your Talk Therapies: Chapter Four

Therapy One: *A Walk in the Garden*

Take your own walk in the garden. If it's summer, find a local garden (or your own background) to walk in. As your feet step lightly on sacred ground, contemplate the beautiful gifts that Mother Earth and Heavenly Father have provided for your personal joy. If it's winter, take a walk through a snowy park or an indoor garden, contemplating how beloved you are that God has created such wonders for your human senses to enjoy. Realize how blessed you are to participate in this grand experience or experiment we call "life." Absorb the various fragrances and colors which a benevolent creator has designed to thrill you with delight. Allow your heart to be filled with appreciation and gratitude for the relationship between your senses and the sensibilities that this male/female creator has created for your rapturous enjoyment. This world—and all that it contains—was created for *you!* Learn to "take time and smell the roses" but more than that—learn to be completely present to the beauty that surrounds you. As you appreciate all of the gifts of life God blesses you with, remember to give thanks always—to whatever you conceive your creator to be.

Therapy Two: *Design Your Own Garden of Eden*

Imagine (image in) what your own Garden of Eden would look and feel like if you could create it. See the beauty of flower gardens growing spontaneously without effort. Imagine the fragrance of rows of lilac bushes, beds of lavender and rose bushes—all planted for your enjoyment. Taste the fruits of all the various trees you would chose for your garden. Feel the peace of being in harmony with your creator and having that intimate relationship you enjoyed before the fall—your fall into separation within or sin. Feel the joy and bliss you would feel as your loved ones—dead and alive—surround you with love and peace as they partake, along with you, of the Garden of Eden delights. There is no threat of war, no terrorism, no commercialism, no conflict, no pain, no guilt, no remorse. Everyone has evolved past the need to partake of the Tree of Good and Evil and desires only to partake of the Tree of Life. What would you be doing? What would you be experiencing? What would your life be like?

Now create your own drawing or vision board of what that would look like. Clip pictures from magazines or create architectural drawings of the buildings you would live in or landscapes you would design. Make it as detailed and creative as possible. Put your feelings and emotions into it so it becomes "real" for you. You can actually see yourself living there—along with all of your loved ones. Now post the vision board in a place that you will notice daily perhaps above your desk where you work, on your computer or on your refrigerator door…somewhere where you will be sure to look at it and contemplate it daily. As you do this, truly believe (be live) that this Garden of Eden is coming into your life. Your life is continually aligning itself with the energy of your own creation. If possible, get others—including your family and friends—involved in creating yours and their Garden of Eden paradise. Now release it to the universe and God to allow it to happen. Know that it will!

Chapter Five

Dancing with the Serpent

There are some people you meet in life who you know right from the start were "friends from our heavenly home." This is how it was when I first met Jodi, the niece of a dear friend, Lorraine, living in Manti, Utah.

When I first walked through Jodi's front door and our eyes met, there was an immediate spiritual recognition that went well beyond this lifetime. I believe that we must have been sisters in some other place and time, and perhaps someday we will both be able to remember.

As for Jodi, the first thing she said as her eyes got wide with surprise was, "I can't believe you are here!" (I hadn't a clue as to what she meant, but I'd gotten this reaction from others who've met me for the first time.) Then she told me that she had found a photo of me in a book she had just taken back to the library. Actually, it was a snapshot of me standing next to a large rock with the same hair-wrap, so Jodi was convinced it _had_ to be me.

I then asked her the name of the book, as I didn't remember a picture of me in any book I'd written or otherwise. She told me that she couldn't remember the exact title of the book, but that it was a book about "_Kundalini._"

I laughed out loud as the spirit is always playing these types of tricks on me. I was at that particular time involved in an extensive study and practice of awakening the _Kundalini_ or "serpent power."

Jodi then related that the spirit had witnessed to her that the person in the photograph was to be a great teacher and friend to her. That's why she had delightedly exclaimed when I walked through the door, "I can't believe you are here!"

As it turns out, Jodi and I soon became fast friends and, as for me becoming a her teacher, I think we have been teachers for each other as we have shared many learning experiences together. What Jodi was able to teach me (and eventually Kurt) was some yoga and breathing exercises that helped us both to open up and experience the full awakening of the *Kundalini*, or "serpent power" of energy.

But before we get into all *that*, let's back up to where we left off in the last chapter and discuss the significance of the "crime and punishment" of the serpent in the Garden of Eden.

The serpent has been the source of great controversy throughout the ages for both those of religious and of non-religious views. Throughout the world, we see the occurrence of the serpent symbol as representing profound power as well as a universality of religious mysticism. In the book, *The Great Cosmic Mother* by Monica Sjoo & Barbara Mor it reads:

> The snake was, first of all, a symbol of eternal life since each time it shed its skin it seemed reborn. It represented cosmic continuity within natural change—spiritual continuity within the changes of material life. Gliding as it does in and out of holes and caverns in the earth, the serpent also symbolized the underground abode of the dead who wait for rebirth. Its undulations symbolized the serpentine earth currents of the underground waters. The serpent path on earth was the terrestrial energy-flow; the serpent path in the sky was the winding spray of stars in the galactic spiral arm, or Milky Way.

It's interesting to note that the Hebrew word for angels is *seraphim*— bright and shining angels, a flying dragon, and it's derived from the root word "serpent." In Joe Sampson's enlightening book, *Written by the Finger of God,* he states:

> For centuries Jews and Christians have wrestled with the meaning of the unusual thorny phenomenon of fiery serpents biting the children of Israel during their exodus from Egypt to the promised land, and the subsequent raising by Moses of a brass serpent on a pole which allowed those who looked at it to live (see Numbers 21:8-9; John 3:14-15; Alma 33:19.) This strange incident has not caused most Jews and Christians to lose faith in their scriptures. Nor has the Lord's turning Moses' rod into a serpent been considered a reason to discredit the story of the prophetic calling of Moses. (See Exodus 4:2-4)
>
> When the first white settlers witnessed the American Indian make use of the serpent or the snake in their religious ceremonies, the white men undoubtedly thought native beliefs in the serpent were pagan

superstition or demon inspired worship. This is furthest from the truth in Native American reasoning.

The symbol of the serpent legends has over-shadowed the whole western hemisphere as an object used in religious ceremonies, and as well used as temple decor for Aztec and Toltecs. Furthermore the ancient mythology of the flying serpent was seen amongst most other Amerindian tribes. These traditions go back centuries, having their origin and foundation from the Holy Scriptures. Moses, by command of the Lord raised a brazen serpent before the children of Israel, in similitude of the fact that Jesus Christ would be lifted up on the cross. (See Numbers 21:4-8 *cf.* John 3:14-15) This brass serpent staff was used by Moses so to illustrate to the children of Israel the saving grace and powers of their God Jehovah—Jesus Christ, if we believe on Him.

In both the Eastern and Western Hemisphere the ancient ones used the serpent, a Judaic-Christian symbol representing the saving powers of the Savior that saves men from their sins. To this extent the gospel principal was so simple, that men would overlook and fail to see it.

The question I have is this—if the *serpent* was originally a positive symbol perhaps representing Christ, then why was Eve "beguiled" by a *serpent* in the Garden to partake of the forbidden fruit? And why do we Biblically and historically believe *that serpent* to be Satan or Lucifer (the Son of the Morning) who was cast out of heaven onto this earthly plane? (See Rev. 12:9)

A dictionary definition of the word "beguile" is: to cheat (out of): to wile (into): to divert attention from (anything tedious and painful). Could it be possible that Eve was "beguiled" in the real sense of the word in that she thought Satan was Christ, *the messenger of truth and light* sent forth from the higher realms to reveal to her further light and knowledge? I'm sure Eve with her innate mothering instincts had a compelling desire to bring forth the children she had been promised. And so what do you know—here shows up a "bright and shining angel" to give her further instructions on how to go about doing this process called "procreation." The only sad part about it was that she had to break one of God's commandments to do it. Add to that the fact that she was willing to do it on her own without the mutual consent and approval of her partner and soul-mate, Adam.

In listening to the counsel of the "wrong serpent" and partaking of the forbidden fruit alone, Eve created a tremendous chasm of separation between her and her husband, Adam—not to mention the chasm of separation that was ultimately created between God and man by Adam subsequently partaking of the fruit of the Tree of Good and Evil.

Obviously, there are some significant lessons to be learned here if we, as Adam and Eve, want to learn from their (our) "mis-takes" (missed opportunities) and make "restitution" (restore that which was lost). Let's go back to the serpent symbol and see how it could possibly be a symbol for both Christ *and* Satan.

Throughout the history of mankind (perhaps because of its shape and its ability to glide in and out of holes) the snake has come to symbolize the phallus, or male sexual energy. The Zohar relates this concept to the idea that this organ (the penis) contains the light or flame of life and it is the "fruit of the tree yielding seed." (Gen 1:11) All of these concepts were combined by Isaiah:

> And there shall come forth a rod out of the stem of Jesse, and a branch shall grow out of his roots.
> And the spirit of the Lord shall rest upon him, the spirit of wisdom and understanding, the spirit of counsel and might, the spirit of knowledge and of fear of the Lord. (Isaiah 11:1-2)

The Zohar goes on to explain that this male energy or "rod" is the light or spirit of life and intelligence in the living creature which is carried in the male seed. It is that attribute which says, "I see, or I know." It is consciousness of mind (or the Christ consciousness, so to speak).

As we look back on the story of the serpent in the garden, we see that God cursed the serpent after he had tempted Eve with a sore curse "to crawl on its belly." Could this perhaps have been the curse of "impotency" or the inability to procreate or create which Satan heretofore was given the ability and knowledge to do? Obviously, he was left in a different state or condition after God cursed him.

On the other hand—isn't the greatest power or blessing given to mankind the ability to procreate or sexual potency? And to go a step further ... isn't the one identifying characteristic of God His ability to have eternal increase? Therefore isn't it logical to assume that Christ, the son of God, would represent to all mankind, through his obedience to the laws and covenants of God, the ability of eternal procreation or creation? Doesn't "omnipotent" mean "forever powerful or forever potent?" Perhaps this symbol of the rising serpent, or a winged serpent, may also represent the erect male penis or male potency. And perhaps the important thing for the male gender to remember is that this power to procreate must be in accordance with the laws and covenants of God.

Perhaps that's why God gave such strict laws regarding sexual activity and also gave Abraham the covenant of circumcision (see Genesis 17:10, 11), so he would not abuse a God-given ability. It's interesting to note that Abram's name was changed to Abraham only after he had entered into the covenant of circumcision. Interestingly, the name "Abraham," anciently was symbolized by the "flying" or angelic snake. The blessing that God placed upon Abraham is encoded in the name "Abraham."

Through the covenant of circumcision, (which was a Mosaic law which Christ transcended; see Colossians 3:11) God gave Abraham and his descendants power over the transcendental plane. The most obvious case in which this occurs is in conception where a soul is brought down into the world. Since the mark of the covenant is on the sexual organ, it gives the individual access to the highest spiritual realms from which he can bring down the most lofty souls.

The covenant of circumcision also represents the channeling of sexual energy. The sexual drive is one of the most powerful psychological forces in man, and, when channeled along spiritual lines, it can help bring on the highest mystical states. In giving the commandment of circumcision, God indicated that the emotions and desires associated with sex could be used for the mystical quest of the Divine on a transcendental plane. But this can happen on a spiritual level without the necessity of cutting one's foreskin— which was considered a "blood-sacrifice" back in the time of Moses. Many of the Mosaic "laws" were given for sanitation and hygiene purposes because of the living conditions back when there was no clean water or refrigeration. Those laws are considered obsolete in our modern-day society.

So one might ask: If men were given the covenant of circumcision which was a ritualistically-imposed blood sacrifice which somehow provided "access to the highest spiritual realms," what was the female equivalent of the circumcision covenant?

The Bible doesn't seem to give any indication of what women needed in order to obtain to this spiritually enlightened realm. Perhaps not in the Bible, but in the Gospel of St. Thomas in the recently translated Nag Hammadi scrolls, the following exchange occurs in the presence of Mary Magdalene.

> Simon Peter said to them "Let Mary leave us, for women are not worthy of Life."
>
> Jesus said, "I myself shall lead her in order to make her male, so that she too may become a living spirit resembling you males. For every woman who will make herself male will enter the Kingdom of Heaven."

So what is the process Jesus talks about of making a woman male? If we truly understand the process of "becoming one," we'll understand the significance of the marriage act in which a man "knows" a woman and a woman "knows" a man. In legal terms it is defined as "carnal knowledge." Could that be the process Jesus refers to in the Gospel of St. Thomas?

When we realize the significant role Mary Magdalene played in the life of Jesus, it's not difficult to understand that their relationship went beyond what the Bible mentions and was more intimate than the relationship between Jesus and his disciples.

For example, wasn't it Mary who anointed Jesus with oil as a symbol of her love and also her astute understanding of Christ's divine mission? Of all his beloved followers, she *alone* knew and accepted his required sacrificial death and thus anointed him beforehand for his imminent burial.

And who was the first person Jesus appeared to after his death and prior to his ascension to Heaven? His beloved Mary Magdalene who identified him, addressing him as "Rabboni," or "My Master." In some cultures this could be interpreted as "my husband."

A significant occurrence took place at the time of Jesus' death which is documented in three gospels, but the *real* meaning behind it is left unexplained. The renting of the temple veil in two as described in Matthew:

> Jesus, when he had cried again with a loud voice, yielded up the ghost.
>
> And, behold, the veil of the temple was rent in twain from the top to the bottom; and the earth did quake, and the rocks rent;
>
> And the graves were opened; and many bodies of the saints which slept arose,
>
> And came out of the graves after his resurrection, and went into the holy city, and appeared unto many. (Matt 27:50-53)

In the Kabbalistic tradition, it's indicated that the physical "temple" was meant to be a microcosm that represented the Universe. If that was the case, perhaps the veil rent in the temple represented the veil between the spiritual or heavenly realm and the physical or earthly realm. In other words, it was the final domain or dimension which Christ broke through—the veil between life and death. By his infinite act of atonement, he claimed victory over the final separation or enemy which is death... "For as in Adam all die, even so in Christ shall all be made alive." (1Corinthians 15:22)

So if the renting of the veil in the temple represents the macrocosm or spiritual domain, the victory over death or the "cutting a path" from the realm of physical death into eternal life, what does the veil represent in the human body?

In the female, it can most likely represent one thing—the hymen. We read in Exodus about where the veil is placed in the temple.

And thou shalt hang up the veil under the taches, that thou mayest bring in thither within the veil the ark of the testimony: and the veil shall divide unto you between the holy place and the most holy. (Exodus 26:33)

If our bodies are living temples of the most high God, then where within this temple (our body) is the "holy of holies" (our most sacred place) located? Could it be that the renting of the veil that protects the holy of holies represents the marriage act itself wherein man and woman "know" each other and become *one in flesh?*

And, he answered and said, unto them, Have ye not read, that he which made them at the beginning made them male and female.

And said, For this cause shall a man leave father and mother, and shall cleave to his wife: and they twain shall be one flesh? Wherefore they are no more twain but one flesh. What therefore God hath joined together, let not man put asunder. (Matt 19:4-6)

Obviously, the act of *becoming one flesh* is a tremendously important one, or it wouldn't have been mentioned so many times in the scriptures. It's also a reoccurring theme in almost all religious and non-religious systems where the sacredness of the marriage act is recognized for its spiritual empowerment.

Ancient tribal people believed that power resided in images themselves—or rather in the resonance between the image and the thing imagined—and this belief still lives in all of us; symbols continue to have great power over human emotions.

In Indian mythic symbolism, the multiplicity of this world is shown by the integration of the upward male triangle (phallus) and the downward female triangle (vulva)—the ascending and descending vortices of creative energy. Again, this is not just a Hebrew symbol but an ancient symbol found in India.

Another interesting symbol in many ancient hieroglyphics is the *circumpunct* that represents eternity as the point within the circle—or the microcosm within the macrocosm. It can also be represented by a column, or phallic symbol, surrounded by a circle at its base, intended for the vagina or female generative organ. This union of the phallus and the vagina, which is represented by the point within the circle, was intended by the ancients as a type of prolific powers of creation, which they worshipped under the united form of the active or male principle and the passive or female principle.

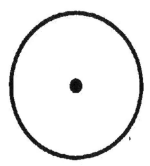

As we've seen, the symbol of the serpent has mythically and mystically come to represent several powers. In its connection to the phallic symbol, it represents male potency or the power to produce offspring. In its association with the Goddess, the serpent is a universal symbol in several cultures that represents the feminine powers of generation and regeneration. Through all of these aspects it has come to symbolize health or "wisdom."

Even today, the *caduceus,* a staff around which two snakes are entwined, is recognized as the general emblem of the medical profession. These snakes are the female and male serpents that intertwine in the body, the source of an energy flow that moves from center to center (chakras) up the spine. When these "snakes" have risen to the top of the spine in the rising *kundalini* experience, some people say they sense an opposing downward force which is called *sushumna.* As sensation moves downward, one has an experience of complete awareness of all *chakras* "awakening," and the energy flowing freely between them. Pictorially, the caduceus can be seen to represent the awakening of the seven chakra centers by the rising serpent power of the *kundalini.*

In ancient Hinduism, the symbol of the "serpent swallowing its tail" is represented in their practical and mystical approach as awakening the *kundalini* or *serpent powers*. In this image of the *uroboros* (shown below) both the male and female organs are implied. This process of awakening the kundalini starts in the base energy center located in the genital area of the spine, and in the Hindu belief system the process of awakening it is an essential element to obtain "enlightenment." This awakening of life force or "primal energy" and its subsequent path up through the *chakra system* is an element in the ancient alchemical mysteries. According to believers it's how we find our way back to the most ancient of all—God, the Oneness, the Omniscient.

The worm, snake, serpent or dragon biting or swallowing its own tail is a powerful symbol of infinity, and also of our universal nature, of completion, perfection and totality. Parallels abound—the figure-8 symbol of infinity (quite possibly derived from the uroboros), the Chinese yin-yang symbol, the Buddhist wheel of Life, etc. The Serpent biting its own tail appears in New Kingdom Egypt (1600 years b.c.e.). It was taken up by the Phonecians and then to the Greeks, who called it the Ouroboros (or uroboros), which means tail-devourer. They considered it the Great World Serpent encircling the earth, associated with the world-ocean. Uroboros became an important Gnostic symbol, later taken up by Western Alchemy. The following is a Theosophical Society's symbol which includes the Uroborus or "serpent swallowing its tail" along with other mystical symbols.

If you've ever been involved in any of the holistic healing arts or have ever visited a chiropractor, you're familiar with the term "*chakra.*" Or perhaps, you are familiar with its Western traditional term "energy center" of which there are seven located at different areas of the spine and that relate to the various glands in those areas. These "energy centers" or *chakras* ("wheels of light" in Sanskrit) are at their optimum health and power when they are perfectly aligned and "opened," so to speak.

This "opening" or activating the *chakra system* or "energy centers" can be accomplished in several, if not unlimited of ways. The discipline of yoga and deep meditative practices in Hinduism is a formal approach to the opening up of these *chakras.* Since this book is about *relationships*, and in particular the male/female *oneness relationship,* we will cover in detail the process of opening up the *chakras* (energy centers) through the practice of *tantric yoga* (or "marriage bed" yoga as I've chosen to call it).

Although I've been a student of yoga and in particular tantric yoga for a good part of my life, I will still utilize the helpful information from the book *Wheels of Light* by Rosalyn L. Bruyere. I'll finish up with some of my own experiences with awakening the *Kundalini.*

The First *chakra* or the base of the energy centers is called the *kundalini chakra*. It is what generates life. This chakra holds the very mystery of life as well as the drive for procreation. Maintaining physical life is its most basic function.

Men and women's first chakra is placed about two inches differently in the body. In men it is towards the surface of the body, whereas in woman it is internal for the most part. Ultimately what this means is there is a physiological difference in terms of how energy and information are processed through the pelvic region of each sex—where the base chakra or kundalini is located.

The movement symbology of the first chakra is "in and out." It has serpentine, undulating movements and if we breathe into those energies, moving with them and are conscious of them, then we are aware that we have a first chakra.

It is vital to remember that movement and energy cannot be separated. The movement of energy in the body and physical movement go hand in hand, so when we get into the area of the first chakra, the kundalini, we are always dealing with movement of some kind, usually the movement of vital energy or of life force itself.

Another name for this vital energy or life force is *prana* or *chi (lei)* energy. Breathing is the way of accessing prana. When we breathe, we should feel movement. Ideally, we should feel breath from the hips, expansion in our trunk, and breathing throughout the entire body, even in the feet. We should feel fully alive.

The experience of "the rising" or the awakening of the "sleeping snake" of the kundalini can make us feel so incredibly alive because more energy is tangibly available to us than we have previously had access to. Right after the kundalini opens, the second chakra opens and connects to the third eye, so that everything we feel, we see. This is a highly visual state. The right and left hemispheres of the brain come into synchronization, and at this point, we are highly programmable. Most importantly, when the kundalini opens, we have an activated awareness throughout the body. It is really all right to feel this alive, this aware, this good on a regular basis. That sensation is our life force moving through us, and it is very important, and it is very powerful.

The kundalini is the primary energy source for our spiritual vehicle. If kundalini energy is limited, that limitation will be reflected in every part of our consciousness, until ultimately the realization of our sense of touch, our sense of feeling is limited. The first chakra allows us to feel *ourselves* and to feel what we feel. This function is different from that of the second chakra, which is the seat of the emotional body and which allows us to sense what others are feeling. As a whole, our culture suffers from a condition of kundalini dysfunction; when the kundalini does not work in us, we do not feel who we are.

The next capacity that is limited is our ability to perceive others. The kundalini center's function is providing energy or sourcing. If it is not developed and therefore lacks power, all our interactions are limited. For instance, the ability to perceive the quality and dimension of another's feelings is dependent upon how much of ourselves we feel with; if our own feeling level is very low, we will always perceive another's energy to be at maximum level, when, in reality, it is not.

Third, a diminished kundalini limits our intellect. We can only hold as much information as we can hold energy. Without kundalini we have neither a long-term nor a short-term memory. A limited short-term memory means *nothing* is stored. Consequently, when the kundalini flow is diminished, trying to retrieve information from short-term memory is very difficult. The mind is a field, therefore, it is everywhere. It is a vast and complex data base composed of many smaller energies (bits) stored throughout the tissues of the body. It is the kundalini that allows a flow of energy to locate the information and bring that information up to the conscious level.

Diminished kundalini also affects the heart. It inhibits circulation and breathing. A limited kundalini restricts the warmth we feel toward others and the warmth and affection others feel toward us. In addition, it limits the awareness and expression of freedom in our lives. Without power, which originates in the kundalini, we have no sense of freedom, no awareness that it can be taken away and no ability to experience or express it in our day-to-day existence.

Next, a diminished kundalini inhibits the throat. No zip, no zing, no voice, no projection. The voice could be considered the kundalini for the spiritual center. The lower three centers, the physical, emotional, and mental bodies, are replicated in a way in the upper three centers, with the voice being the physical aspect of the spiritual world. In all creation myths, sound or the voice or the word calls the earth into being.

It is the kundalini that carries us from the three-dimensional world into the next dimension. Once we enter the spiritual world, the kundalini manifests first as sound (fifth chakra) and then as light (sixth chakra). If there is little kundalini, there is little imagery, little visualization, lack of creativity and inspiration, and no sense of the future.

Finally, and most importantly, the last thing inhibited by diminished kundalini is the ability to move beyond physical reality through sleep, trance, or other altered states. The crown chakra can be considered the gateway to the other world. When kundalini is diminished, the crown chakra does not have the power to open sufficiently to allow us "out" far enough to sleep peacefully. For those of us with sleep disturbance, the problem is often lack of power. Similarly, this lack of power can prevent us from reaching those states of consciousness wherein we reconnect to our spiritual source.

People exchange energy in many ways. Anytime there is an energy exchange of some kind, there is sexuality. Energy, by virtue of its electromagnetic nature, has a positive and negative flow. This back and forth movement or rhythm, this ebb and flow, registers in our bodies as sexual. As a result, our culture tends to interpret many types of interaction as sexuality. The primal life force, the energy of creation, blood, "fire," power, survival—all vibrate within the red frequency band. Because the frequency band is the kundalini, the body has an awareness of these interactions on a physical level. Furthermore, there is a sense of anticipation, a feeling of excitement, with every energy exchange, which further confuses the system, since these feelings are also associated with arousal. But when energy is moving, and we feel it moving, it is not an indication that sexuality is the next step. It is an indication that every part of us is alive.

To the degree that the first chakra is open, one will be tactually aware and feel alive. When the kundalini is flowing, one has a powerful physical presence and impact on others. Then it is often said that one has "charisma." Some people who carry this quantity and quality of energy are frequently misunderstood and considered to be overly sexual or too sensual by a society born of a puritanical consciousness. Life force is life force. In energy terms, there is little difference between the force of artistic creation and that of procreation, between the power needed to give life to a child and that needed to create a political system or even to give birth to a spiritual path.

The exchange of energy in lovemaking is an aspect of the first chakra, the true purpose of which has long been misunderstood. Orgasm is a trance-like state; the purpose of sexuality is the expansion and empowerment of one's partner through an exchange of energy. Often what is conscious in one partner lies hidden in the other. The partner's energy has the power to ignite in us those aspects of ourselves previously unexplored. The beauty and function of sexual intimacy is in encompassing the "opposite," in becoming more than we are alone. Sexuality allows every living being to know that there is "other" and that mergence with that other is possible; that all of us can attain, even briefly, One Mind.

The quality of one's sex life, of how well one merges, also depends upon how well one can communicate with one's partner. Communication needs to be verbal, nonverbal, and tactile. Ultimately quality again depends upon quantity: One must be able to move enough energy to put the partner into a trance, an altered and higher state of consciousness. If, for example, one stimulates the partner but does not put him or her into a trance, the result is not orgasm but an anxious state in which performance becomes impossible for either partner, male or female. Trance-like states are tidal; they ebb and flow, push and pull. Without a rhythm, communication, or abundant energy, there can be no altered state—no orgasm.

In the final analysis, one's ability to achieve orgasm is not dependent upon one's partner. Rather, the experience is limited by an individual's issues around sexuality. If sex is associated with violation or coercion, achievement of mergence with another will be next to impossible. If the experience of oneness is associated with a particular kind of sexual encounter, response might be inhibited simply because the "ideal" circumstances will never be repeated. Ultimately, the degree to which one is able to achieve sacred mergence with another is related to the limitations—physical, emotional, or mental—placed on that union. The quality and quantity of energy necessary for a complete and fulfilling sexual experience is essentially dependent upon one's views and experiences of sexuality.

The mergence or oneness of sexuality is intended to be a heightened awareness, not a deadening, a numbing, or a sleep state. Besides empowerment and mergence, the goal of sexuality is to enter and maintain a simultaneous state of deep relaxation and expanded consciousness. In our culture relaxation usually means sleep; people go to sleep rather than becoming more awake. A common experience after engaging in sex is to fall asleep. Contrary to some popular thought, when one is "exhausted," when one has little or no energy, sleep in not possible. For sleep to occur, there must be sufficient energy to allow the astral body to leave the physical body. In sexual intimacy, once the agitated energy is transformed through orgasm, the energy accessed is abundant enough to allow this to occur. This is fine for the physical body. However, we would grow more in power and consciousness if we "stayed in" the body, stayed present, as the energy expands and increases.

Orgasm is the sense of being a single organism, a signal cell. The ideal of sexual intimacy is to stay in that "single-celled" feeling, that heightened state of consciousness, for as long as possible. This expanded trance-like state lasts only as long as energy can be held and not released from the system. Sexual partners can assist each other in maintaining energy—and thus extend orgasm—by preventing the kundalini energy from leaving the other's system. This can be done by placing one's hands on the partner's back to direct the energy flow as well as by holding those areas where energy tends to "leak out". One can keep one's mate in the body—and thus maintain the energy in the region of the third eye—by putting one's hand on top of the other's head.

The emptiness one frequently feels after making love is indicative of an inability to stay in the expanded state long enough to produce neurotransmitter activity in the brain, of a failure to maintain that "single-celled" feeling. Once again, the quantity of energy one is capable of carrying determines the depth and quality of the sexual experience. If one's usual energy field is rather small, the extra energy accumulated during sexual activity will likely be too much for the system to process, resulting in a "loss of consciousness" as one is pushed out of the body. The minute the energy accumulated during sex puts one to sleep, the meaning of the experience, the feeling of oneness, of empowerment, the potential for growth and consciousness, has been lost. Once this happens, there is a constant need to merge again, a feeling of loss and separation as partners pull apart from each other.

Sexuality is part of the rest and regeneration cycle of those who live on this planet. Sexuality becomes particularly essential to those in service because by and large they will be spending most of their lives in the presence of negative energy fields—disease, depression, addiction. If people who serve do not stay "filled up," those negative fields will attach to them. When kundalini is not flowing and the field is depleted, a vacuum is created. Such a field will tend to attract other fields of greater or larger energy. If we are constantly around negative fields, those fields will impact us. When people are tired, when their energy feeder systems are closed, when they are out of their bodies, they are fair game for all the negativity around them. The obvious way to avoid such situations is to be open enough to keep the kundalini always flowing, the system always conscious.

Whether it is within the act of mergence in sexuality or by means of the rising kundalini of sacred initiation, the purpose of the first chakra and first-chakra energies is awareness: awareness not only of our own life force as it moves through us, but an awareness of our connection to the Force that creates and maintains life throughout the entire universe. As the chakra that allows us this awareness, the first center is the main chakra in which our karmic journey begins.

Kurt and I were able to experience this incredible "awakening of the kundalini" after we were taken through a few yoga postures and breathing exercises taught to us by Jodi. During this process, we were able to merge on all three levels of being—spiritual, mental and physical and obtain the *oneness* spoken about. It was (and still is) an incredible experience which I invite all to seek and obtain in your intimate relationships with your marriage partners.

But one word of caution—this type of energy and power isn't something you should experiment with outside the safety of a committed relationship. It is *that* delicate and *that* powerful, and if it's not directed under the guidance of Holy Spirit energy, it could destroy you.

It is my personal belief, that this is what caused the fall of mankind in the first place—when Eve listened to and then participated in a program designed by the *wrong serpent*. The *seraphim* or "angel of light" given for our guidance and direction is that Christ light which resides in each of us. This awakening of the Christ light—the flow of energy which is pure and holy which resides in all of us—is the *only way* we will we achieve the *oneness* with the Father which we *all* seek.

In the Gospel of St. John, he speaks of who Jesus Christ *really* is:

> Then spoke Jesus again unto them saying, *I am the light* of the world; he that followeth me shall not walk in darkness, but shall have the *light of life.* (St. John 8:12)
> In *him was life*; and the *life* was the *light* of men. (St. John 1:4)
> Jesus saith unto him, *I am the way, the truth, and the life: no man cometh unto the Father, but by me.* (St. John 14:6)

And then in the Book of Mormon we read:

And now my brethren, I have spoken plainly that ye cannot err. And as the Lord God liveth that brought Israel up out of the land of Egypt, and gave unto Moses power that he should hear the nations after they had been bitten by the poisonous serpents, if they would cast their eyes unto the *serpent* which he did raise up before them, and also gave him power that he should smite the rock and the water should come forth, yea, behold I say unto you, that as these things are true, and as the Lord God liveth, there is *none other name given under heaven save it be Jesus Christ*, of which I have spoken, whereby *man can be saved*. (2Nephi 25:20)

In my own mind and heart there is *no question* as to the identity of the *serpent* who possesses the *kundalini* power. *It is the power or light of Jesus Christ,* and it is within each and every one of us.

I stand as a witness of the joy that can be experienced when we contact and awaken the love of God within us and grow our own "tree of life." It is the most delicious fruit to the soul! The *chakra* system or the "energy-center" system is really the "tree of life" which resides in each and every one of us. For some of us, it lies dormant waiting for the "seed of faith" to be planted. In others, it's a fully awakened, thriving tree which awaits the fruit to be plucked from its branches and eaten. It's up to us to awaken this seed of faith to grow the tree of life within us by following the path of spirit and doing the necessary work. The following is an illustration in which all the symbols of the "tree of life" are integrated. I found this symbol on the front cover of the book, *The Middle Pillar* by Israel Regardie. What a beautiful metaphor for oneness! It also represents the balance between the outside pillars of the temple—our temple. Israel goes on to explain in his book:

Just as the Temple represents in miniature the whole of life by which we may ever be confronted, or, rather, the manifold parts of our own inner nature, so these two pillars symbolize some aspect of these phenomena. They represent light and darkness, heat and cold. In man, they stand for love and hate, joy and pain, mind and emotion, life and death, sleeping and waking. Every pair of opposites conceivable to the human mind find their representation in the implication of these two pillars...

It is unwise to swing to opposite poles of life's pendulum. Unbalanced power is the ebbing away of life. Unbalanced mercy is but weakness and the fading out of the will. Unbalanced severity is cruelty and the barrenness of mind. Either of these qualities when carried to an extreme, unmodified by the other, is conducive to an unhealthy state of psyche. Thus it is, that in so religiously authoritative a book as the Bhagavad-Gita, which some consider one of the finest pieces of devotional and philosophical literature yet penned, we find it stated "Be free from the pairs of opposites."

As noted in the above symbol, the middle pillar represents the chakra system (the body's energy system) and the two serpents represent the rising of the kundalini energy or the caduceus (physician's staff of health and well-being). This is how powerfully important it is to gain a "gnosis" or knowledge of the serpent-power (the Christ-power) within and to learn how to activate it for oneself. Or as Israel Regardie states on the back cover of his book, "Integration of the human personality is vital to the continuance of creative life. Without it, man lives as an outsider to his own true self."

Scriptural References: Genesis 3:1-7,14,15; Numbers 21:8,9; Isaiah 14:29; Matthew 10:16; St. John 1:4,5, 3:14,15, 8:12, 14:6; 2Corinthians 11:3,4; Revelations 5:1-5; 2Nephi 25:20; Alma 33:19-22; Helaman 8:13-16.

Walk Your Talk Therapies: Chapter Five

Therapy One: *Activating the Chakras (Energy Centers)*
Find a private, quiet space where you can create a sacred space. Sit in a comfortable lotus or half lotus position. Close your eyes and breathe in deeply through your nose, visualizing your breath flowing down into your base or first chakra. Now hold the breath there while contracting and releasing the muscles connected with the base chakra. Visualize the breath and muscle contractions awakening, energizing, and balancing this chakra area. Now

release the breath through the mouth as you relax. Next, breathe in deeply through your nose, visualizing your breath flowing down into your second chakra or sexual chakra. Again, hold the breath there while contracting and releasing the muscles connected with the second chakra. Visualize the breath and muscle contractions awakening, energizing and balancing this chakra area. Now release the breath through the mouth as you relax. Continue this process of breathing into each ascending chakra and contracting and releasing the muscles connected with that chakra area until you reach the crown. With the crown chakra, simply visualize white light coming in through the top of the head with the breath and radiating each color down through each of the chakras, awakening and energizing each one. Practice this sequence until you can complete the whole process in just two breaths.

Therapy Two: *Awakening the Kundalini through Tantric Practices*

With a partner (marriage partner preferably), create a sacred space that will ignite the romance in both of you. Make sure any children are tucked away in bed so that you won't be disturbed. Start by getting naked and sitting across from each other—face to face and holding hands.

Now, both of you close your eyes and start to visualize the "breath of spirit" breathing in and out of you as you begin to awaken each energy center. As you are able to feel the energy awakening, get close enough to each other that you are able to feel your partner's "breath of life," softly tickle your face. Now visualize the spiritual essence of your partner entering into your spiritual being by way of *breathing* in their *breath*.

Now concentrate on surrendering yourself to their breath and visualize yourself becoming "one in spirit" with them, as you *breathe in and out the breath of spirit*. This may take a few sessions of practice, but eventually you'll start to feel an immense *awakening* that you've never felt before. Don't be afraid of these exquisite feelings of love and passion—they are beautiful and Godly. The more intimate and open you are with your partner, the more you will feel this energizing flow, circling and spiraling up and down your chakra system opening up all of your chakras in an incredible expansive way.

You may even feel sensations of *spiritual orgasm* as every cell in your body is becoming one with your partner and one with the Universe. If this happens, don't forget to praise God and thank each other for the incredible experience you have shared.

Chapter Six
BALANCING MALE AND FEMALE

Before I get into how we can learn to balance the male/female relationship in order to understand what God is about, I'd like to begin with some quotes by one of my favorite authors on relationships, Leo Buscaglia, from his book, *Living, Loving and Learning*:

> An investment in life is an investment in change. When you are changing all the time, you've got to continue to keep adjusting to change, which means that you are going to be constantly facing new obstacles. That's the joy of living. And once you are involved in the process of becoming, there is no stopping. You're doomed! You're gone! But what a fantastic journey!

> I think the loving person must return to spontaneity—return to touching each other, to holding each other, to smiling at each other, to thinking of each other, to caring about each other… Hugs are good, they feel nice, and if you don't believe it, try it.

> We've got to learn to trust again, to believe again. Of course it's a risk, but everything is a risk. We need to begin to go beyond just "being" again. We've got to get in touch with being *human* and there's a difference.

A favorite saying when I was a child was, "A friend is a gift you give yourself." As an adult, I've morphed it to, "A lover is the *best* gift you can give yourself." Yet "to have a lover is to be one" just as "to have a friend is to be one," and so the best gifts we can give each other are our loving, beautiful selves. That means when we get into intimate relationships, the best thing we can bring into them is the best "I am" we can be. It may take a little effort clearing up the "garbage" we've been carrying around inside of us, but we all pack around some trash. Ideally, the more garbage we can clean up, the better is our gift to the person we love.

I tell people who are continually searching for their "soul-mate" or "true love" to *stop looking* for that soul-mate and *start being* that soul-mate. That means creating the most perfect, wholesome *you* possible. Then the law of attraction will automatically magnetize the perfect, wholesome person *to you*.

So, imagine you get into a marriage relationship with someone who isn't your *soul-mate* (which I'd say about 99.9% of the population are). Then things start getting a bit tough as issues come to the surface for you to recognize the garbage that's been hidden inside you. Are you going to "bail-out" because you can't deal with the issues that are crying out to be resolved? Or are you going to "dig-in" and uncover the trash so that you can "clear it up" once and for all?

Did you know that in reality there's no such thing as divorce? Just read Matt 19:3-9 if you don't believe me.

> What therefore God hath joined together, let not man put asunder.

Also in the Gospel of Thomas in the Nag Hammadi scrolls we read:

> Jesus saw some babies nursing. He said to his disciples, "These nursing babies are like those who enter the Kingdom."
> They said to him, "Then shall we enter the Kingdom as babies?"
> Jesus said to them, "When you make the two into one, and when you make the inner like the outer and the outer like the inner, and the upper like the lower, and when you make male and female into a single one, so that the male will not be male nor the female be female , when you make eyes in place of an eye, a hand in place of a hand, a foot in place of a foot, an image in place of an image, then you will enter (the Kingdom.)"

Yet, somehow we've created the illusion that because we hire a lawyer to whom we pay lots of money that we'll get a "bill of divorcement" and then we'll be separated from each other *forever!* What a bunch of B.S! So we continue under the illusion that because we get divorced that we no longer have a "relationship" with a person with whom we had been married to.

Most people who've ever been through a divorce can tell you that that's absolute B.S. You still have to maintain a "relationship" with your "ex" even though you don't want to, so you can finish out the "contracts" you made with them. Whether they are implied or otherwise, the "marriage contracts" we form with each other are *very real* and *very binding*. They can't be broken just because we have a piece of paper saying that it's over. *All* relationships are *eternal,* and the important thing is to move through the conflict that is polarizing us and into resolution…and *love.*

This *doesn't mean* we need to get back to sexual intimacy with our "exes." Separation is often a way of healing physical addictions or co-dependency behaviors we've fallen into. But this *does mean* we need to resolve the anger and the bitterness of "fall-out" caused by emotional separation or polarities that inhibit us from pure, unconditional love and unity.

If we don't get beyond the "polarization" we feel towards each other, we'll recycle it in the next relationship—intimate or otherwise. And "divorce" isn't just a term we use as an illusion of separation between two married persons. I've heard of children divorcing their parents and parents divorcing their children. In fact, I know of one person, very dear to me, who's "divorcing" her whole family—brothers, sisters, Mom, Dad and everyone, because her therapist told her that this was the best way for her to heal. That she should "avoid anyone who would trigger her emotions and cause her to recycle them." "What a "great" therapist," I thought. He (or she) should consult their own shrink!

Our relationships *are* the best way to heal and the more loving and intimate they are the quicker and more effectively we can heal. So let's not run away from those relationships in life that will teach us the most about ourselves. Let's embrace them! But let's try to make them as healthy as possible. Yes, there are times we must move away from abusive relationships to give them a chance to heal, but ultimately our desire is to come into a wholesome or holistic relationship with *everyone!*

When I was into the first cycle of marriage (relationships go through cycles), I met a wonderful man who taught me a lot about relationships. His name was John Lund, and he wrote a book entitled *Avoiding Emotional Divorce* in which he states:

> Of what value is a gift if a person chooses not to receive the gift? The answer: "It is of little value." An important part of any relationship is the ability of each partner to receive what the other has to give. A synonym for "receive" is "accept." Acceptance is the most basic human emotional need. After the basic physical needs of air, food, water, clothing, shelter, and physical security, comes the emotional need for acceptance.

When you care for someone deeply and sincerely, there springs forth a desire to give of yourself. Sometimes that desire is so strong and compelling that it manifests itself in a shower of affection. Poems are written, flowers are purchased, songs are composed to express the feelings of love. What frustration then exists when the loved one has eyes, but chooses not to see; has ears, but chooses not to hear? The object of the love does not receive the gifts of self offered by the loving one.

The art of receiving is the art of being gracious. The ability to receive is the ability to be appreciative.

Some have mistakenly thought they must return like for like. This is seldom the case. Most great artists or poets do not demand equal performance, just equal commitment. One such talented person explained to his wife: "If I write a deeply moving poem that expresses the song of my soul, I do not expect you to reciprocate. I only ask that you read it or listen to me intently as I read it. It is my offering of love."

When we are *not* fully awake and fully alive in our relationships, we *not only cheat* the other person—we *cheat ourselves* from the gifts of love that are offered. When our minds are on someone else or something else while our partner is expressing heart-felt love towards us—whether our mind is on the children, the woman next door, or the garbage that desperately needs taking out—then we are engaged in a form of "fornication" (mental separation).

We must learn to be completely alive and present in each moment—especially in those we spend with our loved ones—and particularly when making love to our spouses.

I enjoy the truth that sometimes comes out in popular songs. This one was a hit when I was a teenager and helps illustrate my point:

> If you can't be with the one you love,
> Love the one you're with.

If we could comprehend even in a minuscule way the capacity of God to love us, we could understand the expansiveness we have within ourselves to love others. As children of God and seeds of His love, it's our heritage to be able to love others completely, fully, and with no conditions or restraints. When we are in this pure, unconditional love, we begin to touch God. When we learn to be in this rapture of pure love during every moment of our lives, we cut a pathway to the eternal, Celestial realms. Love is the only reality because God is the only reality. "For God is love." (John 3:8)

There are several excellent books out about life cycles and, in particular, marriage cycles. (Have you seen the movie, "The Seven Year Itch" with Marilyn Monroe or read *Passages: Predictable Crises of Adult Life* by Gail Sheehy?) I've come up with a cycle chart of my own I'll share as I believe it's relevant to the discussion about how to balance the male/female relationship.

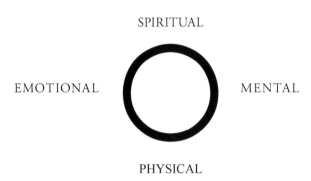

When you first begin any relationship, it always starts in the spiritual realm as perhaps you've contracted with the other person to be a "helpmate" during this life. Then you meet up with them in this earth plane at the same time and space as you are and you *connect.* Your first connection (or "spirit-linking") is that first eye contact when one or both of you might think, "I've seen this person before, but not on this planet."

Or it could be that you first connect through verbal contact. "There's something about that person's voice that connects with my soul," you might say to yourself when you hear them sing or speak. You then attempt to connect with them mentally by talking with them, perhaps listening to them describe their vision of how the world works and their part in the eternal scheme of things.

Then you ask yourself, "Do I have a part to play with this person?" or, in other words, "Have we spiritually contracted to do a work together?"

Then you realize, "Yes, I do have a work to do with this person—so what is it?" But this is where most of us make a terrible mistake. We often jump right into the physical part of the relationship before it's time—before we've had a chance to figure out all the dynamics of what our spiritual agreements are. It's important, however, to discover the *exact* nature of our intended *work,* which may be to simply "mirror" some of our "blind-spots" to each other.

Often when we move too quickly into physical intimacy (signing the contract, so to speak), we don't realize what we've gotten ourselves into, and then we go looking for a fast way out or "divorce" (the illusion of separation).

My recommended way to "avoid emotional divorce" is to *not* get into sexual intimacy before the cycle of "spiritual oneness" has been completed. But before I get into how we do that without getting "stuck" in the physical aspects of the relationship, I must tell you a story concerning my Shaman friend, Patrick (Speaking Wind).

Have you ever had a *spiritual* argument with someone? These can become very interesting especially when you have a lot of other things to do like taking care of a house full of children.

Well, one day Patrick and I got into an interesting (spiritual) argument about the efficacy of "one night stands." Patrick argued that spontaneous hook-ups can be very beneficial and healing as long as both parties understand and agree that their sexual relationship is nothing more than temporary. I countered that *all relationships are eternal,* and it's not the coming together that causes problems but the act of separation. (Separation always causes "fall-out" and "fall-out" always leads to disintegration of the oneness.)

I also told him that in the female mind (the holistic mind), the *wisdom* of having a "one night stand" is an absolute illusion or absurdity. A woman gives herself completely in the act of love-making when she gives herself to a man. That is why women are usually more capable of committing to long-term relationships than men are because in her *wisdom mind,* she commits herself to the marriage act and signs a contract to be with that person *forever!* That's also why women, more often than not, suffer more than men from "fall-out" as the feelings of separation are more "real" to them.

Whereas the male mind (the dualistic mind) attempts to *understand* or "rationalize" that one night stands can be very exciting and healing (for a moment). It tries to ignore the illusion that *"there is no pain in separation."* Have you ever known anyone who *hasn't* suffered some sort of "fall-out" pain when going through a separation or divorce? I certainly haven't!

So to "avoid emotional divorce" or divorce of *any* kind, it's best *not* to get into an intimate physical relationship until you are a "whole person" yourself. This also prevents co-dependency and/or physically addictive behaviors.

So, let's get back to our cycle and see how we can avoid getting "stuck" in the downward swing without enough momentum to get us back up to the top—which is actually the spiritual and physical oneness combined. Because often when we have physical relationships when we're not completely conscious or aware, we can get caught up in a co-dependent physical relationship requiring some healing.

Yet everyone likes to feel physically close to someone, especially when you're "in love." But there are a thousand and one ways to be physically close to someone without having to experience sexual intercourse. In fact, I've found it to be more pleasurable and rewarding (and often exciting) to enjoy another's physical closeness by just cuddling or by giving each other a "full body massage." And, of course, the ecstasy of spiritual lovemaking *far* surpasses that of physical lovemaking which is precisely the level that *all* relationships desire to achieve—*spiritual/physical connection or oneness.*

So how do we get to that level of oneness and connection if we're "stuck" at the bottom of the cycle in the "physical position?" There are many ways of balancing the polarity we get trapped in, and one is through "emotional communication."

"Com-uni-cation" (the process of coming into unity) is a fascinating subject, and there are many books on this subject alone. One of my favorite authors on communication and community building is M. Scott Peck. The following is a quote from his book, *The Different Drum: Community Making and Peace.* He describes communication as the form in which we get to community.

> The overall purpose of human communication is—or should be—reconciliation. It should ultimately serve to lower or remove the walls and barriers of misunderstanding that unduly separate us human beings from another. The word "ultimately" is important. Confrontive, even angry communication is sometimes necessary to bring into focus the clear reality of those barriers before they can be knocked down. In the process of community-building, for instance, individual differences must first be allowed to surface and fought over so that the group can ultimately learn to accept, celebrate, and thereby transcend them.

Open, and oftentimes, emotional (energy in motion) communication is vitally important in order for resolving the differences between the male and female mind. It's interesting to observe how the male and the female parts of the brain function and how scientists are just beginning to learn that some of us (mostly women) are learning to use their *whole brains* to communicate.

"Gray Matters" was an article in the March 27, 1995 *Newsweek* that discussed scientific technologies like functional magnetic resonance imaging (FMRI) and positron emission tomography (PET) that can photograph brains in the very act of cogitating, feeling or remembering. Researchers reported that men and women use different parts of their brain when thinking. Ideally, when both sides of their brain are functioning and integrated, they begin to have "whole-brain thinking" which is much more expansive and effective. It shows that because women are now engaging in the "male world" they are developing "whole-brain thinking" quicker than men are. Perhaps it's time for men to get into the "female world."

So let's take a look at just how each side of the brain works—the male and female sides—or the left and right hemispheres of the brain.

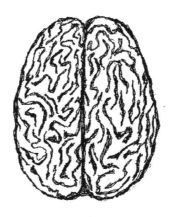

Brain Hemisphere Functions

For those not familiar with the functions of the left and right hemispheres of the brain, the following will help. The lists, however, do not include all brain functions. To keep them as simple as possible, the functions listed are those most important to our discussion.

Left Brain (CONSCIOUS)	*Right Brain* (SUBCONSCIOUS)
THINKER	CREATIVE
LOGICAL	FEELING
ANALYTICAL	INTUITIVE
PRACTICAL	ARTISTIC
MOVER	NURTURER
SEQUENTIAL	EMOTIONAL
DUALITY	UNITY
WORDS	IMAGES
WILL	POWER
MATERIAL	SPIRITUAL
CELEBRATION	REVERENCE
EXPRESS	SILENT

Remember, when we *think* something and we *feel* the same thing, we're functioning from our whole brain. We're no longer at war inside (at least as far as that one thought/feeling is concerned.) We no longer experience inner turmoil. We're no longer double-minded. We're single-minded in that area and on that particular issue. The internal conflict is over and life responds by offering us peace of mind.

So once we've become single-minded and balanced within ourselves, how do we start communicating with one another in the male/female relationship to reach and maintain a complete balance of *integrity?* It begins by simply *communicating using the same part of the brain!*

Communication breakdown usually occurs when one partner is using one side of their brain to communicate with while the other partner is using the opposite side. Let me give you an example:

Once Kurt and I were discussing the efficacy of killing mice in mousetraps. It had become a real *emotional issue* for me as that morning I had discovered a mouse that had been trapped in a mousetrap overnight but was still alive and suffering. What compounded the problem was that my son, Jared, discovered (after putting it out of its misery) that it was a nursing mother mouse, and that somewhere in the house was a brood of baby mice squealing for their mother. As a nursing mother, I can only say, that my heart was in anguish at the feelings of suffering I'd helped to inflict on the mouse kingdom through my passive complicity. I hadn't set the traps myself, but I was aware of them being set and didn't object at the time.

The issue of "killing mice" had surfaced in our relationship, and when we discussed it, I had been in the *female* (emotional) mind. Unfortunately, when we discuss issues in an "imbalanced" state of mind, it usually throws the other partner into the opposite part of their brain so they can somehow bring things back into balance. So Kurt had countered from a defensive *male mind* position with, "Well, what do you want us to do then? Just let the mice overrun the entire house with their friends and offspring? Or maybe you'd prefer to raise mice and sell them to the pet stores for a profit."

Past experience teaches that this type of conversation, if allowed to continue back and forth between the male and female minds, gets you nowhere but *polarized!* I immediately tried to shift back into the balanced mind—the Christ-mind—by replying, "Okay, I *understand* we have a problem with the mice overrunning the house, but I don't *feel* that killing them is the solution to our problem. Perhaps we could figure out another way to resolve this issue that works for both of us."

This helped put us both into a balanced mind so we could discuss the matter *rationally,* yet *sensitively,* and come up with a balanced solution. We decided to let Christy borrow our neighbor's cat for the week we'd be gone to

Aspen so it could chase off the mice. It was a "natural" solution since neither of us wanted to own a cat. (I've heard that just the smell of a cat in the house keeps mice away.)

I hope this simple example illustrates how important it is to get into the "balanced" mind to discuss and resolve issues—especially in marriage. As I mentioned earlier, relationships bring our issues to the surface so we can mirror (reflect) them to each other and realize (real eyes) what they're supposed to teach us.

Often, however, we feel it's our duty to mirror issues when the other person is unwilling or not prepared to discuss them. That's like reflecting sunlight into someone's face with a mirror. We've all heard of "constructive criticism," but there's no such thing! It's always perceived as "sunlight in the mirror," and we should think about it next time we're tempted to criticize. The Lord will bring issues to the surface in a natural way when it's time for them to be resolved. Remember this little saying about reflection: *Internal* reflection is a lot more pleasant and effective than *external* reflection.

So let's say you're having a problem with one or both of you reaching a state of balanced mind? Usually (but not always) there's one person in a relationship who's able to transfer into that part of the mind from which the other person is communicating, allowing them to discuss issues without creating polarities. And I'm *afraid* (it's not a great word, but I'll use it anyway) that if we are ever to find balance in our society, it might be up to the women of the world to cross over into the male mind…the logical mind…to help our husbands move into the female mind…the emotional mind.

As I mentioned earlier, the article in *Newsweek* detailed how women are already beginning to use their "whole brains" and achieve a balanced mind. Now it's up to women to teach men how to do it. But, women, you don't have to *act* like a man or take on a man's nature to get into the male mind and gain balance (whole brain-ness). That's a "mis-conception" (missed concept) many women have accepted as they try to compete with males in the workplace. Some tend to overcompensate in their attempt to "rebalance" the male/female polarization. But it's not necessary to discount the value and power of a woman's femininity. Women simply need to use *logic* (understanding) with men until they can experience the *sensitive* (wisdom) female side of their brains.

I loved what Kenny and Laura Loggins had to say in their presentation at the 1995 Windstar Symposium about "balancing their male and female relationship." Laura (who was pregnant and absolutely radiant at the time) expressed that a woman doesn't need to be or act like a man in order for her to be "empowered." Her empowerment comes from her own blossoming and becoming that full flower of feminine womanhood that she was meant to be. And when the fully blossomed lotus flower joins with the fully awakened Kundalini power (serpent power), there is synergistic empowerment! Isn't it exciting that there are couples who are actually becoming awakened and enlightened to the principles of balancing the male/female relationship?

It's ideal if, when we do come together in marriage intimacy, we bring our "completed circle" or our fully healed and awakened self. When we come together without wholeness in ourselves, we usually get stuck in the physical "down-side" of relationship. That's when most of our phobias and fixations come to the surface. And more often than not, those inhibitions polarize the relationship and keep it from reaching a oneness of spirit and body.

Suppose you're in a relationship that's "stuck" in the downward side of the physical. Do you just give up and walk away because your partner *isn't getting it*? Does a mother give up on a child just because he doesn't *get* potty training after the first attempt? Or the second, or the third? It took one of my sons until he was three and a half to finally catch on to using the toilet.

We sometimes want to withdraw ourselves from our partners just because we feel that *they're never going to get it!* But as Matthew Fox suggested in his presentation entitled, "Dreams, Visions and Choices for a Viable Future," we must "stay close to the unweaned." This means that there are some of us that still need "breast-feeding." (And how many in our generation got the literal opportunity to do that to our hearts content? Very few, I would say.) It's important that we nurture each other with oodles of love and affection to fill up our "loving cups" that may have run empty or was never filled when we were young or into adulthood. I've heard it said, "You can't teach anything to someone who is starving."

The same is true in relationships. You can't cure a physical addiction to sex by going on a 6-month abstinence fast. (Believe me, I've tried and it doesn't work.) We must learn to fill each other's "loving cups" until they're overflowing with other types of love besides sex so that the person is satisfied and ready to move onto something more enlightening.

It's important to be the best "help-mates" we can be without getting into playing too many games. Games are OK for kids, and some games are still fun for adults. (Frankly, I love playing many of those old childhood games like Old Maid, hide-and-seek, spin-the-bottle, kick the can, Scrabble, etc.) But the games we may want to get-out-of playing are the ones we play that cause polarization and damage to our relationship.

Some of the games I've encountered in my personal relationships that I've chosen to stop playing are:

1) The "one-up" game is when we try to put ourselves into positions of power and control over another person. Another similar game is the "get-

even" game where one person gets hurt and feels justified in striking back at the other person. This can turn into a real down-ward cycle of retaliation. Forgiveness is key here.

2) The "I'm-going-to-take-my-blocks-and-go-home" game happens when things aren't going as well as we'd hoped, so we pack up and take off. It's not very helpful for resolving relationship issues. But if the relationship becomes too dangerous either physically or emotionally, we may need some time-out and outside intervention to help put things back on track.

3) The "stroking" game operates on the principle of "if you rub my back, I'll rub yours." Granted, there should be a give-and-take in any relationship, but whenever we get into expectation in a relationship, we're outside of pure love (God's love) which is unconditional love no matter how imbalanced we feel the relationship is on the "give-and- take" scale. We need to give our 100% to make a relationship work because if our partner isn't giving at least 50%, we need to make up the difference. But a powerful relationship is one where both parties give 100% making it a 200% relationship. *Now that's empowerment!*

4) The "P.L.O.M." game means "poor little old me" and is a power play that uses the opposite strategy from the "one-up" game. This is where we become "martyrs," so to speak, and perhaps a "door-mat" for a partner to walk on in an attempt to make the relationship work. When we find ourselves in this situation we need to pick ourselves up and dust ourselves off and start becoming "help-mates" and not "door-mats."

5) The "protect you from yourself" game is when we hide our true feelings by covering them up with "little white lies." But there is no such thing as a "white lie." Lies are lies, and they all lead to dishonesty in a relationship and ultimate disintegration. If a relationship *isn't* based on *total honesty and commitment* (unity based on correct principle), it has diminished integrity. Be *completely* honest with each other even when it hurts. But don't get into the "blame game" that makes your partner's habits the source of your unhappiness. *We are responsible for our own happiness.* Trying to get someone else to change so that *we* can become happy is a "dead end road." It *never* works, so don't even try it!

6) The F.U.S.U. game or "fuck up, suck-up" game is played when we neglect to "show-up" for each other and then resort to "sucking up." It's human to make mistakes and neglect another person's needs, but when it becomes a pattern or habit, it becomes destructive. There is some truth to

the romantic phrase, "Love means never having to say you're sorry" but when you're constantly apologizing for your mistakes (missed opportunities to love)—then "love is not spoken here."

7) The last game is kind of fun to play and can be either beneficial or destructive to a relationship. It's called the "bait-and-hook" game, and it can often get us what we want by promising a reward at the end of the game once we resolved the issues. Another variation on this game is the "kiss-and-make-up" game where we can come together in love *after* we've resolved the issues that are polarizing us.

I read a beautiful story in a book called "Kabalah," by Z'ev ben Halevi which illustrates some of the benefits of the "bait-and-hook" game.

A certain young man once saw the figure of a veiled girl at the window of a palace. At first only curious, he went each day to catch a glimpse of her. After a while, she would look in his direction as if expecting him. Slowly he became involved in what appeared to be a relationship if only at a distance. In the course of time the girl lowered her veil to reveal something of her face. This so increased his interest that he spent many hours at the palace hoping to see the fullness of her beauty. Gradually he fell deeply in love with her and spent most of his day at her window. Over time she became more open with him and they conversed, she telling of the secrets of the palace and the nature of her father the King. Eventually he could bear it no longer and wished only to be joined with her in marriage so that he might experience all she spoke of. The man in this allegory is the soul, the princess the spirit, the palace existence, and the King—the King of Kings.

The gospel of Jesus Christ is the most beautiful, precious gift we've been given. It is like a bouquet of flowers that we send to a loved one to say, "I love you. Have a nice day." The gospel or "good news" too often is used as a two-edge sword to divide and separate us from each other. Instead of the path of the warrior, let's find the path of the flower that shattered the stone—the soft, feminine path which shatters the illusions which keep our hearts as stone.

And one final note about soul-mates…every element and cell of our physical and spiritual beings cries out for the re-union (returning to oneness) with our soul-mates. It's innate in each of us to want to join with our soul-mate in intimate union to again become one and find out who we really are. This perhaps is our final link with our God/self because only through our soul-mates can we again reconnect ourselves with the God within—to complete our own circle of oneness and integrity. This is the beauty of the soul-mate reunion. The greatest work we have contracted to do in life is perhaps to be done with the help of our soul-mates.

The only problem I've noticed with most soul-mate reunions is that they come together in a physical relationship before it's time. That's what happened with David and Bathsheba, Gwenevere and Lancelot, Romeo and Juliet. They came into their "covenant relationship" before it was time (God's time) to do so. If soul-mates come together before their individual circle is complete, it can cause insurmountable polarities and consequent "fall-out," sometimes for the entire human race as in David and Bathsheba. This "soul-mate connection" is *that vital*, and it can be *that detrimental* to the scheme of things when soul-mates come together before God's timetable. We need to be patient and willing to wait for God to bring us together when we are ready and have completed our own "sacred circle."

Otherwise we become like magnets stuck in that polarized position which magnets get into just before they connect to form that strong magnetic bond of oneness. (If you've ever played with magnets you know what I mean.) God teaches us in each of our relationships about unconditional love—*His love*—which is that glue, that magnetism, that binds us together. Until we've learned what this type of unconditional love is, we have no business looking outside ourselves for our soul-mates. God will bring us together in His own due time and place. You can count on it!

So in the meantime, why not strive in our relationships with ourselves and one another to find that unconditional love and unity which is so nourishing and vital. This is what keeps us young and vibrant until that day we become the soul-mate someone else is waiting for. It's then that the connection of oneness will flourish until the end of time and become a Celestial relationship.

The following are the lyrics to a beautiful song that was sung by an extraordinary man, at a magical place in the heart of the Rocky Mountains. He shared it with us at the 1995 Windstar Symposium in Aspen, Colorado. It describes the commitment of Spirit to the soul-mate reunion.

The Wandering Soul

In this magic hour of softening light
The moments in between the day and the night
The instant when all shadows disappear
The distance in between the love and the fear
There's a longing deep within a wandering soul
It's like the half that understands it once was whole
Like the two who only dream of being one

Like the moon whose only light is in the sun
There's a danger in forever looking outside
You start to believe that all your prayers have been denied
And you'll forget the sound of your own name
Thus begins the suffering and the pain

I wanted an answer, I wanted a way
I want to know just what to do and what to say
I wanted a reason, I want to know why
Can there never be heaven right here on earth and peace inside
Inside my heart, deep in my soul
Within each part, and in the whole

There's a promise in the journeys of the mind
You begin to believe that there are miracles you will find
And that someday you'll remember who you are
The seed within a bright and shining star
It's like the flame that lives within a hungering heart
That only awaits the gift of love for it to spark
Into a fire that burns forever, endlessly
Like the river that can't help but meet the sea
In this magic hour between the dark and the dawn
In this space between the silence and the song
Suddenly the mystery is clear
That love is only letting go of fear

Love is the answer, love is the way
Love is in knowing just what to do and what to say
Love is the reason, and love is the why
And love is in heaven right here on earth and peace inside
Inside your heart, deep in your soul
Within each part, and in the whole
Love is the answer, love is the way
Love is in knowing just what to do and what to say
Love is the reason, love is the why
And love is in heaven right here on earth and peace inside

(John Denver)

Scriptural References: Genesis 2:24; Matthew 19:3-9; Mark 10:3-9;

1 Corinthians 6:15-17, 7:10-17; Ephesians 5:22-33; D&C 49:15-17; Moses 3:23, 24; Abraham 5:17, 18.

Walk Your Talk Therapies: Chapter Six

Therapy One: *Learning to Communicate Love*

In *Avoiding Emotional Divorce,* John Lund describes the three ways couples learn to communicate *love*. He calls them the "Three Ts"—Touch, Talk, and Task. Although some individuals and couples may show a predisposition towards one or two, it's important to develop all three to be effective and balanced communicators of love. Let's look at each to understand how we can more effectively communicate them.

Touch Therapy

Often when we're sharing love with our partners, we don't effectively communicate that love because the other partner isn't open to receiving it. One way of opening your partner up to love is to give each other a *full body massage* without any anticipation of sex. It's an incredibly intimate way to practice sharing and receiving love through sensual touch.

You can start by making the massage as romantic and as sensually stimulating as possible by adding candles, romantic music, and fragrant aromatherapy oils. Focus on communicating to each other what *feels good* and what *doesn't* so you can respond to each others deepest desires in the *touch* area of communication.

If you'd like to release trapped negative energy in each other, "pressure point therapy" works well. Here's how to do it. If you come across an area of the body that's painful or sensitive, work the area deeply until you get a release of pain. *Pressure point therapy* releases energy blockages that keep the *kundalini* from circulating completely up through your "energy centers" or *chakras*.

There are also "secondary chakras" found throughout the entire body, especially in the hands, feet, and ears. You may wish to study books on hand and foot *reflexology* to better understand how the various pressure points affect different areas of the body. There's nothing quite like a good foot massage and reflexology treatment to keep all the systems working and the channels open.

Talk Therapy

This may be the most impacted area because we haven't learned to effectively communicate in the *balanced brain* or "Christ-centered brain." When we communicate in the *male side of the brain* we tend to be aggressive or forceful. When we communicate in the *female side of the brain,* we tend to be passive or defensive. Unless we are utilizing both sides of the brain, we remain ineffective communicators of love.

For example, a husband may come home from work, tired and exhausted, needing some extra nurturing. So he grabs his wife who's busy making dinner in the kitchen, draws her close and whispers, "Did you miss me today, dear?"

The wife, holding a sharp knife in one hand and an onion in the other, cries out, "*Did I miss you*? Of course! What kind of question is that? Here finish up the dinner while I nurse the baby whose been screaming for the past hour!"

But what a beautiful transformation she could make if she could pause for a moment and reply in her *balanced mind,* "Yes, dear *I did miss you*, and maybe tonight after dinner and after the children have been all tucked in bed, I can show you just how *much I missed you.*"

Learning the language of love is a difficult skill to acquire. Here are a few exercises for working both sides of the brain so you can effectively communicate in the balanced area of the brain:

Cross-crawl therapy: One reason we don't communicate with the whole brain or balanced brain is because it hasn't been developed on both sides. This could be due to lack of stimulation during infancy and childhood when we weren't given enough opportunity to crawl, take dance classes, or participate in sports which exercise both sides of the brain. And oddly, this happens more often in males than in females…perhaps because boys were apprehensive about taking dance classes.

However, there are still ways as an adult can re-stimulate those neurons that were underdeveloped in childhood. One is called the *cross-crawl* method. It doesn't mean crawling on the ground like a baby (although some therapies include that especially with autistic children). Simply march around the house lifting the opposite arm than leg for 5 minutes or so; then 5 minutes of lifting the same side arm as leg; and then another 5 minutes of lifting the opposite arm than leg. That's it—for 15 minutes a day, you can stimulate neurons in the brain that were underdeveloped in childhood and left you one-sided or "half-brained."

Another *whole-brain therapy* is to learn to write with both hands (not at the same time, of course). If you're right-handed, learn to write with the left. You can learn to play hand-ball or other ambidextrous sports which use both sides of your body and involve both sides of your brain. Or you can learn to French-braid hair or to play a musical instrument. I believe most musicians and artists are more effective at communicating love in a balanced way because they have developed their *whole brain* through the use of both hands.

Any exercise, sport, or hobby that teaches you to utilize both sides of the body will also teach you to use both sides of the brain and help you to learn to communicate in the balanced brain.

Task Therapy

This can be the most creative way of communicating—and the most fun.

Doesn't everyone enjoy a bit of romance? Well, why not have some every day?! It could be as simple as placing a small note saying "I love you," inside the pocket of your husband's shirt or lunch pail as he goes off to work; to as spontaneous as "fixing dinner with only an apron on." (Isn't there a song about that?) Since life is full of unexpected surprises, why not try to create the most enjoyable, romantic ones possible?

Kurt has kept the fire of romance kindled by spontaneously bringing home flowers just to say, "I love you, and I was thinking about you today, dear." He never neglects to give me a thoughtful card for each special occasion—birthdays, Mother's Days, anniversaries, etc.—he has *never* missed a single one.

And there are the special times when we leave the kids with a baby sitter and "go out on a date" just to *celebrate life* and especially our *life together*.

But the *real task* part of the relationship consists of the "honey-dos" we do without being asked. Taking care of children; fixing things when they break; arm-in-arm escorts to the movie or out to dinner; always looking and acting your best; are some of the little things in life that really add up in the long run.

If you compare your relationship and the ways you communicate love to each other to a cake, it would stack up like this. The body of the cake would be the *task* part of your relationship or make up the main part of the cake. This is where you spend the most time and effort communicating *love*.

The *talk* part of your relationship is the icing on the cake...the sweet part where expressions like "I love you," and "I enjoy our relationship, sweetheart," come in and can be spread on as thickly or as thinly as desired.

The last aspect of the relationship is the *touch* part...the fun little sprinkles or messages on top that make it fun and exciting—and extra special. And those can be applied according to taste. But remember, these aren't an essential ingredient. It's the *task* and *talk* parts where we should focus most of our energy and effort. The sprinkles are simply decorations for added enjoyment.

As you can see, building and maintaining a loving, eternal relationship can be fun *and* challenging, but the more we invest *all of our hearts, minds and souls*, the more we receive in return.

It's also important to remember that all relationships are different, and you can't compare *your* relationship with anyone else's. There are apples, oranges, and bananas and they're going to look different, feel different and taste different. Just *relish* the enjoyment of partaking of the "fruit of the tree of life" each relationship offers, and then *eat it up*, savoring every bite. You worked hard at growing the tree that produced the fruit—so you deserve to enjoy it!

Chapter Seven

The River of Religion

Our belief systems or "religions" are interesting things. They are, in a sense, what make us who we are. It's been said that "what we believe is what we become." In other words—*our beliefs become our reality!* If this is a true statement, then isn't it about time we examine what we "believe" (be live) so that we can "realize" (real eyes) who we are and who we are becoming?

Growing up Mormon or LDS (Latter-day Saint) I was marinated in a whole menagerie of beliefs. From: "If you don't pray over your food (out loud) it is inedible. (Try that on a first date and see where it gets you.) To: listen to your Priesthood head (mine being my husband) and everything will turn out okay. (So what if your husband wants to try-on polygyny?) Or being a Bible-basher I held onto the Pauline Gospels for a long time. The ones that say "Women should be silent in Church" or that "It's best for a man not to touch a woman." (Do we have cooties or something?) Or that a woman shouldn't leave her husband for *any* reason—that it's better to put up with the physical, mental or spiritual abuse rather than to get a divorce. I'm sure St. Paul never had to deal with any of these issues himself being a celibate male. Thank God he didn't turn any of those beliefs onto his children—except for the billion or so God-fearing Christians!

And so after examining many if not all of my beliefs which held me hostage (the latest being that if I suspend my joy and bliss for another person until they "get it" that we might share in that joy and bliss together) I found that I'd been totally tyrannized by my *own self.* That I had the power to oppress myself by adhering to beliefs which keep me hostage in a system of my own tyranny. There was marriage tyranny (someone else is responsible for my joy), occupational tyranny (I can't practice my chosen occupation of Tantric therapy in Utah unless I want to get arrested), friendship tyranny (I have to be nice to people in order for them to like me), spiritual tyranny (If I'm a good girl, God will reward me), personal tyranny (If I act out or do something deviant—like walk around naked in my own home and yard—that everyone will see me as nuts), mental tyranny (It takes a lot of time and effort to be successful; and if anything's going to get done I have to do it myself). I have spent a lifetime of tyrannizing and terrorizing myself by my own system of beliefs! "So when does this all stop?" I asked myself. "RIGHT NOW!!" I screamed back.

So as I've examined my own religious roots (Mormonism), many beliefs have come to my attention that I've had to re-examine as an adult. I've knowingly and unknowingly been a victim of "religiosity" (great movie, by the way) because I've been programmed from infancy in certain doctrines which contain both truths and untruths. I call these programs "isms" for lack of a better term, because they cause "schisms" (divisions or separations) that keeps us apart. These polarizing "schisms" are the ego's way of diverting the stream of truth from its perfect course—oneness with God and each other. Humans *love* to divert or change streams. We build canals, dams (damns), add chemicals to it, pollute it with corrupt ideas, and basically annihilate most of the value that "pure stream of truth" was meant to provide.

If you study any belief system and trace it back to its purest source, you'll find its seeds of truth. This truth is what resonates in us when the Holy Spirit witnesses this truth to us. Religion is like a stream that starts out pure as a clean, mountain "glacier of truth." But then it travels down the mountainside mixing with other streams or tributaries from other mountain glaciers. The stream continues to remain pure and clear even as it mixes with other streams that are pure and clear, but then what inevitably happens? Humans get involved in the process. For some reason, every time man's ego (edging God out) gets involved it causes "pol-lution" (a system of getting into polarities). So we struggle with these polarities that pollute the stream, trying to find the balance between them. This then becomes the "pol-itics" (another system of polarities) of religion.

But after living in the mountains of Montana and having a pure glacial stream that comes directly from the mountain wilderness running a few yards from our front door, I realize the value of pure drinking water. This coincides with the value of pure truth obtained directly from the source—God—or gnosis—to know God for oneself.

Religion became a way of defining or "labeling" a spiritual experience. That's where all the secularization began as we looked at God with an "eye of judgment," or from the perspective of the Tree of Good and Evil. *Labeling* is also a way of limiting our perspectives and one that keeps us "stuck" in categories or boxes. But just for the "hell of it" (hell being a place of damnation—or limiting beliefs) let's examine some of these labels or *schisms* that keep us apart.

Here's my own personal list of "isms," although many are recognized philosophical or political systems. It would take volumes to cover each one, but this is neither the time nor place for that. However, I'll briefly describe where each one leads:

1. Elite-ism
2. Excuse-ism
3. External-ism
4. Human-ism
5. Exclusive-ism
6. Inclusive-ism
7. Existential-ism
8. Recycle-ism
9. Liberal-ism
10. Conservative-ism
11. Individual-ism
12. Commun-ism

1) Elite-ism covers a lot of territory (and you'll find most "isms" overlap to some degree), so let's break down elite-ism into some of its nasty tributaries.

A) Religious elite-ism keeps us stuck in the illusion that we have to belong to one particular religious sect or organization (a good ol' boys club) to be "saved" or that we have to be taught by a "Master Guru" to really "get it." The reality is that *all* pure religion or spirituality will bring us to that great ocean of oneness which is the "Christ Consciousness," "Krisna Consciousness" or the God within—*which is love!*

B) Power elite-ism is the illusion that we're better than certain others because we are rich, famous, beautiful, talented, educated, etc. Granted, much of this illusion is generated by so called "fans" who subject themselves to the power of the guru or celebrity. But still these people are responsible for "buying into" the *illusion* that somehow they are more "special." But the *reality* is very clear that we are *all one* in the eyes of God. In fact, one of my favorite Mormon scriptures (which I've included at the beginning of this book) is, "I say unto you, be one and if ye are not one ye are not mine."(D&C 38:27)

I like the analogy of a bucket of water. When you put your fist (yourself) into a bucket of water (the world) and then pull it out again, what impression do you leave? *None* except for a few ripples. You may be placed in a position of power or influence because *God* puts you there or allows you to be there so

His/Her perfect will may be done. But all of our gifts (talents, money, fame or otherwise) are gifts from God and are only useful for the building up of the Kingdom of God on Earth.

C) Race elite-ism is the illusion that one human group is superior to another or that one color is better than another. A brief story illustrates that this isn't the case.

As Kurt and I were traveling to the 1995 Windstar Symposium, we had the exhilarating experience of seeing two of the most spectacular rainbows I'd ever seen. Each color was brilliant and distinct from the rest—separate and distinguishable. It occurred to me that each race or culture also has a distinct beauty and brilliance of its own. Just as each flower, each tree, and each rock has form, function, and beauty; each race has its own particular color and flavor.

I used to believe that for all races to live in peace, we'd eventually learn to integrate ourselves through means such as desegregation laws. Where racism is a societal problem, it needs to be addressed through proper legislation. Because I'd come from a very "race elitist" background (Mormonism and even more so in fundamentalist Mormonism), I wanted to change that belief pattern. But then I had an awakening that challenged all that. It involved a family heritage that goes back two generations.

At the end of his life, my grandfather Callister was given a vision that he was to assist the "Lamanite" (Native American) people using the wealth with which the Lord had blessed him. He thought the best way was to educate the Indians to the White man's "superior" way of life; so a large foundation was set up for Native American college scholarships using his multi-million dollar estate. Monies were also set aside in a missionary fund for Native Americans to go on LDS missions—again embracing our culture and our religion.

But what's the result of this so called "desegregation of the White man and the Red man?" For one, a whole magnificent spiritual culture has been lost due to this so called "blending of colors." The shamanic ways of many Native American peoples have been devalued and destroyed, causing us to lose sight of amazing and authentic spiritual paths. I've since come to realize what happens when you blend several colors of paint. You don't get some original, beautiful color? You just get *gray.*

It is one of my visions to heal this "broken circle" which my ancestors helped create by sharing some of the Native American traditions, customs, arts, crafts, and spiritual ceremonies with the White man so that he can be enlightened in the Red man's way of life. (Red man and White man are colloquial terms and I mean both men and women of each particular race.) And thus we can both benefit from each group of "Native Americans" (as I am also native to America) by celebrating each other's cultures. It really isn't about *blending* cultures—it's about *sharing* our cultures and the distinct qualities or flavor that keep them unique.

2) Excuse-ism: We all have our excuses. We're not rich enough, not young enough, not good looking enough, not talented enough, not strong enough—we all have excuses—and many of them are quite valid. (Mine is that I don't have enough time in the day to do everything I'd like. Would any of you lend me some of yours if you're just wasting it by sitting in front of a TV?)

Tom Crum, an Aikido master and author of the books, *The Magic of Conflict* and *Journey to Center* said, "It's time we cut through our story and start living our vision." In other words—let's stop making excuses for ourselves for not living our visions (mine is of building Heaven on Earth). I have a few of my own "ex-cuses" (not useful anymore). Do you want to hear some of my favorites to see if they're familiar?

A) I come from a dysfunctional family background. (It would take an entire chapter to describe all of my family's dysfunctions—believe me, I can "one-up" most anyone.)

B) I have too many mouths to feed and not enough time or energy to do it. (I have ten children and live in the mountains with no electricity or phone. That means no spin-washer, dryer, dishwasher, microwave, TV, blender, etc. I do everything by *hand*. Well, I do have an old wringer washer I plug into a gas generator that helps me with laundry.)

C) I've had too many tragedies in my life. (I lost an infant son due to whooping cough, and all of my family and church have rejected me because of my "spiritual" beliefs. I was in a near-fatal car accident to where the passenger was killed and I was confined to a wheelchair for six months.)

D) I'm not very attractive, (I had a long, crooked nose with a deviated septum which I chose to have surgically altered for cosmetic and functional reasons.) But I don't think anyone, anywhere is completely satisfied with what they see in the mirror each day. My motto: Accept the things you cannot change and change the things you can.

E) I don't have enough money. (What can I say? We have 14 mouths to feed and are trying to stay out of "Babylon" (babble-on), living strictly self-sufficiently and by the spirit. That means *no regular paycheck*. But praise God, He provides "sufficient for our needs.")

I could go on and on with my list of "exc-uses" (not useful anymore), but I think you get my point. But the best story I've heard about someone "cutting through their story and living their vision" was told by a beautiful man named Mitchell. He shared it at a Windstar Symposium, and I was absolutely inspired by it. (Thanks, Mitchell for sharing your story.)

Mitchell isn't what you would call "beautiful" if you were to look at him with the natural eye. His face is a jigsaw puzzle of scars from perhaps hundreds of plastic surgeries to replace the charred skin that left him "faceless." Not only was Mitchell left "faceless" from a tragic accident in which over 60 per cent of his body was burned, but he was also left fingerless. Where hands should be, Mitchell has a pair of scarred and gnarled stumps. But despite Mitchell's physical deformities, he is indeed a beautiful man. Even though he spends his life in a wheelchair because he is paralyzed from the waist down due to another tragic accident, Mitchell has a remarkable success story about how he has "cut through his story and moved into living his vision."

Today, Mitchell is a multi-millionaire, is the former mayor of Crested Butte, Colorado, has won many awards for public speaking and owns a thriving business. But even more remarkable, Mitchell radiates a spiritual quality that is rare in most people we call "handicapped." There is no reason to feel sorry for Mitchell—he's simply amazing! So is there any reason we should feel sorry for you?

3) External-ism: This is a belief system which keeps us in the illusion that we need someone to "pull us out" from the hole we've gotten ourselves into. In reality, however, we've gotten ourselves into the messes we're in, so *it's up to us to get ourselves out!* Granted, there are many "therapists" out there who are willing to help us through the healing process. But as my shaman friend, Speaking Wind, always says, "A true friend is someone who stands beside you to offer his support, but allows you to do your *own work."* Let's have none of this "damsel in distress" mindset while waiting for the perfect "knight in shining armor" to come and rescue us. *You are your own knight and shining armor.* Isn't it about time *you* came to *your own* rescue?

4) Human-ism: This is the belief system that creates the illusion that "we can make it here all alone." There's no doubt about it—we *do* need a "savior" to get us out of this mess we're in. And *He* has already come and has paid the price for our "sins" (separations within) and "mis-takes" (missed opportunities to learn), and it would be foolish of us not to partake of His free gift of "at-one-ment" which brings us back into the integrity of God. I don't know about you, but I can use all the help I can get in this difficult challenge we call life, and I personally look to our Savior, Jesus Christ, for that help. (Thank you for sharing *your story* and *your life* with us, Jesus. My love for you and your love for me is beyond my present comprehension. Please teach me more about this love in the days to come.)

5) Exclusive-ism: This "ism" puts us into the illusion that we must *exclude* ourselves from other relationships besides our primary partner that

are pleasing to the physical senses or to the flesh. That the flesh is corrupt and whenever we cater to it in any sensual (or sexual) manner, we're corrupting the spirit. In actuality, "When the spirit and the body are inseparably connected, there is a fullness of joy." (D&C 93:33) Also, in the *Bhagavad-Gita*, Krishna consciousness teaches: "I am sex life which is not contrary to religious principles."

Often the spirit feels strong connections with those outside the limits of a monogamous relationship. Should we deny those strong spiritual connections simply because our monogamous belief system tells us it is "wrong" to have more than one marriage partner? If we are truly living a spiritual life, we should be open to the guidance of the Holy Spirit in manners of intimacy and marriage. And if we truly believe the Bible to be the "word of God," we realize that most, if not all, of the prophets who talked with God had more than one marriage partner. And didn't Mother Mary have more than one marriage partner when she married Joseph after the conception of Christ? (More on that in Chapter Nine.)

6) Inclusive-ism: This belief system leads us into the illusion that "anything goes" and we can have relationships with *anyone* at *anytime* without any type of commitment—that *all* desires of the flesh are of God so we should satisfy them regardless of the consequences of breaking prior contracts or agreements. Another word for this ism is "hedonism" which is defined as: a philosophy devoted to the idea that pleasure is the highest good or the source of moral values. But we can pretty well see where *that* elusive ism has gotten us. Straight into chaos and perhaps into contracting a terminal STD. Because each partner you connect with sexually, you sexually connect with every one of their partners. So be careful about intimate-contract-making as a form of pleasure.

7) Existential-ism: This goes hand-in-hand with the inclusive-ism illusion that we can "eat, drink and be merry, for tomorrow we die." It attempts to remove any sense of responsibility for our actions which is an illusion because "what we sow is what we reap". Even some Christians adopt an existentialist attitude when they believe that they can "sin today and repent tomorrow." This belief system is responsible for the out-of-control consumerism rampant in our society wherein we are "feeding the gluttonous woman at the sake of depriving our own children and our children's children from having enough." (Quote from Lou Gold from the 1995 Windstar Symposium.) But the true definition of an existentialist is one who "takes responsibility for their own actions and shapes their own destiny whether or not they believe in a divine purpose."

8) Recycle-ism or Reincarnation: This belief system perpetuates the illusion that if we don't "get it right" this time we can "recycle" and try things again. Unfortunately, many of us get trapped in recycle-ism, feeling that some how, some way, we're going to make it up or pay for the "karmic debt" that we've incurred in this life or previous lives. Perhaps this belief alone keeps us in the "recycling" pattern. But Jesus Christ *paid the price for all of our karmic debt—for everyone who exists, has existed or will exist on this planet,* and it would be foolish for us not to partake of his gift of the "atonement" or at-one-ment. It's simply ours for the asking.

9) Liberal-ism: A lot of us don't understand the *true* definition of a liberal. It's "not restricted, free; bestowing in a large and noble way." What would the world look like of we all became liberals and bestowed generous amounts of love (not money) to one another and searched out those "truths" that would indeed "set us free?" I vote for liberalism, in the true sense of the word. But then there's the "down-side." Liberals are famous for spending other people's "hard-earned money" in order to "bail everyone out" of their mishaps. Sometimes this leaves people unaccountable (not accounting for their choices) and forces our economic system into a welfare state.

10) Conservative-ism: The dictionary definition of conservative is "preserving; within safe bonds, moderate." Doesn't that sound like something necessary to save our planet? We need to reconsider unrestricted expansion that takes us out of "safe boundaries" and toward the annihilation of our sacred Mother Earth. (Did you know that most environmentalists are really conservatives?) But conserving the Earth is one of the wisest things we can do for ourselves and for all other living things that share this planet. On the other hand, we can't be so conservative that we don't allow for expansion and growth especially in our minds and in our relationships. Sometimes a change in the status quo is necessary for a change for the better.

11) Individual-ism: This belief system sets us up for the illusion that we are *not* connected and that our *own* individual, unalienable rights are the *only* ones that need to be respected and preserved. "Survivalists" will even extract themselves from society to preserve their individual rights and freedom. (We've been labeled "survivalists" just for the fact that we've chosen to relocate our family to the pristine mountains of Montana.) But my need to express myself to a broader community has compelled me to write this book and share my passion with others. My desire to connect with other like-minded people

has led me out of individualism and into forming a "Zion" (pure in heart) community. That's one of the reasons I left Montana.

12) Commun-ism: Actually, I'm more attracted to "commun-ism" than to "individualism" because I believe living in "com-munity" (living in unity) is the ideal. But I believe true community can only be established on correct principles and balanced forms of government.

As a child I was taught that the only correct or "balanced" form of government was that found in the United Order. I wanted to know more about the workings and economics of that "social order" which I discovered from the book *Liberalism, Conservatism and Mormonism* by Hyrum L. Andrus. In it he described the United Order and the Law of Consecration this way:

> While socialism is founded upon the state and its power, the law of consecration and stewardship is based upon mature individualism, where free and mature men covenant with God and with each other to support an economic program that develops the individual while promoting brotherhood and economic well-being among men. Compulsion is not to be exercised within the system. Instead, the appeal of truth and the stimulus of spiritual powers in the lives of humble men promote the needed spontaneity to motivate each individual to fulfill his covenant obligations to God and to others within the system. Under the influence of enlightening spiritual powers, men are blessed with the spirit of love and of truth; and in loving their neighbor as themselves they willingly sustain an economic order of free and mature individuals where each man holds himself obligated to see that every other person has the necessary where-with all to care for his temporal needs and achieve the good things of life.

I believe that the "United Order" or as Jesus taught "the community of all things common" is the ideal form of government and way of life. But as you have just witnessed neither religion nor politics is the answer to this type of community of oneness.

So now that we've taken a tour of some of my favorite "isms," let's move on to something new. It can be fun to swing between the extremes of the various "isms" to gain a broader perspective, but if you're looking for peace and *oneness*, "isms" are not the answer. So what is? It's simply by walking the spiritual path.

One night while lying in bed in our tepee in Montana, I was discussing the idea of following the path of the spirit with a dear friend, Ranelle. She was trying to get her book *Living Joy* published, and we were expressing how we knew for a certainty that we were following the path of the *Holy Spirit* and not a *dark spirit* or our *own spirits*. We both admitted that we'd been guilty of following the "wrong spirit" on occasion, and we didn't want to fall into that illusion again.

I shared with her my "fail-safe" method to "test" the spirit that was guiding or directing me. I told her that whenever I have a question about whether or not the spirit of God is guiding me, I do four things:

1) I make a decision about it.

2) I take the decision to the "Christ-center." If I get a warm, "burning within" feeling or an expansion of the heart chakra, it's a positive indication that my decision is correct.

3) I then take the decision to the "Universal Mind" or "God-self." If my decision is something that would serve the whole of humanity (and not just me), *that* is a good indicator.

4) If I still have a doubt about whether my decision comes from light or darkness, I pray to the Lord and ask that if the decision is *not* of God to remove it from my heart. God *always* answers prayers.

Ranelle really connected with this "Four-step method of discerning spirits." She also shared something very profound that I'll share with you concerning grace.

She asked, "Janae, what is your understanding of grace?"

I related to her the popular metaphor of the "nail in the board"—how *grace* comes along and fills the hole in the board after we've done everything in our power to remove the nail that we put in the wrong place. She enjoyed it and shared an understanding of her own.

"Janae, have you ever struggled with a concept in your mind trying to understand the deeper meaning that it's trying to teach you?"

"Of course, I have, Ranelle. You know it!"

"Well, to me *grace* is that instant, that subtle instant, between knowing and not knowing when all of the sudden it's there—when you can grasp it with your mind and understand it. It's that instant of 'aha' when it all comes together and you have a knowledge of the concept. That's my understanding of grace."

At the 1995 Windstar Symposium, I met a truly enlightened man whose understanding of "grace" was phenomenal. Here's an excerpt from a talk given by Brother David Steindl-Rast on "Nurturing Our Spiritual Selves." (Thank-you, Brother David for sharing. You helped me have another one of those "aha" moments.)

Spirituality rightly understood is aliveness—*super aliveness...* It is the Holy Spirit—the life breath of all of creation. Whenever we are alive on every level, we are spiritual. And we are fully spiritual when we are alive on the highest level—in our caring for one another and caring for this planet.

Brother David went on to say that "Religion is an inevitable process of learning to articulate what spirituality means so that we are able to understand it. The understanding is a process that happens when (you) so completely give yourself to the word that it takes you into the silence out of which it comes, and you understand. And when you give yourself so deeply to the silence and the silence comes to word and you can express it. That round dance—of word into silence and silence into word—that round dance is understanding. And our understanding of the word is what makes up religion."

If only *all* religions could remain so pure.

Scriptural References: Mark 9:23, 11:24; St. John 3:34-36, 6:29, 11:25, 26; 1 Corinthians 13:7; Romans 10:9, 10; Hebrews 13:8; James 1:22-27; 2 Nephi 28: 3-14; D&C 134:4.

Walk Your Talk Therapies: Chapter Seven

Therapy One: *Bridging the "Ism" Schism*

A dictionary definition of "schism" is "a split, as in a church, because of difference of opinion, doctrine, etc." These schisms I call "isms" or belief systems that keep us apart.

I'm sure each of us owns some favorite "isms" or belief systems we feel are important and that give us the "substance" of who we *think* we are. For example, someone might look at me as a "female, white, separatist, conservative, who is big on Gnosticism, women's rights to their bodies, and preserving the rights of the unborn." This would be the "box" or category I could be put into through *labeling.* What this does, however, is put an illusionary wall between me and someone who, let's say, is a "male, black, interracial, liberal, who is big on patriarchal rule and pro-abortion."

Obviously, if this other person and I were to live in the same community, we'd have a difficult time finding some "common ground" in which to carry on a constructive conversation. By virtue of our *labeling* each another, we would have caused barriers for each other which are very hard to bring down.

But those barriers *must* be brought down if we are *ever* to realize that we are *all in this together* as children of God and part of His/Her human family. So how do we accomplish this? One way is to identify those we feel the *most* isolated from and connect with them in some way. This may mean writing a sincere letter to a member of Congress who we totally disagree with on every issue and share with him or her (in a *nice* way) our views on a particular issue.

Or it could mean phoning your father-in-law who is a cattle rancher and sharing with him (in a *nice* way) your views on the negative aspects of the beef industry. (Or you could do like I did and send him one of John Robbins' books, *Diet for a New America*.)

Anyway, find some way to cross over those barriers and "link-up" with others on the opposite side of the fence, so we can start tearing down fences and resolving issues once and for all. But first, find some common ground to start communicating.

Therapy Two: *Dealing with Offence (a fence)*

How often are we offended by the words and deeds of others? It's easy to get trapped into judging them and become offended if their actions don't meet our expectations. Like the driver who cuts you off as you're trying to change lanes—and you're in a hurry to get somewhere. Or your significant other who doesn't follow through on *anything* you ask him to do. It's easy to get offended (off-ended) and build up resentment towards the people around you who don't always perform the way you'd like them to.

So how do you get around the nasty habit of building offence (a fence) between you and your associates—and especially those you love? Forgiveness is key! But even more important than forgiveness is non-judgment. Because if we *never* judge another as being *wrong* or *evil,* but simply see them as a brother or sister on the path of enlightenment, then we will *never* be offended by their "less than perfect" actions. Then we will never have to forgive them.

Realize, of course, that this is easier said than done. So try this exercise the next time you become offended by the actions of another. Take a deep breath and try to visualize this person as *your very own child.* See them in their stages of infancy trying to take their first steps and falling down again and again. Do you get offended because they haven't learned to walk? Or do you have the patience of a parent whose only joy is watching their child develop and succeed?

We can never know what's in the hearts and minds of others and so it's good practice to do what the Native Americans advise and "not judge a man before you've walked a mile in his moccasins."

Chapter Eight
FACING OUR FEARS

Let's look at some other belief systems that keep us separated or cause "dis-integration" (not together) in our relationships. These can be labeled our "fears."

In his book *Journey to Center*, Tom Crum shared two acronyms for fear. FEAR=False Evidence Appearing Real or FEAR=Fuck Everything And Run. Both are considered valid depending upon the circumstances. If a large, wild animal was coming toward you at top speed, it would be appropriate to *fuck everything and run!* But in terms of relationship dynamics and our path to oneness, fear is simply the absence of love. These two emotions—fear and love—cannot exist in the same place at the same time. So if we constantly hold fear in our hearts concerning our loved ones, isn't it time to "let go and let God?" And not just for their sake, but for our own sanity.

Jerry Jampolsky in his ground-breaking book, *Love is Letting Go of Fear* explains about fear and love:

> Fear always distorts our perception and confuses us as to what is going on. Love is the total absence of fear. Love asks no questions. Its natural state is one of extension and expansion, not comparison and measurement! Love, then is really everything that is of value, and fear can offer us nothing because it *is* nothing.
>
> Although Love is always what we really want, we are often afraid of Love without consciously knowing it, and so we may act both blind and deaf to Love's presence. Yet as we help ourselves and each other let go of fear, we begin to experience a personal transformation. We start to see beyond our old reality as defended by the physical senses, and we enter a state of clarity in which we discover that all minds are joined, that

we share a common Self, and that inner peace and Love are in fact all that are real. With Love as our only reality, health and wholeness can be viewed as inner peace, and healing can be seen as letting go of fear. Love, then, is letting go of fear.

I first read Jerry's book when I was in high school facing the scary transitions life offers at that critical time. I can honestly say that reading his book literally changed my outlook on life. It was one of those "aha" experiences when it all comes together and you finally "get it." So when I heard that Jerry Jampolsky was going to attend the 1995 Windstar's Choices for the Future Symposium as one of the presenters where I could meet him in person, I was elated!

And so at this particular Windstar Symposium in Aspen, after listening to Jerry and his life partner, Diane Circione, speak about "Changing your mind, changing your life," I knew I *had* to meet him in person—*no matter what!*

As we broke into discussion groups, I made sure I was at the one with Jerry and Diane. We engaged in discussion about "fostering community," and I kept "spirit-linking" with Jerry through eye contact hoping to elicit a response. I wasn't disappointed! At the end of the session, I caught Jerry alone after he'd finished speaking with some other "fans."

Our eyes met, our hands grasped, and then came an unexpected hug and a kiss on the cheek as we shared an incredible "spirit-linking" exchange. I expressed my love for Jerry and how he'd been one of my favorite authors along the path to enlightenment. In fact, Jerry's book and presentation inspired me to write what follows about "letting go of our fears."

The best way I've found to release fears is to face them smack in the face. Whether they're fears of the known or of the unknown, we all need to face our fears and pass through them, or they will show up at an inopportune moment to paralyze us from moving forward in our relationships of oneness.

Everyone has their own set of fears; whether they're fears of the dark, fears of the future, fears of failure, fears of confrontation, fears of death or dying, fears of separation, fears of rejection, fears of confrontation, so on and so forth. Since I can only write from my own experience, let me share with you some of my personal fears and how I learned to overcome them.

One of my greatest fears as a parent is losing a child to death—one of the greatest "separation" fears we have as humans. When we lose someone to death, we can't see them or share this life with them, which is a very difficult issue for most people to deal with.

In February of 1985, I became pregnant with my fifth child. At the time I wasn't especially excited about the prospects of having another child as I already had an eight-month-old baby, Ariel, who I'd wanted to continue nursing until she was at least a year old (as is my usual practice). I'd gotten pregnant, you might say by "default" (neglecting intent), and I was somewhat angry at my husband, Kurt, and at God for allowing another "soul" to be conceived inside of me when *I wasn't prepared.* I wasn't physically ready, emotionally ready, or spiritually ready to take on the prospects of contracting with another soul to care for when I already had my hands full with four. (Little did I know that this was only the beginning.)

One day when I was suffering from symptoms of morning sickness *and* hypoglycemia (as I was still nursing Ariel), I knelt down and prayed wholeheartedly to the Lord "to take this baby from me and perhaps wait until another time and place when I was more healthy and prepared." Well, God *always* answers the prayers of the heart, but often in ways we don't expect.

I continued to carry this spirit/soul within me, still somewhat reluctant as I felt God had deserted me in not answering my prayer for a "spontaneous abortion." I ended up weaning Ariel at nine months for my own health.

Then on October 9, 1985, I delivered a beautiful, eight-pound baby boy we named Jadon David King, in the Hamilton hospital in the heart of the Bitterroot Valley of Montana. My heart swelled with joy as I held him in my arms for the first time after a very difficult labor and delivery. An immediate love affair between the two of us began.

But this love affair (in mortality) was to be short-lived. Within a month my sweet baby, Jadon, contracted whooping cough (from a teen-aged neighbor) and ultimately passed away. I won't go into all the details here (they're in my book, *Heartsong*) but the point of this story is: (Actually there are many points to this story.)

We bring into existence those things we fear because we unconsciously *desire* to overcome those fears and move through them. Perhaps the story of Job would have turned out differently if Job hadn't had fears about losing everything. "For the thing which I greatly *feared* is come upon me, and that which I was *afraid of* is come unto me." (Job 3:25, italics mine)

Another thing I learned through all of this is that we need to be *very careful* about what we pray for as the Lord will sometimes answer prayers in ways we don't expect—perhaps to teach us a lesson. And the lesson I learned, which I want to touch upon briefly, is about an issue that has polarized us as a nation in ways which have become severely violent and destructive. And that issue is abortion. In my opinion, the highly polarized debate over abortion is best summarized by the bumper sticker: "Pro-choice before conception—Pro-life after."

Now I don't want to get on a "high horse" and guilt you by telling you how deeply sorry I feel about my own "abortive thoughts" towards my own son, Jadon. I know God has forgiven me for them. But I also know that God has *zero tolerance* for the atrocity of destroying innocent human life—or any life for that matter. And so I dedicate the following poem to you, Jadon, which is also included in my book, *Thank you, Mother Nature:*

Respect

Oh God, who dwells within all things
Giving life to all liberally
Your beauty's contained in every flower
Each bird's song a perfect melody
Who can deny your majesty?
When gazing at heaven through cedar boughs
Your grace expressed in watching does
Lead their fawns through bramble roughs
Your tender love is most revealed
In Mother's smile when tear's concealed
Oh Blessed Creator, my heart is full
Of love, respect and praise for you

Each time I chance upon a flower
And ponder upon the seed within
One tiny grain of awesome power
Brought forth this beauty to my view
And when my son goes climbing trees
And comes upon a Robin's nest
He knows to leave the eggs untouched
For Robin's song is what we love best

Exploring ancient cedar groves
Where dwarfs and elves and fairies dance
My foot steps lightly on sacred paths
For cone and sapling become rich romance
When frost appears on forest hills
And buck and doe run fast with fear
A shot is heard, a silent prayer
For buck and doe—and unborn deer

Precious newborn babe of mine
Red and wrinkled, still wet from womb
Some say it was not you I felt
And make your former home a tomb

But even my young child of four
Was given sense enough to know
The tiny brother she now holds
She felt kick so long ago

Dear God, whose infinite love is full
For living things both great and small
And in your image of supreme majesty
Created man—the choicest of all
Yet of all your creatures you have born
None have shown a lesser respect
To take the life of their own unborn
Your greatest gift they crudely reject

I pray each time I hear a Robin sing
Or when wandering down each sacred path
Collecting herbs and flowers and things
And chance upon a fresh fawn's track
Holding tight my young child's hand
I shed a tear as I look in his eyes
And pray he and God will understand
That I have won the grandest prize

Another fear that I had to overcome is the fear of pain. Any pregnant woman knows that when she approaches her due date (especially if she's had children before) that there's a luminous fear of pain in the back of her mind. As she starts into labor and the fear of pain becomes a reality, she has two options. She can either choose to resist the pain by struggling against it (or even denying it by having an anesthetic), or she can choose to embrace the pain and pass through it, thus making it a learning tool for later growth.

As I was approaching the delivery of my tenth child, Jenny Pearl, I was filled with anticipation as I was determined once and for all to conquer pain (at least the fear of pain) by transmuting it into positive energy. I had determined that by sending out praise and thanksgiving to the Lord for this great *Vision Quest* of childbirth, I could transmute the pain into joy. Through giving birth, a woman brings herself to the threshold between mortality and immortality to receive a new life into her arms.

To make a long story short, the quick, "painless" delivery I had anticipated didn't happen. Instead I "suffered" during transition for over an hour waiting for the cervix to dilate completely, perhaps because of a very large placenta positioned right next to the opening of the cervix. (Praise God I had overcome my fears of a *placenta previa*.)

During the long hour of suffering through transition (the longest I'd ever experienced) the thought of Christ hanging on the cross at Calvary overcame me. For the first time, I experienced a window of insight into what Christ suffered that He might offer me "life eternal." I wept tears of joy for this blessed experience of suffering—for just one brief hour—so I could offer "life" to my sweet, Jenny Pearl. I realized that as a mother, the greatest gift we can give Spirit is to offer tabernacles of flesh so our children can progress towards their own *celestial integrity*. And Christ's gift of the at-one-ment is the greatest gift he offers mankind to assist us in obtaining that Celestial Integrity. I've always felt that if there were some way I could "suffer on the cross" so humanity could be saved, I would.

But we *already* have a Savior who did that, and His only requirement is our broken heart (open heart) and contrite spirit (penitent spirit). "Blood sacrifices" were done away with in Christianity. Although I'm very touched by those who feel that *they* need to suffer for the sins of humanity (like polygamous wives stuck in abusive situations who feel that they will be "blessed" for staying in these dysfunctional relationships), all I can say to them is: "Get off your cross—we need the wood to build Zion."

Another fear I was able to face is the fear that lurks deep within each of us—the *fear of death!* So here's what happened.

In the late summer of 1995, some family members and I went berry picking on the back side of "Marriage Mountain" at our home in "Higher Ground." Our hillsides are *very* steep and the roads are often treacherous. Christy (my sister-wife) and I were in our Subaru Brat pick-up truck with some of the kids (I think there was eight of us in all), and we parked it to go pick a bush of blackberries. I'm usually careful to park on a flat spot as the Brat had no emergency brake (and no reverse either). I'm also very careful not to leave the keys in the car with any of the kids—just in case. But this time I was negligent and left my two-year-old, Kelsey May, in the car along with the keys.

I was up the road picking blackberries when suddenly I heard the engine start, and out of the corner of my eye I saw it lurch forward as standard transmissions do when started in gear. My heart leaped into my throat, and I panicked as I saw the truck rolling forward towards a steep incline with Kelsey in the driver's seat.

"Oh my God! What do I do now?" I screamed to myself as I sprinted towards the truck.

My fifty-yard dash brought me to the passenger's side of the truck and ready to jump in. I grabbed the door to open it. *It was locked!* "God help me," I prayed as I was losing momentum. Thank God, the window was open, so I reached in and unlocked the door from the inside. With the door open, I jumped into the truck—but who jumped in alongside me but my four-year-old son, Jordan, who'd been running alongside with me to "save the day." He jumped in and I lunged over him to grab Kelsey who was still in the driver's seat and braked the truck just *inches* before it went over a steep embankment.

My whole body was shaking with fear and exhaustion by the time Christy and the other kids arrived. She carefully removed Jordan and Kelsey from the truck before I dared lift my foot off the brake as we were tipped as far sideways as a vehicle could go before rolling. I gently removed my foot off the brake while my leg shook uncontrollably. Praise God the truck held, and I was able to get out before it could roll. (Thank God it didn't roll and Kurt was able to pull it out with his skidder. And praise God that He was watching over us and answered my petitions in a time of dire need!)

Near fatal experiences have taught me some of the greatest lessons I could possible learn. One of those is *how precious life is!* It is truly the greatest gift God has given us, and we do well to not waste a single moment of it in self-pity, doubt, fear, regret, anger, bitterness or in any other emotion that blocks us from enjoying life fully and completely. I intend to enjoy every moment of my life!

Another thing I learned was about the nature of fear and why it keeps us paralyzed and impacted from moving forward. I could have chosen to let this "fear of death" inhibit me to the point where I'd be afraid to ever go berry-picking again. But such activities bring great joy into my life, and I don't want anything to inhibit me from enjoying the "fullness of joy" which *is* our inheritance as children of God.

So the next week I decided to go berry-picking in the exact same spot along with Kelsey and the kids (but this time I was certain *not* to leave the keys in the car.) Fears, like any other belief, hold us hostage until we willingly choose to "walk through them" and turn weaknesses into strengths.

But there is *one more thing* I learned from it all. I needed to start a work-out program to get in better shape in case of another dramatic incident that Involved sprinting!

Scriptural References: Job 3:25; Isaiah 41:10; Romans 13:7,8,10; 2Timothy 1:7; 1John 4:18,19; Moroni 8:16-18

Walk Your Talk Therapies: Chapter Eight

Therapy One: *Facing Fears*

Find a quiet, sacred spot where you can do some deep breathing and visualization. As you enter a deep meditative state, think about some of the past *fears* you've faced and overcome. Start from the present and travel backwards to visualize the exact moment you faced a particular *fear* and moved past it. Focus on *that particular moment* until you can experience the *feeling of fear* as you did when facing it not knowing whether or not you were going to walk through it to the other side.

Now re-experience the *feelings of victory* you felt when you moved past that *illusionary fear* into the *reality of faith*. Realize that your *faith* moved you through and past the fear until it no longer existed.

Now confront your present fears that are paralyzing you from moving forward on your spiritual path. Visualize the worst-case scenario that could occur from each particular fear. Make it as specific and dramatic as you can, visualizing in detail the worst that could possibly happen. Next, try to experience the *feelings of fear* you would be experiencing if you were faced with this particular fear. Make it as *real* and *dramatic* as possible.

Then as you are experiencing overwhelming feelings of fear, visualize or imagine in your mind a beautiful, *bright angel of faith* standing beside you, helping you walk through the fear (holding your hand perhaps) and moving you past it to the other side of it. With that beautiful, *bright angel of faith* by your side, celebrate in the *victory* of overcoming that fear just as you have overcome other fears from your past.

And then, if there are any "real" fears that have paralyzed you from moving forward on your spiritual path, take the first opportunity you can to face up to them and move through them to the other side where there is *victory, celebration, and peace*. I did this with my fear of heights by parasailing in Cabo san Lucas when on vacation there. What a true sense of celebration and victory I felt as I was flying through the air hundreds of feet above the water. I exuberantly laughed out loud the entire time!

Therapy Two: *Working the Bowl*

This is a therapy I borrowed from Patrick (Speaking Wind), and with his permission I'll share it with you. (I've changed it a bit to suit my "come-from" as a Christian.)

As the spirit directs, find a spot in nature next to a "standing person" or tree where you can sit quietly, undisturbed for about an hour. This needn't be an impressive tree like an ancient Cedar "grandfather standing person" like we have up at Higher Ground. It can be a favorite apple tree or a withered, old pine tree. (I've done this in front of one of those, too.) Bring along a bowl preferably made of a natural material like glass, ceramic, clay or wood.

As you sit in a comfortably position in front of "the standing person" with the bowl in hand, allow yourself enough time to reach a state of meditative silence. Now visualize yourself as a pitcher pouring out all the ugly "sins" of disharmony—those deep, dark thoughts that lie buried within your soul that are preventing you from following your true spiritual path. As you think about those thoughts (some may be abstract, others concrete) allow them to pour out of your soul like a pitcher pouring out dirty water into the bowl. Visualize filthy water being poured out and collected into the bowl in front of you. Make it as specific and as imaginative as possible.

After pouring out all the darkness and "dis-ease" contained in your soul, hand the bowl to the tree in front of you since the tree represents an important person or figure in your life. It is the "tree of life" or *Jesus Christ* who made that great atonement (at-one-ment) between you and God. *He is God* and therefore *He alone* has the power to redeem you from the fall or the dark state you've been in.

Trust in Him, and He will take your bowl full of filthy water and transmute it into pure light. And this pure light, He will then pour down upon you and fill you with joy, peace, beauty, love, enlightenment—all of the characteristics that He is as the "tree of life."

When you feel at peace with your soul, go over to that "standing person" and give him a big hug as if you were hugging the Savior, Jesus Christ, who hung on a wooden cross or *tree* and died so that you could have eternal life. *Believe in Him, love Him, worship Him*—not the *creature*, which is the *tree*, but the *Creator*, who is *in all things* and gives us our *life* and *being*.

Chapter Nine
SURRENDERING TO LOVE

God is love! And that just about sums it up in my book. Even though this one statement may seem terribly simplistic to some, the implications are so significant and profound that they cannot be comprehended by the mortal mind. The magnitude and eternality of God's love for us is so exquisite that even when we touch upon it in our relationships with each other, our spouses and our children, we can only conceive of a particle of the beauty and immensity of it. The love of God or "God's love" is the electricity or magnetic charge—the "glue" if you will—that holds the Universe together. It is this "glue" that binds us together in our relationships one with another. A poem quoted by Rolland Smith, the Master of Ceremonies at the 1995 Windstar Symposium in Aspen, Colorado really emphasizes this point:

> Consider this inquiring friend
> There's no beginning and no end
> There's only balance out of time
> A mystic concept much sublime
> It is within our intellect
> To understand and then reflect
> That something holds us in a grace
> To freely move from place to place
> Let us assume this universe
> Is perfect balance and diverse
> And in the form of symmetry
> There comes a knowing certainty
> All atoms, quarks and humankind
> Have orbits that are intertwined

To all the other's frequency
A masterpiece in artistry
Now take the step of further thought
What keeps this balance from onslaught
Of random pandemonium
Disturbing equilibrium
There only is one answer to
This complicated spirit-glue
A cosmic field, unified
By something simple undenied
It's love.

All the love that we feel for each other is generated by the God within us and is a gift of God. We should never hide or feel ashamed of the feelings of love that we've been given. *All love is of God.* But often we get confused or mixed-up in our minds about what these feelings are really telling us or what God is trying to tell us about ourselves.

Each relationship, intimate or otherwise, teaches us something about ourselves and who we are. Whether it's with a spouse, our children, with that nosy neighbor down the street, a boss or co-worker—each relationship teaches us more about our ability to love.

The more we become God-like and understanding of His/Her love, the more our ability to love unconditionally expands. When our capacity to love is impaired or inhibited, there's something inside us blocking unconditional love. It could be from unhealed wounds from the past, unresolved conflicts of the present, or fears about the future—each causes impairments in our ability to love as God loves—*unconditionally.*

Perhaps the greatest reason for us to come into relationship with one another is to unblock these blockages or impairments. The more intimate the relationship, the greater the opportunity for those blocks to surface so we can examine them or "realize" (real eyes) what they truly are so that we can then get rid of them. It's the process of "enlightenment" or bringing the darkness into the light.

If you have not yet discovered it, one of the best ways to expand love (in my life, anyway) is through plural marriage (I now call it "polyamory" or *many loves*). Talk about having to pass through one of the greatest of all fears—sharing the person you love with another person you love. This could certainly involve "the fear of letting go."

Here's why my first husband, Kurt, and I decided to "try on" this life-style. When I first set eyes on Kurt my spirit whispered, "If I ever get married, it will be to someone just like you." I was sitting in the Student Union Center at Utah State University in Logan during my freshman year, 1976. I was between classes and decided to observe the people walking by (which has been a past-time of mine since youth) until my next class. Suddenly, in walks *the best looking guy I'd ever seen!*

He was tall (6'2" to be exact) with blonde hair and blue eyes and sported a confident smile that would melt the coating off of any piece of candy. And what happened next? This "Greek Adonis" chose a seat *right across the hall* from where I was sitting!

I couldn't believe it—here I was sitting straight across from "the man of my dreams," but I lacked the courage to make the first move and introduce myself. I sat nonchalantly *staring at him,* hoping beyond hope that he would notice me—but not notice my staring. Finally, our eyes met followed by a responsive smile—but neither of us was brave enough to make conversation. I sat for awhile with butterflies fluttering in my stomach playing the "bait and hook" game—flirting with my eyes. (Kurt, by the way, was also busy flirting with a group of gorgeous girls which added to his charisma.)

But then the bell rang signaling the start of my next class so I left *before I had a chance to talk with the "man of my dreams!"* I was devastated! Yet, I wasn't willing to risk making a fool of myself (especially in front of all those "rival" girls) and introduce myself. (Isn't it silly the games we play that cause the spirit to work overtime and make "coincidences" happen so two people can connect?)

That evening, I walked to the dormitory with mixed emotions. Half of me was ecstatic at having seen the man of my dreams. My other half was kicking itself for not having *done* something about it!

The next week I kept hoping (*and praying*) that I'd somehow run into this "mysterious stranger" so that I could find out who he was.

One week to the day later, I was coming around a blind corner after buying art supplies from the school store when suddenly I ran right into a guy who was moving the opposite direction. Now I don't mean that "I ran into him" in the figurative sense. I mean we had a *major head-on collision!* My books dropped, my art supplies went flying, and it took everything in my power to remain upright and not wind up sprawled across the floor.

As I looked up to see who I'd run into, *I couldn't believe my eyes.* There standing smack dab in front of me was *him*—my Greek Adonis, my mysterious stranger—the man of my dreams!

His face was a bit redder than I'd remembered, and he graciously helped me pick up my books and things. He apologized for having run into me, but I wasn't one bit "sorry" that I'd run into him!

Then came the "line of the century." I mean it was a classic, and to this day I still tease Kurt about its originality. After all my things were back in my arms, Kurt asked, "Haven't I seen you somewhere before—and not from this planet?"

The first part of the question was kind of romantic (even if a bit cliché), but the second part was definitely "quirky." If I hadn't had those same feelings myself, I would have retorted, "Well, frankly I haven't traveled to Mars lately, have you?" But at that point I didn't know *where* this guy's head was at, and I didn't want to spoil the perfect moment. I responded that I thought I'd seen him a week ago in the Student Union Center sitting across the hallway talking with some girls.

He then explained that those girls were "friends" from a dance troupe he was in, and they were just talking about the rehearsal schedule for a performance.

Bingo! We hit common ground, and I told him I'd auditioned for the same dance troupe at the beginning of the year but hadn't made it.

He asked if I'd like to go to a rehearsal that evening, and of course I said, "*I'd love to!*" This was the beginning of the "mental" phase of the relationship which lasted close to a half-hour until the class bell ended our historic "first conversation."

I could sense that "destiny was in the making" (and Destiny would become the name of one of our eleven children, by the way), and I "floated" home to tell my roommates of my unexpected close encounter with "Mr. Right."

But isn't it interesting how there's always something that interferes with our "prime directive." It tells us, "You've just met someone who somehow connects with you to form part of your section of the puzzle. All there's left for us to do is find out what the connection means so you can begin putting it all into place with the vast, beautiful picture of heaven or the integrity of God."

What also appears at those critical times of connection and integration, however, is the "dark side" whose sole purpose is to prevent us from making those connections and cause "dis-integration." But isn't that part of the challenge and excitement in the game of relationships—to see if we can "beat the Devil at his own game?" And for those of you who don't believe in the Devil or "dark side," I found an enlightening quote in C.S. Lewis' book, *The Screwtape Letters.*

> Two equal and opposite errors of thought exist concerning devils. One is to disbelieve their existence. The other is to believe and to feel an excessive and unhealthy interest in them. Demons themselves are

equally pleased by both errors and regard a skeptic or a magician with the same delight.

The rest of Kurt's and my love story is in another book, *Heartsong*, if you're interested in the details. It's more of an autobiography told as a "fantasy based on a true story." *This* book is more the practical application of my life's experiences. So on with the story.

Most every couple has their favorite song or songs which paint a picture of their romantic relationship. There are many songs that illustrate the deep affection we feel for each other, but this one best describes the eternal commitment we share—*to love.*

Their First Touch

Their first touch at seventeen
Was in the park...
And the moon was full...
She was beautiful to him,
And her hair was long
And her eyes were blue
And her skin was warm
And she turned to him,
And he thought that he knew
What love was...what love was.

Another touch at twenty-two
On their wedding night...
And the stars were bright...
She was beautiful to him,
And her hair smelled sweet
And her lips were full
And her skin was warm
And she turned to him,
And he thought he knew
What love was... what love was.

And then again at twenty-five
When the baby came...
And the sun was high...
She was beautiful to him,
And her hair was damp

And her fingers shook
And her skin was warm
And she turned to him,
And he thought that he knew
What love was … what love was.

Later on at fifty-four
Sitting on the porch…
All the children gone…
She was beautiful to him,
And her hair was gray
And her forehead lined
And her skin was warm
And she turned to him,
And he thought that he knew
What love was … what love was.

Their last farewell at eight-five
Was by her bed…
And the moon was full…
She was beautiful to him,
And her hair was thin
And her eyes were closed
And her skin was cold
And she turned to him,
And he knew that he knew
What love was … what love was.

After sixty-eight years
Of laughter and tears
He knew that he knew
What love was…

It takes years of commitment and sharing to come to *truly know what love is.* After twenty years of life with a partner, here are some thoughts about what I think love is. (I hope to someday *truly know what love is.*)

First, *love* is a *verb*—not a *noun.* A "noun" is "a person, place or thing"; whereas a "verb" is "an action."

Love is definitely an *action word!* It's something we *do,* something we *feel,* and something we *work at* every day to keep it alive and growing. Love is never a "thing" and *never, ever* a "possession." I've heard it said that "we receive love the more we give it away."

But that makes it a "thing," doesn't it? But the saying could also go, "We are loved more, the more that we love." That's because love is something we *do*—not something we *own*. If love were a commodity we could have or own, it wouldn't grow, diminish or stay the same without us needing to *do* something about it. But it isn't a "thing"—it's an *action*. It has to be worked at every day to grow.

And so it is with loving relationships. They're like gardens that we plant but they also must be attended if we expect them to bear fruit. You can't just throw "seeds of love" onto the ground and expect them to grow and produce without nurturing and caring for them. But seeds of disharmony seem to grow spontaneously like weeds that can choke out the seeds of love we've carefully planted. These weeds must be "pulled out" each day to clear the way for love to grow. We must nurture our loving relationships with the greatest amount of T.L.C. so they can grow into lifelong relationships and even into eternal ones.

I suppose now is as good time as any to talk about the principle of plural marriage. As I mentioned in the first chapter—*integrity* is *unity* based on *correct principle*. I truly believe, (actually it goes way beyond belief) that plural marriage or "polyamory" is a correct principle ordained by God. If you were to take it through the "three witnesses to truth" process outlined in Chapter One to determine if it meets the criteria for being a correct principle it would definitely qualify—no question.

First, it certainly passes the test of nature, because all God's laws are manifest in nature. Most animals (at least herbivores) live in polygamous situations such as herds, flocks, packs, and broods. It's part of the instinctual drive for animals to live in community which creates a sense of safety and security. It's also part of the law of "natural selection" for the female to select the sire of her offspring.

This may be why in the animal kingdom males, rather than females, are usually the more ornate and "attractive" ones—equipped to "attract" their female mates. Except when the females are in "heat" or ovulating—then their pheromones or scents attract the males for the purpose of reproduction. And a female will usually mate with *any* available male—although she allows a favorite or "primary" male to mate with her first. That male is usually the one to impregnate her and is her "natural selection." This is how most primates (gorillas and monkeys) reproduce, and they are genetically our closest relatives.

On the human side, most indigenous peoples around the world have lived or are living in more or less polygamous relationships called "tribes." That is how humans "instinctually" live when societies don't dictate otherwise. Consider the Native Americans. Most tribes were considered "pagan" by the early Christian missionaries because polygamy was one of their beliefs and practices. Most of the great Indian chiefs who ever lived had more than one wife. One of my ideals, Chief Joseph of the Nez Perce tribe in Montana, had three wives and this was perhaps part of what made him great. (If you've ever lived in a polygamous situation you'd understand what I mean. It definitely is a "refiner's fire.") As for a woman, when she became discontented living with a man, she would simply place his "things" outside the tepee door to indicate she was "done" with him. (Boy, just think of the money they saved on divorce lawyers.)

In the science of biology, the human hormonal system is geared up to be polyamorous. It is in our "hard-wiring" to desire more than one partner in order to maintain perfect balance and health in our endocrine system. When we first meet someone we are attracted to, it causes the "infatuation hormones" to come into play which are the chemical endorphins and dopamines which make up the "pleasure hormones" that create the "juiciness" in a relationship. This "juiciness" starts to diminish in "half-lifes" each year until by the seventh year it's practically gone. That is why most couples go through the "seven-year-itch" cycle during their seventh year of marriage. However, these "infatuation hormones" are replaced by other "contentment hormones" which create the feelings of peace and well-being. These are the chemical serotonins and oxytocins (hormones found in lactating mothers) which give us the feelings of security and contentment after the juiced-up pleasure is gone.

If we consider polyamory (polygamy) from the scriptural or doctrinal standpoint of being the "word of God," we find the principle revealed over and over in the Old and New Testament.

In the Old Testament, practically *all* the prophets who ever talked with God were polygamists—Abraham, Isaac, Jacob, Moses, Solomon, David—the list goes on and on. Well, this is all fine and dandy if you are *male!* (Is that perhaps why there are no females recorded in the Bible as having spoken to God? Because they weren't living the law of plural marriage! At least nothing is recorded in scripture—except perhaps Mary who was married to both God and Joseph.) But the real question here, for me as a Christian, is—how did Jesus live? Wouldn't he be our greatest example?

Unfortunately, there's been a huge "cover-up" regarding these issues, but a lot has recently been discovered concerning Jesus being married. The best book I've found on the subject is called *Jesus Was Married* (now there's a positive affirmation), written by an ex-Mormon Fundamentalist, Ogden Kraut. His in-depth research revealed evidence that Jesus was not only married to Mary Magdalene, but also had other wives like the two sisters, Mary and Martha of Bethany, the woman at the well who received "the living waters" (I'm curious to know what that might mean) and others who were known among his female followers.

One curious thought concerning the case of Mary Magdalene or the "woman taken in adultery." (John 8:2-11) This story actually took place *inside* the temple. Was Mary Magdalene perhaps this woman who was actually a "temple priestess" performing temple rites? Why was she brought before Jesus if he wasn't intimately connected to her as a "husband" as it is the husband's right (in the laws of Moses) to stone his own wife if she is guilty of adultery? Why did Jesus *not* condemn her if she was *indeed* committing adultery? Interesting.

Another curious case is that of the Samaritan woman at Jacob's well. (John 4:5-30) If she was committing adultery by having five husbands and not being married to the man she was presently living with, what an excellent opportunity for Jesus to publicly condemn her. Instead, he gave her the "living waters, which shall spring up into everlasting life"—a most precious *blessing* rather than a *cursing* because perhaps she was "doing the works of Abraham." Something to think about.

But what exactly does Jesus say concerning marriage, if he's the expert on the subject? One of the best known discourses is in Matthew 22:23-30 and retold in Mark 12:18-25:

> Then come unto him the Sadducees, which say there is no resurrection; and they asked him, saying, Master, Moses wrote unto us, If a man's brother die, and leave his wife behind him, and leave no children, that his brother should take his wife, and raise up seed unto his brother. Now there were seven brethren: and the first took a wife, and dying left no seed. And the second took her, and died, neither left he any seed: and the third likewise. And the seven had her, and left no seed: last of all the woman died also. In the resurrection therefore, when they shall rise, whose wife shall she be of them: for the seven had her to wife. And Jesus answering said unto them, Do ye not therefore err, because ye know not the scriptures, neither the power of God? For when they shall rise from the dead, they neither marry, nor are given in marriage; but are as the angels which are in heaven.

So is Jesus telling us there's no marriage in heaven? But if it's true that it is "on earth as it is in heaven" then why get married anyway? Again we go to the words of Jesus found in Matthew and Mark.

The Pharisees also came unto him, tempting him, and saying unto him, Is it lawful for a man to put away his wife for every cause? And he answered and said unto them, Have ye not read, that he which made them at the beginning made them male and female, and said, For this cause shall a man leave father and mother, and shall cleave to his wife: and they twain shall be one flesh? Wherefore they are no more twain, but one flesh. What therefore God hath joined together, let not man put asunder. (Matt. 19:3-6)

So here's a big clue to the mystery of eternal marriage. "What therefore *God* hath joined together, let not *man* put asunder." That could be the missing clue to the first marriage question. But I didn't finish the quotation. Jesus goes on to say in Mark 12:26, 27:

And as touching the dead, that they rise: have ye not read in the book of Moses, how in the bush God spake unto him, saying, I am the God of Abraham, and the God of Isaac, and the God of Jacob? He is not the God of the dead, but the God of the living: ye therefore do greatly err.

Hum, does this mean that God is only acknowledging known polygamists as being "the God of the living." This is curious until you relate it to some of the Gnostic scriptures found at the Nag Hammadi describing Jesus' relationship to Mary. In the Gospel of Philip we read:

The companion of the (Saviour is) Mary Magdalene. (But Christ loved) her more than (all) the disciples and used to kiss her (often) on her (mouth). The rest of (the disciples were offended by it...). They said to him, "Why do you love her more than all of us?" The Saviour answered and said to them, "Why do I not love you as (I love) her?'" (Note: The parenthesis are the "fill in the blanks" by the translators as many of the scrolls were badly damaged by fire.)

The book *The Second Messiah* by Christopher Knight and Robert Lomas goes on to explain:

The Gospel of Mary tells us that she was favoured with visions and insight that far surpassed Peter's. Another document, the *Dialogue of the Saviour*, describes her as the apostle who excels all the rest... "a woman who knew the All." Gospels that refer to the equality of women were rejected by the Roman Church under the catch-all accusation of being Gnostic, but in these versions it is clear that there was a power struggle between Peter and Mary Magdalene. In a document called "Pistis Sophia," Peter complains that Mary is dominating the conversation with Jesus and displacing the rightful priority of Peter and the other male apostles. Peter asks Jesus to silence her, but he is quickly rebuked. Mary Magdalene later admits to Jesus that she hardly dares speak to Peter because: "Peter makes me hesitate; I am afraid of him, because he hates the female race." Jesus replies that whoever the Spirit inspires is divinely ordained to speak, whether man or woman.

And then in the Gospel of Thomas we read:

Simon Peter said to them, "Make Mary leave us, for females are not worthy of life."

Jesus said, "Look, I shall guide her to make her male, so that she too may become a living spirit resembling you males. For every female who makes herself male will enter the Kingdom of Heaven."

Wow! That's powerful stuff when you put it all together. Does that mean all I have to do is become like a male (and a polygamist as were Abraham, Isaac and Jacob) in order to become a "living spirit?" Or do I just need to be married to Jesus? Perhaps they are one and the same as this truly could be the "Bridal Chamber" Jesus spoke of that's only available to those who have oil in their lamps or have obtained the "Holy Spirit" for themselves. This is a Gnostic Christian concept, by the way, and was also supported by many Mormon prophets including Joseph Smith who stated, "I would that we could *all* be prophets!"

So this question of plural wives was a *good question* Joseph Smith posed to God one day when he was asking concerning Solomon's "many wives and concubines." And God's answer is found in Doctrine and Covenants 132. I won't quote it here, as it is a *very long* quotation. You can read it for yourself if you wish. But the whole debate, both inside and outside of the Mormon Church, is whether or not the "new and everlasting covenant of marriage" *is* "Celestial plural marriage." That's where Mormon Fundamentalists come into the picture and argue that they *definitely* are the same. And then the debate becomes "keys, keys, who holds the keys?" It can become very confusing for any student of Mormon theology.

Of course, much controversy has arisen in the LDS Church and elsewhere as to the expediency and efficacy of plural marriage and whether or not it has been ordained by God in modern times. Most members of the LDS Church believe that the *Manifesto* did away with the principle of plural marriage—at least as a practice for the church today. But I would counter that "correct principle is correct principle" for "Jesus Christ (is) the same yesterday, today and forever." (Hebrews 13:8)

This brings us to our third witness—the Holy Spirit. Both Kurt and I received a spiritual witness that we were to live the principle of plural marriage back in 1982 after we read the book, *The Most Holy Principle* by Rulon Allred. We each received a personal witness by the Holy Spirit that it was a "correct principle," so we decided to "unify ourselves on correct principle" by living it.

Suffice it to say after having lived it for over six years that I've received my own personal witness and testimony that *it is a correct principle.* The principle of polygamy will bring you closer to *oneness* or a state of Godliness than any other principle. It has brought Kurt, Christy and I closer to the divine unity of love and spiritual oneness than anything else. I'm not saying it can't be achieved it any other way, but if you want an accelerated program in *loving unconditionally* without jealousy or possessiveness, this is the *one principle* which teaches you to do so. Not only that, but the sense of community that develops gives you the freedom to do other things besides just domestic duties (like writing books). It's a comfort to know that my children are cared for by another caretaker referred to as their "other mother." This is just one of the beautiful aspects of the principle of plural marriage.

"By their fruits ye shall know them" and the fruits of plural marriage (though challenging at times) are very delicious as I have tasted them. So shall the fruits of the "Oneness" be when both males and females are evolved enough to submit their EGOs (Edging God Out) to God and can live in polyamorous relationships with each other. Because as the saying goes—what's good for the goose is good for the gander—and correct principles are required by both sexes to live. But I believe this is the divine evolution of the planet and when we give ourselves over to "divine evolution" rather than "violent revolution" then Zion (the pure in heart) will be gathered. Then Zion will be redeemed by the Lord as he receives her to his bosom. But first Zion must be established within the hearts of men.

When we choose to submit ourselves to the covenants and promises of the "New and Everlasting Covenant of plural marriage" as the Holy Spirit dictates, and not by the dictates of outside authorities or mandates, the "keys of the kingdom of God are committed unto man on earth" and the promises thereof shall roll forth.

> The keys of the kingdom of God are committed unto man on earth,
> and from thence shall the gospel roll forth unto the ends of the earth,
> as the stone which is cut out of the mountain without hands shall roll
> forth, until it has filled the whole earth. (D&C 65:2)

John Denver sings of a beautiful metaphor for this scripture in his song,
The Flower that Shattered the Stone:

> The Earth is our Mother
> Just turning around
> With her trees in the forest
> Roots underground
> Our Father above us
> Whose sigh is the wind
> Paint us a rainbow
> Without any end
>
> As the river runs freely
> The mountain does rise
> Let me touch with my fingers
> See with my eyes
> In the hearts of the children
> A pure love still grows
> Like a bright star in heaven
> That lights our way home
> Like the flower that shattered the stone
>
> Sparrows find freedom
> Beholding the sun
> In the infinite wisdom
> We're all joined in one
> I reach out before me
> And look to the sky.
> Did I hear someone whisper?
> Did something pass by?
>
> As the river runs freely
> The mountain does rise
> Let me touch with my fingers
> See with my eyes
> In the hearts of the children
> A pure love still grows
> Like a bright star in heaven
> That lights our way home
> Like the flower that shattered the stone

Scriptural References: Matthew 22:23-30; Mark 12:18-25; St. John 3:16, 8:2-11, 14:15, 15:9-14; Romans 8:28,35-39; 1 John 4:7-12; Alma 13:27-29; D&C 38:27; sec. 132.

Walk Your Talk Therapies: Chapter Nine

To truly *surrender to love,* it's important to have your "house in order," so to speak, so the perfect, pure love of Christ can flow through you unimpaired. Here are a few of my favorite therapies for putting your own house in order.

Therapy One: *Cleaning House*

One of the best ways I know of clearing congested energy is to do some serious "house cleaning." I don't mean just straightening up a few things at home—I'm talking about *house-cleaning* on three different levels of environment.

The first and most crucial is that of our own "temples"—*our bodies.* One way to clean up our temporal bodies is to go on a *cleanse.* There are multitudes of detoxification cleanses available, and one of my favorites is Dr. Christopher's "Three Day Cleanse." Also, detoxifying the liver through high retention coffee enemas are a good way to go. I do them every other day just to cleanse myself of all the accumulated toxins in our environment. I've included the instructions below:

High Retention Enemas

Enemas have been used for centuries for the purpose of cleaning out the large intestine. The Essenes used them anciently for self-purification. (See *The Essene Gospel of Peace*) Movie stars have used them as part of their daily routine. There is even an enema named after a movie star, "The Mae West" which uses coffee, sea salt, and baking soda. Garlic enemas have been known to kill parasites. I know of a friend who actually cured herself of Leukemia with the daily use of coffee enemas. As for me, I recommend a weekly coffee or herbal enema for good colon management. (Some people prefer daily enemas, but for me that seems a bit excessive unless you have a chronic disease.)

How to Administer a High Retention Enema

1. Prepare your enema by filling an enema bag with water, coffee, or herbal concoction (I prefer fresh-pressed herbs if possible). Make sure the liquid is pure, strained and at body temperature (around 100 degrees).

2. Fill the tub with warm water (you will want to be comfortable, as you will be lying in the tub for up to 20 minutes).
3. Hang the enema bag above your head (a showerhead works well) making sure the clamp is clamped tight.
4. Lubricate the insertion tube with a natural lubricant to glide smoothly.
5. Climb into the warm tub of water and insert the enema tube. Use the clamp or your fingers to adjust how quickly you allow the liquid into your bowels. Too quickly will cause cramping. Allow a small amount to clean out bowels initially. Void on toilet.
6. Next, allow the rest of the liquid to fill up your bowels completely. Do circular massage in a counter-clockwise motion starting from the lower left hand side, up and across, then down the right hand side (the opposite way the lower bowel moves). Do this for up to 20 minutes. Start with about 5 minutes and work up. Honor your body when it starts to cramp and you need to void. This isn't a contest to see if you can force yourself to hold the enema. Be kind to your body. Pelvic rocks work well to alleviate cramping.
7. Sit on the toilet and allow your body to void the enema completely. Don't force it at any time.
8. Finish with a warm water flush out. You may add a capful of *Min-Ra-Sol Colloidal Minerals* for a purging, rejuvenating effect. This enema you do not need to retain but massage is helpful.
9. I also like to do an additional warm water rinse with a tablespoon each of vinegar, acidophilus and Aloe Vera to balance the pH and introduce friendly bacteria into the colon.

Another way to *cleanse* (which is a bit more radical) is to go on a *fast*. This means *no food* for a few days, or until the spirit directs you that you've been on it long enough. It's interesting to note that most religions teach the principle of *fasting* in preparation to receive further enlightenment. One of my favorite ways of fasting is a Native American "Vision Quest" in which you go to a sacred spot (where the spirit directs) and stay there for a few days *fasting* until you receive "Vision."

A word of caution regarding fasting—be careful not to overdo it, or you can become very sick especially if you're not used to it. Be extra cautious if you're pregnant or a nursing mother. Actually, childbirth and nursing are already cleansing enough and can be a powerful "Vision Quest." I believe God acknowledges women's sacrifice in childbirth.

Another level of "house cleaning" is to do just that—*clean house.* I mean *really* clean house and organize all of your "stuff." Get rid of things you don't use or intend on using. A good method is this: If you haven't used something in the past year, you probably won't need or use it *ever*—so *out it goes!* Take those items to a local "Good Will" or "Salvation Army" to be "recycled" by someone who can use them.

The Native Americans had a Sacred Ceremony called "The Giveaway" in which they would give away *all* of their material belongings. This was usually done by the Elders in anticipation of walking into the next life unencumbered and unburdened.

If you feel overburdened and encumbered by your "stuff," I suggest to you *get rid of it!* Especially if you feel like you have an addiction to "things" (which most Americans do). If you're brave enough, just get rid of *all of it* and wait and see what the Lord brings into your life to replace it.

Give and you will receive. I promise you won't be disappointed.

The third level of "house cleaning" is of your immediate environment. As the popular saying goes: "Think globally, act locally." How can we expect to clear up the planet's pollution problems if we can't keep our own backyards clean? If we were all responsible (able to respond) to our own "ten acres" (or whatever acreage we own), then there wouldn't be a pollution problem. But since we *haven't* been responsible for keeping our stewardships unpolluted, Mother Earth is going to have to go on a cleansing program *herself.* And it doesn't take a prophet to read the "signs of the times" that this time of *cleansing* is going to start in a *big way* very soon. Also, if you happen to see some litter in a restroom, campground, or hiking trail, please be sure to pick it up and dispose of it properly. Make a habit of going out of your way to make sure your environment is cleaner than you found it. Use the Native Americans "to the fifth generation rule" so that our children's children's…. children will have a planet to sustain them on.

Therapy Two: *Being Open to Others*

If you are indeed in an "open" relationship and your marriage contract includes being open to meeting other companions, allow spirit to direct you to opportunities for meeting other "like-minded people." And if you do meet someone or "someones" whom you feel a connection with—allow spirit to direct your relationship into deeper and more intimate levels of love. Yes, it may bring up all of your hidden "fears" which you will have to work through, but this is the fastest and most effective way of "clearing the channels" so that you can get on the other side of fear which is bliss, love, joy, freedom and peace—or literally the Kingdom of Heaven on Earth.

Chapter Ten
CLEARING THE CHANNELS

We all come to earth complete with a *prime directive* or perfect pattern imprinted on our spiritual beings. If you own a PC this would be the hard drive of your computer program. This *prime directive* includes many things which may include: 1) Our individual path of the spirit which will lead us back to the *oneness* or *integrity of God*. 2) The contracts we have previously made in the spirit realm (or perhaps in other lives) which we agreed to complete during this life. 3) The knowledge or imprint of our split-apart or soul-mate with whom we will ultimately be connected, if we follow the path of the spirit. 4) Our life's purpose or gifts which we are destined to share with humanity.

Our *prime directive* is significant, and whenever we go against it, we cause "static" on our spiritual channel, "aberrations" in our mental state, and "disease" in our physical well-being. For the purpose of clarification, I simply call it "sin" or *separation within*. Because these three *bodies* are inseparably connected, whatever affects one also affects the others. That is to say, if the *spiritual body* is out of whack, the *mental* and *physical bodies* are also out of alignment. If the *physical body* is out of order, so are the *spiritual* and *mental bodies*. They are all connected like the legs of a tripod, and if one side is weak, the tripod is out of balance.

And so what happens when we get out of whack in any or all of our *bodies*? First, we will experience states of confusion, distress, and disease, and we will respond or react to these signals differently. But before we examine how we "respond" to the signals of going against our *prime directive*, let's talk about how we manage to get ourselves "out of whack" in the first place.

Before we can gain *integrity* or complete *oneness* with another person, we must obtain oneness or integrity within our own *bodies*. That is to say, all of our *bodies—physical, mental* and *spiritual—*must be *unified on correct principle*. This challenging process of *integration* can only begin after we recognize how *disintegrated* we've become. After we come to that realization, we must feel a compelling desire to gain back the integrity we've lost. And even though much of the disintegration has occured from no fault of our own and without our knowledge, we still must recognize the state we are in, accept it, and desire to change it. In other words—ignorance is not bliss—and if we continue to ignore the imbalanced state of dis-integrity we're in, the longer we will be in the condition of pain and suffering.

We begin the process of disintegration or separation at the time of birth when, in most cases, we are pulled from the womb, slapped on the behind, and handed to an awaiting attendant to be measured, weighed, pulled, prodded and otherwise traumatized.

Whenever we experience *trauma* through separation, pain or distress, it causes an "aberration" (deviation or disorder) in the mind which acts as a monitor for the body and the spirit. The mind consciously and subconsciously receives and sends messages between the body and the spirit. Whenever there is extreme trauma of any kind, the mind has an automatic "shut-off switch," not unlike a circuit breaker, that shuts off any incoming or outgoing information. But what happens then isn't that the mind simply shuts off. The *monitor* or *rational mind* shuts off and any incoming information coming in at the time of traumatization is received and imprinted in the *emotional mind* without being monitored through the *rational mind* or the mind of understanding.

That's how certain experiences like childbirth, accidents, conflicts, illnesses, and abuses are imprinted in the emotional (wisdom) part of our brain. And then when we find ourselves in similar situations or circumstances, the same emotion we felt during the first experience is reactivated. That's why some people experience things like claustrophobia (fear of tight places), hydrophobia (fear of water), pyrophobia (fear of fire) which aberrate them or inhibit them from functioning normally. These aberrations or inhibitions need to be cleared or processed through before we can become integrated on all three levels of being.

If these aberrations are not cleared or processed through, they will inevitably show up and cause us distress when we try to establish intimacy with others. Whenever we "make love" or open ourselves to another, our aberrations will eventually surface. Because in the act of love-making, our ability to connect with the opposite sex and access the opposite side of our brain (male to female or female to male) is greatly increased. We are the most "whole-brained" or in our higher consciousness when we have an orgasm which is a highly opened and programmable state. That's usually when many of our aberrations appear.

These aberrations often appear even before we can reach a state of orgasm as *phobias* or *fixations* depending upon how we choose to address them. These distorted states of consciousness which began during childhood when we were traumatized by separation, rejection, intimidation, brutality, or abuse, can set us up for abnormal behavior in adulthood.

These distortions sometimes appear as *fixations* or "addictions." We can become abnormally fascinated or "addicted" to certain parts of the body such as breasts, buttocks, penises, etc. or to behaviors such as sucking, biting, scratching, crying, or screaming. Or we can become addicted to the sex act itself because we feel a need to "fill-up" the emptiness that was created in childhood when "mother" wasn't around to nurture us. Some of us even enter relationships for that very reason—to be "mothered" or to "mother."

In fact, most people may need certain amounts of "mothering" at times from our intimate relationships because most of us didn't receive adequate maternal nurturing in childhood. This can be a normal and beneficial aspect of relationship—but when it becomes extreme and turns into an *addictive behavior,* it's time to do some serious clearing.

Other abnormalities that can interfere with intimacy as a result of uncleared aberrations are *phobias.* These can manifest when we are abnormally fearful or self-conscious about certain body parts, experiences, or even the act of making love. This usually occurs when parents did or appeared to have abnormal sexual relationships with each other or with their children. Such phobias, more often then not, need to be cleared with the help of a qualified therapist who has experience dealing with such issues.

Another reason aberrations need to be cleared is that each time we get involved in a situation that triggers the emotional side of the brain to click in and the logical side of our brain to click out; we create a state of imbalance. This, in turn, creates a vacuum or magnetic pull for outside entities (spiritual and otherwise) to influence us. This is one of the methods that those on the "dark side" (Satanists) use to *access* people or place them under their influence. Often, they begin when their victims are very young, and they subject them to fearful or painful trauma to *access* them; then they can access them at will by reactivating the trauma using key words or code names used at the time of the initial programmed trauma. It's a sort of "mind-control" which the dark side (even our own government) uses to gain control over people's behavior patterns.

If you feel that you've been programmed by the dark side, you may want to be "cleared" by a professional trained to do this type of work. There are a few self-help therapies I've included at the end of this chapter for less serious cases. All of us have been *accessed* by Satan in some degree or another, but there are those who have actually been programmed for the purpose of destroying God's work. Such individuals have extra need of help—God's help—to get them cleared of this type of programming, and there are counselors, religious and otherwise, who do this type of counseling and clearing.

Unfortunately because there are so many ways that the dark side can *access* us, it's difficult to know by which spirit we are being influenced. Often we can be put into an imbalanced state of emotion by experiencing euphoric states of pleasure. These states can be obtained through physical and sexual stimulation that puts us into an emotionally opened state we may interpret as "love." And if this is done in the proper way with the proper person, it can definitely open us up to profound states of spiritual awareness. But "sexual magic" has also been used by the dark side to bring about demonic influences on individuals and upon the world. Aliester Crowley, also known as "the Beast" or "the most wicked man on earth" used sexual magic to open doors into the dark side and bring about chaos onto our planet.

But *heiros gamos* or "sacred sexuality" can help us "clear the channels" if done in accordance with the Holy Spirit, bringing us to that euphoric state of *oneness* that we all desire. Unfortunately, most of us settle for physical or sexual gratification that leaves us unfulfilled and "in need"—always searching for the next "fix" to take us to that euphoric "high." This is similar to the physical state of euphoria some have sought through drugs, alcohol, kink-sex, etc. and is short-lived and transient (as all physical gratification is).

It can also put us into an emotional imbalance that leaves us wide open for unclean spiritual possession and can be very destructive. But the *spiritual oneness* that transcends all physical states of euphoria can only be obtained when directed by the Holy Spirit. And when the spirit and the body are connected in loving acts of oneness, there is a *fullness of joy!*

It's interesting to note that television has used this process of putting us into states of emotional imbalance in which we are being constantly bombarded by violence and sex. This *"televised trauma"* puts us into a hypnotic state during which we can be easily accessed by the TV programmers. (It would be interesting to know who the writers are of your favorite TV shows and about their moral values.)

One thing Patrick (Speaking Wind) always emphasized to me and others is, "You should never make a decision in the phase of emotion." When we are in *emotion* (energy in motion), we are in a state of mental imbalance, and we may be easily influenced by others (physical or otherwise) who don't have our best interests at heart. This is why it's important that when we do get into emotional states or "phases" that we allow enough time to pass so that we can again rebalance the *emotional side* of the brain with the *logical side*. Of course, we can also get ourselves into an imbalanced state by being too much in the *logical side* of our brain and shutting off the *emotional side*.

I've seen many instances where people (especially men) have been so traumatized by painful intimate relationships that they have chosen (consciously or subconsciously) to shut themselves off emotionally. They become "walking robots," so to speak, with very few remaining emotional responses or desires. This is most often a self-defense mechanism for avoiding hurts and pain by becoming numb to emotion (no brain—no pain), but it's an imbalanced mental state and can be easily accessed by outside influences (spiritual or otherwise).

These individuals are more likely to self-destruct (commit suicide) as they feel they are in a state of hopelessness and not able to respond to their emotional needs, let alone the emotional needs of others. They are the "living dead," so to speak, and are more difficult to clear then those with other types of emotional imbalances as they don't want to admit that they have a problem and, quite often, refuse to enter an adequately intimate relationship where healing can occur.

Another way of getting into states of imbalances or con-fusion (not together) is through unresolved conflict which occurs when our physical selves go against our spiritual selves. Or in other words, we are "out of sync" with our *prime directive* or spiritual path and instead are following the path of the flesh.

Often we put ourselves into a state of imbalance when we have broken contracts (spiritual or otherwise) and reap their negative karma or consequences. An example would be a woman who chooses a career over getting married and having the children she spiritually agreed to have. Another would be breaking a spiritual agreement and physical contract by having an abortion of a child she has conceived. (This wouldn't include rape or incest pregnancies—or pregnancies she didn't agree to.) A man might choose a career that goes against his prime directive or takes him away from his partnership contract with his wife to help raise their children. A relationship partner might break the contract by committing "adultery" with another person.

Adultery is the act of separation from the integrity of the relationship and happens when partners engage in signing intimate contracts with others without the mutual consent of the other partner or partners involved. "Adultery" comes from the root word "adult" which everyone knows is the opposite of "child." So what if we could sincerely become as innocent as children with the same wonderment for our incredible bodies? Would we be afraid to explore the fascinating world of sexuality? Or would the "adult" in us shut us down to such an intriguing exploration? Well, it is the job of the "adult" to create "safe boundaries" for children to play in and that is why our mothers and fathers stopped us from the exploration of our sexuality when it went too far. Perhaps there was wisdom in this. But now, as "conscious adults," could we possibly continue with that fascinating exploration into the "uncharted territories" of human sexuality that we began as children? The very thought of it exhilarates me.

But let's look at another word which is similar in form to adultery—*adulterate*. The dictionary defines adulterate as "to separate from that which is whole." When two people "become one" in the true sense of marriage, anything that causes separation from that oneness or wholeness can be considered "adulterated" or adultery. Clearly, the married partners should be viewed as one unit because what one partner does affects the other *very intimately* especially in terms of expanded relationship. When one partner moves forward into a loving, intimate relationship with another person, the other partner is pulled along—willingly or unwillingly. If it's willingly and with mutual consent—it can be a beautiful, expanded experience which translates into joy! But if it's unwillingly and without *total* consent—it can turn into heartbreak, separation and divorce. These are the consequences of adulterating or "separating from the whole." In other words—a nuclear holocaust—with a lot of fall-out involved.

Whenever we have intimate physical relationships, it's like signing a contract of spiritual agreement to be that person's "helpmate." We are consenting to help the other person work through the karmic debt he or she has incurred. (As in any business negotiation, we not only "access the assets," but we also are "liable for the liabilities.")

Also, when it's a marriage partnership, any of the assets and liabilities incurred in that partnership (children, houses, cars, etc.) *should* be retained by the party who has agreed to fulfill the contract and not by the one who wants to dissolve it. If our systems of justice were based on integrity, more equitable decisions would be made in cases of divorce. For instance, when the wife or husband commits adultery (or breaks the relationship contract) then the assets of the marriage-contract shouldn't go to the party *breaking the contract*. It should go to the party *keeping the contract*.

Although these are very real and difficult states of imbalances that we get ourselves into, there are certainly ways out. The simplest and best is called "repentance." To "repent" means to "turn around" or *change*. Sometimes it takes people (and humanity) a while before they get themselves into such a state of imbalance and "con-fusion" (not together) that it becomes so uncomfortable to follow the present path any longer that they will decide to change. In other words—change is less traumatic than keeping with the status quo.

I believe our society as a whole has reached this point of discomfort at which we either *have to change* or be *destroyed*. It takes each and every one of us as integrated parts of the whole to make that decision to change before we can turn around this march to destruction.

It's like the body that begins to die from a degenerative health condition like cancer or heart disease. It starts slowly at the weakest point or at the organ most congested with filth or poisons. (Usually it's the colon in the human body—the inner cities in society.) As the dis-ease begins to advance, spreading its cancer to other areas of the body via its various systems, a distress signal known as "pain" is sent to the brain. Pain is a signal or symptom of the disease—not the disease itself. If we choose to ignore the pain by simply suppressing it with anesthetizing drugs, we won't do anything to actually cure the disease and heal the body.

We must first realize that there is a problem going on—a *real dis-ease* which is causing us pain. Then we must discover the *cause* of the disease so we can effect a change. If it's cancer, for example, we must discover if the cause is physically based, (wrong eating habits and elimination) mentally based, (stress caused by mental imbalances), or spiritually based, (unresolved or unrepented sin), before we can enlist an appropriate therapy. In most cases of physical disease, all three areas are involved, (spiritual, mental and physical), so it's best to treat the body as a whole as holistic medicine has discovered. Again, we can look at all disease as a type of sin or separation within.

It's the same in society. Its building blocks are our relationships with one another just as cellular relationships are the building blocks of the body. When our relationships begin to break down or *disintegrate* (not connect) as in marriage, family, community, or church, the whole of society begins to break down and disintegrate causing "disease" (not at peace). When *disease* gets to the point that it involves practically every system of the body (every family unit), then it cries out in pain.

Our society has gotten itself to the point of *disease* and *pain* that it's at the brink of destruction. How can we ignore the cries of distress any longer? *We must act now!*

Even though a person may be in the terminal stages of cancer, there is still hope. I have witnessed where terminally ill patients have recovered through radical holistic health programs which involved an intensive clearing and cleansing of *all* the systems of the body.

We, as individuals of our society, (cells of the body) can also cure ourselves through *repentance.* The following are the five steps to repentance or the "5 Rs" we learned back in Sunday School.

1) *Recognize:* We must first *recognize* that there is a problem and a need to *repent.* This is when we become "conscious" of a situation or enlightened to the darkness within. I think most everyone can recognize when they do indeed have a problem and a need to repent or "turn-around."

2) *Remorse:* When we become conscious, the feelings of sorrow in making wrong choices are quite normal. We learn to take responsibility for the damage we've created and have a broken heart about it. This *broken heart* and *contrite spirit* are the sacrifices God requires that we bring to the altar so we can be cleansed and forgiven of our wrong choices or "sins" (separations within). A "broken heart" means an open heart; and a "contrite spirit" means a humbled spirit. Sometimes people need to be "humiliated" before they can become humble. Their EGO (Edging God Out) or their pride must fall away before they are brought to their knees in humility.

3) *Repentance:* We must ask God in the name of Jesus Christ for forgiveness. "For there is none other name under heaven given among men, whereby we must be saved." (Acts 4:12) Until we are *at-one* with our creator, *Jesus Christ,* we cannot be *at-one* with anyone else. "For in him we live, and move, and have our being; … For we are also his offspring." (Acts 17:2) Christ has already "bridged the gap," so to speak, of "where we're at to where we need to be," by making the infinite *at-one-ment* for us. Now it's up to us to choose the path of the spirit which leads to Christ and ultimately to God—which is the infinite integrity of all things.

4) *Restitution:* After we *repent* or make a conscious choice to change the direction of the path we are we are going on, then comes the work of *restitution.* "Even so faith, if it hath not works, is dead, being alone." (James 2:17)

Restitution is doing everything in our power to *restore* that which was lost in the physical realm (like *restoring* nutrients to the body that have been lost through poor eating habits), in the mental realm (like *restoring* balance to the brain), and in the spiritual realm (like *restoring* the integrity, if possible, of contracts we have broken in relationships.) If total restoration is not possible, then we must *restore* to the person that which we have wrongfully taken if we broke the contract.

If we ask the Lord directly in prayer, He will reveal to each of us what is needed to make *restitution* and will put us on the perfect path of the spirit so we can again follow our *prime directive.*

5) *Resolution:* The fifth and final step to repentance is *resolution.* This is when we *resolve* in our hearts and spirit to never again return to the path of disintegration or destruction which we were on. And then we do everything in our power to move forward with full integrity.

Sure, we all make mistakes and slip up, especially if we've been on a destructive path programmed from childhood. But if we *sincerely repent* and turn our lives over to the Lord, He is merciful and will continue to strive with us as long as we try to do our best. That's what counts!

The Anasazi had a beautifully simple philosophy regarding the concept of repentance. Life is what they call "the walk." And there are two kinds of people who are "walking the walk"—those who are walking forward and those who are walking backward. That's it! It's that simple! And what amounts to their "group therapy sessions," is when they gather together and tell stories about the times each of them came to the great "turn-around" when instead of continuing to walk backward, they decided to walk forward. You can't get any more basic than that—and just imagine how much money (or beadwork) they saved on therapists.

When we strive to set our own lives and temples in order and become pure vessels of light and love (qualities of the Holy Spirit), we are on our way to becoming a "soul-mate" to another person and eventually part of a community of soul-mates. It is then that we begin to see the miracles of God made manifest through us and when life becomes *a wonder and a joy!*

Scriptural References: Exodus 19:10; Leviticus 11:44,45; Isaiah 26:7-9; Matthew 11:27-30; Acts 2:38, 4:12, 17:24-30, 26:18; 1Corinthians 6:11,19-20; Colossians 1:16, 17; 1Thessalonians 5:23; 2Nephi 31:17; Alma 9:12; Moroni 7:13-17,47-48, 8:26, 10:32,33; D&C 29:34, 42:29, 59:5-7, 88:123-126.

Walk Your Talk Therapies: Chapter Ten

Therapy One: *The Cleansing Waters of Baptism*

The principle of baptism was instituted before Christ, but where did baptism come from? It was something John the Baptist had practiced with his own followers even before Jesus came on the scene. The Essenes (who some believe John and Jesus were affiliated with) practiced water rituals as reported in *The Essene Gospel of Peace,* translated by Edmond Bordeaux Szekely.

> After the angel of air, seek the angel of water. Put off your shoes and your clothing and suffer the angel of water to embrace all your body. Cast yourselves wholly into his enfolding arms, and as often as you move the air with your breath, move with your body the water also. I tell you truly, the angel of water shall cast out of your body all uncleannesses which defiled it without and within. And all unclean and evil-smelling things shall flow out of you, even as the uncleannesses of garments washed in water flow away are lost in the stream of the river. I tell you truly, holy is the angel of water who cleanses all that is unclean and makes all evil-smelling things of a sweet odor. No man may come before the face of God whom the angel of water lets not pass. In very truth, all must be born again of water and of truth, for your body bathes in the river of earthly life, and your spirit bathes in the river of

life everlasting. For you receive your blood from our Earthly Mother and the truth from our Heavenly Father.

Baptism was and is an *essential* principle of the Gospel (Good News), but how essential? It was important enough that even Christ himself was baptized by John in the Jordan River even though he was without sin and had no obvious need to be baptized. But it must have been to demonstrate to God his willingness to subject himself to *all things* the Father required of him. It was this *outward* ordinance of baptism that demonstrated to us and to God Christ's *inward* covenant or conviction of the heart.

Don't we use water to wash away the dirt on the *outside* of our bodies? Why then should it be considered odd to use the same element of water to wash away the dirt *inside* us? Think about it. And if the principle rings true to your soul, contact someone who has the authority to baptize you; or you can participate in Watsu therapy which I've discovered to awaken Kundalini energies and I've been certified to do.

I've been baptized three times so far as a token of rededication to the commitment of following the path of Jesus Christ—which is my own path of Spirit—and is *all* paths of the spirit. This one path will ultimately lead to the *oneness with God* and each other which is where *all* spiritual paths lead to eventually. Baptism is the gateway to the spiritual path of Christ.

> Wherefore, do the things which I have told you I have seen that your Lord and your Redeemer should do; for this cause have they been shown unto me, that ye might know the gate by which ye should enter. For the gate by which ye should enter is repentance and baptism by water; and then cometh a remission of your sins by fire and by the Holy Ghost. (2 Nephi 31:17)

Carol Lynn Pearson rehearses this principle beautifully in a poem she wrote entitled, "Ritual."

Ritual

Why ritual?
May I not receive
Christ without burial
By water?
If I remember
That he bled,
If I believe,

What need for
Sacramental bread?
Only this I know:
All cries out
For form—
No impulse
Can rest
Until somehow
It is manifest
Even my spirit
Housed in heaven
Was not content
Until it won
Embodiment.

Repent and be baptized every one of you in the name of Jesus Christ for the remission of sins, and ye shall receive the gift of the Holy Ghost. (Acts 2:38)

Therapy Two: *Dealing with Addictions*

There are times when we become addicted to behaviors, to substances, or to people that keep us "stuck" and unable to follow the path of the spirit. Even after we try therapies or take other steps, like repentance and baptism, to clear those addictions, we sometimes need to take more assertive action.

Addictions are those fixed behaviors that have impacted us since childhood and often manifest in our most intimate relationships. These may include oral addictions such as smoking, drinking, eating, sucking, biting nails, grinding teeth, or any "bad" habit that involves the mouth and the need to gratify oral sensations.

Other addictions may also include drugs, sex, television, music, sports, movies, books, and other behaviors which are attempts to escape "reality" and put us into a state of "illusionary oneness" with someone or something outside of the "oneness reality" of ourselves.

For example, many American women are "addicted" to romantic novels or TV soap operas to escape mundane lives or marital relationships. But the "escape syndrome" of addictive behavior results in separation from what is real or "life," and the ultimate disintegration of the oneness relationship with a spouse and children which can result in a kind of "living death."

I see this happen often in marriage relationships where food, alcohol, drugs, sex, TV, jobs, etc. have been used to "escape" the necessary work involved in forming meaningful, long-lasting relationships with spouses or children. Many of these addictions become so severe that they require expert intervention through Alcoholic Anonymous or drug abuse centers. But most addictive behaviors can be cured in a very simple and practical way through fasting. (See Mark 17:21)

If an addiction is to food—don't eat the food you're addicted to until you have overcome the craving for it. If it's ice-cream, for instance; just stop buying it at the grocery store and having it available for consumption in your freezer. Eventually, you'll find something "good" to substitute.

If the addiction is to television—unplug the set for a specified period (perhaps a year or so) to see if you can live without it. We've been without TV for over 10 years, and I can honestly say our lifestyle is richer and fuller because of it.

If the addiction is to sex—take a break from it for a few months and learn to "make love" in other ways besides sexual intercourse.

If the addiction is to cigarettes—find a program that will help you "kick the habit and join the unhooked generation." There are many support groups that can help with this life-robbing habit.

There are hundreds of forms of addictions—some being more or less difficult than others to overcome. We may or may not even know that we have an addiction to them until we go on a "fast" to see if we have uncontrollable "cravings" for them. Like "Big Macs" for instance. I understand they put a chemical in their "special sauce" to create cravings for Big Macs. Just go a month or so without a Big Mac and see if you have a craving.

Or another example is—a few years ago my family accused me of having an addiction to John Denver music because I was always listening to it around the house. I suppose I did use it as an "escape" from some of those mundane chores I disliked, like washing dishes or mopping floors; and those chores always seemed to go by more quickly and seemed more enjoyable when I could listen to John Denver. (Kinda like the commercial where they snap their fingers and say, "I could've had a V-8". That's the way it was whenever I had a task I didn't like doing—I could listen to John Denver and make the time go faster and more pleasant).

The only problem was it was *driving my family crazy!* It got to the point where they were absolutely *sick* of hearing John Denver's voice. Every time I put in one of his tapes, they would exit the room.

I decided to go on a "John Denver fast" to see if *I was addicted.* So, more for my family's sake than for my own, I went for over two years without listening to *any* John Denver music. And do you know what? I survived! And the best part is that my family can now tolerate John Denver music, although I still try not to play it when anyone's around. Plus I'm able to find enjoyment doing those "unpleasant tasks" without needing to "escape" from them.

Chapter Eleven
JOURNEY TO CENTER

We've discussed in detail how we move out of our personal integrity or create sin (separation within) and how we can get back into integrity through repentance. But what happens when we get out of integrity in our relationships with each other? I call this "shout" or *separation without* which usually disintegrates into conflict, confusion (not together), and fall-out followed by yelling, screaming and shouting which is why I call it *shout*. This type of separation usually happens when we do one or more of the following:

1) Going against our prime directive. This is when we're not in harmony with the God within and are following the path of the flesh rather than the path of the spirit. This brings us into a state of dis-ease which is "not easy." When things become difficult in our lives, it's an indicator that our spiritual selves and physical selves are not in harmony but in conflict. And when we're not in harmony with ourselves, we certainly can't be in harmony with others. We may want to choose other behaviors that work that put us back into harmony with ourselves and with others.

2) Battling distractions. We're often beset by large or small distractions that seem to get us "off center." It's often the "little things" that get to us rather than the major crises as illustrated in this poem by Carol Lynn Pearson.

> Guilt
> I have no vulture sins, God,
> That overhang my sky
> To climb, grey-feathering the air,
> And swoop carnivorously.
>
> It's just the tiny sins, God,

> That from memory appear
> Like tedious, buzzing flies to dart
> Like static through my prayer.

Life is full of small distractions whether it's a lost shoe, spilled milk, a job we detest doing, a dog that leaves a mess on the porch, or the peculiarities of someone we love. They all seem to distract us or get us "off-center." I've learned that I can stay centered if I can "praise God in all things" and see each disturbance as a lesson to learn—perhaps in patience, tolerance, and unconditional love.

3) Getting into expectation or anticipation. Whenever we leave the "now" and dwell on past regrets or future expectations or fears, we get "off-center." So whenever we feel the conflict of agitation creeping into our peace, if we will quickly return to the "now," we can usually regain centeredness. If we get into expecting others to do something for us, we also get off-center. "If your happiness depends on what somebody else does. ... you *do* have a problem." (Richard Bach)

4) Trying to complete too many contracts at the same time. Sometimes we catch ourselves "biting off more than we can chew." Like a computer we can develop "circuit overload." (And being a mother of ten healthy, active children and providing an adequate environment for them makes for enough contracts for any one person to fulfill, let alone trying to fulfill my own spiritual contracts of awakening change in the planet!)

Sometimes we just need to better organize our time so we can accomplish everything the spirit directs us to do. Other times we simply need to admit that we're *not* Superman or Wonder Woman and *not* take on the job of "saving the planet." The most important job we can do for ourselves *and* the planet is to stay in our own integrity.

5) Breaking contracts. Even though we may try with all our power to fulfill all the agreements (contracts) we make with people, there are occasions when we break an agreement which causes a loss of our personal integrity. This causes "dis-agreement" (not fulfilling agreements) until we can make it right with the other person. Usually a simple apology will do if it's a simple agreement, but in cases of eternal contracts (like marriage) nothing short of major reconciliation will do. This is where much repentance and forgiveness are required. "A small love forgives little, a great love forgives much, and a perfect love forgives all." (American Proverb)

6) Judging others. When we're in judgment (which includes condemnation) of others we're off-center and our progression toward God stops. "Judge not least ye be judged." (Luke 6:37)

The only one who can judge the intent of our hearts is God. Not even if we've walked in other people's moccasins for a mile, or a day, or a year, or even a lifetime, can we ever be in a position to judge another person's heart.

If someone trespasses against me and causes me to feel badly towards them, the quicker I can forgive them, the faster I can get out of judgment. "I, the Lord, will forgive whom I will forgive, but of you it is required to forgive all men." (D&C 64:10)

7) Trying to fulfill conflicting contracts. This is one I try to avoid at all costs as it is often the hardest to resolve. This can be caused when we break a relationship contract with one person in order to form a relationship contract with someone else.

For example, my sister-wife, Sandy, is going through a "conflict of contracts" situation with her ex-husband. He wants her to live in Utah with "his" kids as he wants to fulfill his part of the partnership agreement of raising them. But in order for her to be in a marriage relationship with Kurt, she must live here with us at Higher Ground as Kurt, Christy and I are unwilling to consent to having a marriage relationship in two different states. (The implications of this "conflict of interest" are mind boggling.)

This is a common conflict, however, among those who undergo the separation of divorce and the consequent "custody battle." Unfortunately, children are often the "fall-out victims" of such conflicts which can be avoided if we're clear when entering into marriage contracts about what we're agreeing to—implied or otherwise. We must learn to "wait upon the Lord" in making these very important decisions and pass through all the "phases of emotion." Only then can we make rational decisions concerning marriage and divorce.

When we're trapped in unresolved conflict, we become disabled—unable to move forward in our relationships and unable to move forward towards God's perfect love. Often we leave an intimate relationship when it starts getting uncomfortable because of conflict. In actuality, this is when the greatest growth can occur. The more quickly we can move through and beyond conflict and into peace, the quicker becomes our progress toward oneness and God.

In 1982, I met a remarkable man who'd written an incredible book, *The Magic of Conflict*. His name is Tom Crum, and both he and his book resonate with truth...and love. We met at a magical place called "Windstar" in the heart of the Rocky Mountains near Aspen, Colorado. He was the co-founder with John Denver of The Windstar Foundation and was John Denver's personal bodyguard. At the time, I was facing some of the worst "conflicts" of my life.

I'd just had a premature baby, Deserae, who'd spent 10 long days in the hospital because of hyaline membrane disease. (She recovered with no ill effects, praise God.)

Kurt and I were facing bankruptcy because a "friend" had embezzled money from our health food store/restaurant called "Livingstream." And we had no medical insurance to pay for Deserae's enormous hospital bills.

We were also both on trial for our church membership in the LDS Church because we were investigating Mormon fundamentalism. Our marriage relationship was also on the rocks because all of these conflicts were hitting us at the same time. Fortunately, God led us on a journey to Windstar where we enrolled in an *Aiki* workshop given by Tom Crum. For an entire week we learned about the "magic of conflict." (God makes no mistakes when we're journeying on the path of the spirit.)

That week was transformative for Kurt and me but especially for me as I was literally "turned on" by the spirit of truth and love I found there. When I first stepped onto Windstar's property, I was "electrified" by the warmth of the Holy Spirit testifying to me that I had great purpose there. It was what I now call a "born-again" experience. And when we first met Tom Crum, his electric smile and personality connected us in a relationship that has lasted through the years and continues to inspire us each time we make contact.

During our "Aiki Week," Tom redefined in new terms the traditional "Christian" concept of *love*. He basically put the "spirit" of the law of love back into the "letter" of the law, making it *alive!* "For the letter killeth, but the spirit giveth life." (2 Cor 3:6)

The first thing Tom shared with us was the philosophy behind his *Aikido* or "Aiki" training which I can best share with you by quoting from his book, *The Magic of Conflict*. It's the story of how the Japanese martial artist, Morihei Ueshiba (1883 - 1969) gave birth to the martial art of Aikido.

In the Orient in the 1920's there lived a master of the marital arts, or the art of dealing with physical conflict. He was, by all standards of the time, a very successful man. Historically, a master had to be prepared to accept and to meet victoriously, many challenges put forth by opponents interested in gaining fame of recognition. Often the loser was incapacitated or seriously injured as a result of these challenges, so there was obviously a high motivation to win.

This particular martial artist was consistently victorious. And yet even after reaching the pinnacle of success, he felt a deep and growing lack of fulfillment within. He took an extraordinary and unique step to discover this essential but missing ingredient by giving up the traditional way of the martial arts and going to the mountains, to return to nature and the land as a farmer and as a spiritual seeker.

After years of ascetic life and personal training, an entirely different state of consciousness permeated his being. He eventually came down from the mountains and astonished the marital artists in the land by declaring, "The true martial art is love." The physically orientated martial artists' typical reply was something along the lines of, "Thank you for sharing; now let's fight!" He found himself having to put his philosophy into practice. Challengers would inevitably find themselves upside down and immobilized in some unique manner, astonished that they were not hurt in the process. And he now met challengers effortlessly and joyfully, without the pain and strain of the past.

Following this introduction to the art of Aikido, the next few days were spent learning the philosophy and techniques of "centering" and the "dance of conflict." I quote from Chapter Four "Choose to Be Centered" in Tom's book, *The Magic of Conflict.*

The Aiki Approach presents conditions that each of us can choose to create at any time. It allows us to break through to a state of artistry, a state beyond success. It allows for conflicts in our lives to be resolved naturally and peacefully, with all sides being mutually supported, and it brings us closer in touch with our true self: a fully integrated mind, body, and spirit.

The first condition of the Aiki Approach is:

CHOOSE TO BE CENTERED

Notice that it doesn't say try or hope. Talking about being calm or balanced is one thing. Being it is something else. The above condition says choose. Centering is a real psychophysiological experience that each of us can choose to have, right now.

We have all experienced centering. It occurs when the mind, body, and spirit become fully integrated in dynamic balance and connectedness with the world around us. There is a heightened awareness and sensitivity, a feeling that everything is perfect the way it is. The truth of who we are as human beings is revealed.

This quality of centeredness is always there during those magic moments of your life. Those could be taking your first successful steps as a young child, being tucked in at night by Mom or Dad, making the big play in sports, conquering your fear in speaking in front of people, sitting quietly by a river, or just being with someone you love.

The centered state is simple, natural, and powerful. Understanding center is useful only if we truly integrate it into our mind and body and use it. More often, however, we intellectualize and philosophize about centering, rarely using it or making it an integral part of our being and our daily life.

Physicists have defined the center of gravity of an object as an infinitely small point upon which the entire object can be balanced. You can take the local grocery store or the car you drive or your own body and balance it on that one infinitely small point. This is not just an intellectual concept, nor is it merely a physical location that can be marked with a magic marker. It is a dynamically active, vibrationally alive center of balance and stability. By understanding and cultivating the skill of centering, you will dramatically affect your ability to live an active and vital life. Those rare moments can become your daily routine. Does it seem outrageous that all this is possible simply by your becoming centered? Maybe so, but it works!

I can't adequately explain in writing what it feels like to be *centered*, but it's both *very real* and *very powerful*. And if you want real-life experience in the practice of centering, take Aikido instruction. Tom Crum's book goes into much more detail on *centering* and you might want to get a copy for more information.

But the practice of *centering* is neither a new concept nor is it only achievable through Aikido or the martial arts. All religious and spiritual paths recognize this process as a path to enlightenment. In Christian terms it may be known as "centering on Christ." It's referred to as the "Christ consciousness" by New Age practitioners. In Oriental philosophies it could be "following the Tao" or the "Way of Life"; and in Hindu it could be "Krsna Consciousness" or the awakening of the Kundalini (or serpent power). Among Native Americans it's known as "the spiritual path" or "following the Great Spirit" or the "spirit-that-moves-in-all-things." Each religion or spiritual path talks about the same thing as "being centered" and it's simply a matter of understanding each unique definition of terms.

Participating in Tom Crum's Aiki Workshop helped me to redefine and clarify "Christ-centeredness." Praise God and "thanks" Tom for sharing.

Tom also helped me realize what conflict is all about. The following is from Chapter Eight in his book entitled, "Be Willing to Change."

Did you ever think, when you held or looked at a beautiful pearl, that its origin was irritation? An oyster, in response to the irritating presence of sand within its shell, creates a thing of beauty. Not only is the conflict resolved but value is created. When we understand that conflict includes the potential for us to create beautiful pearls and contribute to the world and to ourselves, then we begin to open up our shells, less concerned about letting life in. Embracing conflict can become a joy when we know that irritation and frustration can lead to growth and fascination.

The evolution of every living species has been a lesson in change. Witness the aeronautical design of a hawk, the camouflage magic of the chameleon, the killer instinct of the shark, or the pungent defensive scent of the skunk. All living species must adapt to and evolve with their constantly changing environments to flourish. Change in nature is not a philosophical choice. It is a survival choice. It is a choice for growth and flexibility. Conflict is nature's prime motivator for change.

When we fight with our children about a household chore, or with our fellow worker over which approach to take on a particular project, why is it so hard to change our point of view? Most often it is because we are not nearly as interested in resolving the conflict and possibly creating a new pearl as we are in being right. When we perceive conflict as a threat to our ego, our reaction is to defend or attack. All our energy and mind-power are used in the protection of our ego, not in the growth of our being. Fear of failure reigns supreme.

During a physical confrontation, if a person were coming at you with a circular attack, such as swinging a stick or throwing a hook punch or kick at the side of your head, what would your response be? Over my years in the marital arts, I've discovered that most people put up their arms in a sudden and tense motion to protect themselves, and are so frozen by the swing itself that they rarely move from their position. In effect, they are dealing with the attack right at its most powerful point. There are two places where a hurricane's force will not be felt—one is outside its range of power and the other is inside, at the center. In Aikido, both responses are available to you. You can move inside or outside the point of power—in this case, the fist or foot. In addition, the aikidoist moves in the same circular direction as the attack itself, so even if contact is made the impact is minimal. The aikidoist is riding the wave of the attack's energy instead of slamming into it. This requires timing and sensitivity to the direction and intensity of the attacker. The Aiki Approach is akin to dance. It's very difficult to waltz with a break dancer. It's important to be willing to move so that we pick up the tempo of an attack in order to transform it into a dance. The desire to dance with energy creates more awareness and connectedness in every situation.

When we choose to use conflict as an opportunity to change, life becomes a beautiful dance with energy. Even so, it's interesting that when we begin to understand the cause of conflict rather than "just dealing with its effect," we comprehend its true nature. As in holistic healing, it's not enough just to treat the symptoms of a disease but to understand the underlying causes of "dis-ease" (not easy).

So the next time we start showing symptoms of "shout" (separation without) in our relationships, remember to take the "journey back to center." When we are "Christ-centered," or come from a place of pure, unconditional love, the conflict we feel with others can be changed and transmuted into peace, joy and love.

Scriptural References: St. John 3:16, 14:15, 9:14; Romans 8:28,35-39; 1John 4:7-12; Alma 13:27-29; Moroni 7:13,47-48, 8:26, 10:32; D&C 42:29, 59:5-7, 88:123-126

Walk Your Talk Therapies: Chapter Eleven
The following therapies are taken from Tom Crum's book, *"The Magic of Conflict"* (with his permission).

Therapy One: *A Centering Exercise*
Sit in a comfortable position in which your back can be held straight without straining. Close your eyes and take some long, deep breaths through your nostrils. With each long, slow exhalation, imagine you see the tension flowing out of your body from head to toe. Do this for a few minutes until you feel relaxed and comfortable. Let your breathing settle down naturally to its one pace.

Imagine that you have a beam of light extending from your center through the top of your head. Picture your center as being about the size of a basketball. Let the light beam emanating from your center swing from side to side, taking your head and upper body with it as one unit. Let your swaying be easy and relaxed. After swaying back and forth for ten to fifteen seconds to establish a natural rhythm, let the swing and your center become half as large as before. Continue swaying with the same rhythm, but decrease the swing proportionately to the size of your "new" center. Continue in this process, every few seconds decreasing the size of the swing and of your center by half.

Soon your body will cease to move physically and it may be difficult to picture the actual size of your center. Simply focus your attention on the vibration of your center diminishing in size to infinity. It is the vibratory quality of the swinging "pendulum of light" following a single, infinitely decreasing point that becomes the focus of your attention. It allows for a comfortable ride inward to the source of your being.

When extraneous thoughts come into the mind, do not fight or struggle against them. Instead, easily come back to that vibratory quality of the center becoming smaller by half...half...half...and half again, on to infinity. The vibratory quality may be perceived differently by each individual and may change within an individual periodically throughout the exercise. It may be perceived as a feeling, a sound, or an image. Allow it to take whatever form it chooses.

Continue this process for fifteen to twenty minutes. When ending the exercise, bring your awareness back to the breath and breathe deeply into each and every area of the body. Take a few moments to do this, as it allows you to come out of the process easily and brings your awareness back into your body and the immediate surroundings.

Therapy Two: *The Change Exercise*

This simple exercise will illustrate how change—getting off your position—can alter the way you look at a conflict. Have another person stand behind you, put her hands on the back of your shoulders, and start gently but consistently pushing you forward so that you must start walking. As you start walking, have her continue increasing the pressure. After several steps, spin to one side, in the same speed or rhythm as the pusher, rolling along your partner's arm, maintaining contact, so that you end up in back, pushing the person who was just pushing you. The exercise demonstrates clearly that as soon as you are willing to get off line and to change, you find yourself in a powerful position of choice.

Chapter Twelve
RETURNING TO ONENESS

There are some people and events which completely shift your consciousness. That's what happened when I met Speaking Wind or "Patrick" as I will refer to him. Patrick was a Native American Shaman from the Pueblo Tribe with an Anasazi heritage. His shamanic title was "Spirit Caller." I won't go into all the details of how we met and became "one in spirit." My other book, *Heartsong,* has all those details. I'll just say that it was an earth-shattering or should I say shifting experience and took me into a spiritual dimension that I didn't know existed until then.

As another witness to this book on becoming one, I'd like to share some of Patrick's spiritual teachings from his book, *The Message.* This "message" was given to Patrick by the Ancient Ones (with all due respect and permission):

> These steps that we are now willing to share with you are meant so that others will have a path to follow. And this path will bring them to see themselves for who and what they are.
>
> However, we will caution you and those who would be willing to accept our message that there will be a great change that will come to all. And this change that will come to them will be one of a great surprise.
>
> Whenever one will begin to see themselves for who and what they are, Speaking Wind, there will be a great awareness that will come to them. And it will be from this first awareness that will cause them to fall into this place we call the awakening.
>
> The awakening will come to them when they will first learn to go within themselves and search for those same things that they share with

all of their brothers and sisters. Those things that will cause them to feel a great love that is within themselves.

For it is this love that is within them and comes out for no material reason. It is this love that will guide them to their spirit path in the domain of the Earth Mother's.

When they can stand in front of one of the standing people and feel a part of themselves that is covered with this love of sharing, there will be a recognition of what will be returned to them.

For this standing person will return this part of their love to them, and they will know that this has begun a part of a great adventure. An adventure that will lead them to know who and what they are and know that this is good.

Within all of the two-legs, there is a place of the spirit. And it is from this within place that they must reach into very deeply in order to find this love we are speaking to you of.

For it is this love that has no limitations and no boundaries that has been used to bond all spirits together from the one. And in finding it once again, there will become a beginning bond that will be felt...first from the standing person, then from the others.

Once any two-leg will find this part of themselves that holds this love that we speak of, this love that is within their own spirit they will feel as if they have uncovered a great truth. One that will now allow them to feel a part of all living that is within this domain.

And as they have this doorway opened up to them, there will be a great awareness that they are, in truth, a part of all things that exist. And as truth begins to fill them in their empty places, there will be a great joy that will come over them. One that will allow them to feel alive and no longer in a place where they do not know what they are to do.

Many of the two-legs will attempt to find this love that exists within them, but they will not find it. For there has only been for them a part of their living and seeing that has existed on the outside of their selves. There have not been the necessary acknowledgments of who and what they are from their within.

You see, Speaking Wind, one of the truths that must come to be... before they will be allowed to experience this love that is within them, is that there are two parts to themselves. And it is these two parts that must be brought into balance before they will be allowed entry into their own place of the spirit. This place of the spirit that is holding their love for them.

It is holding this love of theirs in a good way though, for if it were to be given to them before they had been prepared, they would not know what to do with it anyway. And it is great, Speaking Wind…greater than anything they have yet found on their path.

So it is that before this small doorway will be opened for them, they must travel within themselves and find their other half. This other half of themselves that will be just the opposite of who they see themselves as being on the outside.

For many of the two-legs you will see, little one, this will be a very strange experience for them to hold. And one that my prove difficult for them to embrace…but it is truth and they should follow it if they are to come to any place of understanding themselves and this path that is being offered to them.

If they will have the face of a female on the outside, then there will be their other face of the male that they carry on the inside. And if there is the face of the male on the outside, they must travel within to find their face of female… these are the other sides to all living things and must be brought into balance.

It is only when one will find the balance from the inside as being the same as the balance from the outside that they will come to know the meaning of the one. And it will only be when they will have become this one of themselves that their spirit will share with them the secret of this great and unconditional love that resides within them.

And Speaking Wind… this is the love of creation. For it was through this love that Great Mystery created all that you see before you. It was through this love that we were created…and it is through this love that the two-legs will once again learn to create for themselves. To create for themselves in a way that was once held by all of them. This way that they have forgotten to remember but still have the chance of learning once again.

I have had this mystical experience during which I contacted the Great Mystery. It's what the Gnostic Christians called "gnosis" which literally means "to know God for oneself," and it has become an essential part of my life and is what's directing me as I write this book. It's the total surrendering of oneself to following the path of Spirit.

In the Gospel of Thomas, one of the Gnostic gospels found at Nag Hammadi and translated in 1945, we read:

The Kingdom is inside you and outside you. When you know yourselves, then you will be known, and you will understand that you are children of the living Father. But if you do not know yourselves, then you live in poverty, and you are poverty.

When we come to know ourselves as spiritual beings enjoying an earthly existence, our physical bodies simply become vehicles for us to follow the path of the spirit. But following the path of the spirit is an interesting concept that is very difficult to describe in words. Patrick stated in one of his lectures that:

> There are two paths that we can choose to follow—the path of the spirit and the path of the flesh. These paths are diametrically opposed to each other, as one follows the "lusts of the flesh," while the other one follows the "desires of the heart." We must learn to follow the path of the spirit if we are to survive into the fifth world (next world).

The only counsel I can offer about following the path of Spirit (the Holy Spirit) is *just do it!* If there's *anything* in your life that's preventing you from following the path of Spirit, get rid of it or change it so you can.

I'm not saying that if you feel like your spouse or children are holding you back that you should get rid of *them*. It's absurd to think that *anyone* or *anything* can hold us back from following the path of Spirit. Obviously, some relationships are easier to maintain when they are on the same spiritual level, but the idea that we need to separate ourselves from intimate associations because we aren't all on the same spiritual progression is an illusion. The reality is this—we are *all on our own separate spiritual path* until we reach that ultimate *oneness with God.* We will *all* arrive at the same place at different times just as in the example of mountain climbers who ascend to the top of the mountain on different routes. We start out at different places at the bottom of the mountain and take different paths to get there. But ultimately, if we don't give up, we *all* reach the top of the mountain and celebrate our *oneness together* on the "peak of enlightenment" of our *ultimate oneness.*

Just keep following the path up the mountainside which is your own individual path of the spirit. And remember—don't let anything get in your way. If it happens to be other people standing in front of you blocking your progress, just politely say "excuse me" as you pass them by. Better yet, grab their hand and help them up the path along with you.

A wise man once said, "It's about time we realize it, we're all in this together; it's about time we find out, it's all of us or none." That same man was also inspired to sing a song about the power of gentleness when he sang about "The Flower that Shattered the Stone." Perhaps John Denver was yet another prophet, prophesying concerning the last days—our day—the New Day of Enlightenment when we will walk with God.

And I will give them one heart and I will put a new spirit within you and I will take the stony heart out of their flesh, and will give them an heart of flesh:

That they may walk in my statutes, and keep mine ordinances, and do them: and they shall be my people, and I will be their God. (Ezekiel 11:19, 20)

Just to give you a personal example of how the path of the spirit works in the physical realm, I'd like to share with you a few days' excerpts from my own personal journal to include in this chapter on "Returning to Oneness."

Friday, July 28, 1995 around 6:30 a.m.

I woke up in the pre-dawn to the sounds of Jenny Pearl stirring next to me. I turned toward her, lifting my pajama top to bare my breast so that she could nurse back to sleep. I fell back into a light sleep, listening to the sounds of our nearby creek and roosters crowing in the background.

In a half hour or so, I was again awakened by the sounds of Jenny making her baby cooing noises (not unlike a kitten purring), signaling that she'd had her fill of nursing and had gone back to sleep. I turned over onto my back to look out our "picture window" to the scene of morning sunlight filtering through the lacy cedars and tall pine trees. Suddenly the words to a John Denver song came to mind that I'd been listening to (and singing with) on the way to Frenchtown pond yesterday. It was on his "Rocky Mountain High" tape that I'd played on the car stereo. The words that came to mind were these:

> Silently the morning mist
> Is lying on the water
> Captive moonlight
> Waiting for the dawn
>
> Softly like a baby's breath
> A breeze begins to whisper
> The sun is coming
> Quick you must be gone
>
> Smiling like a superstar

The morning comes in singing
The promise of
Another sunny day

And all the flowers open up
Together in the sunshine
I do believe that
Summer's here to stay

And oh, I love the life within me
I feel a part of everything I see
And oh, I love the life around me
A part of everything is here in me...

"Perfect," I thought to myself. "How could the words of any other song fit so perfectly?"

I wondered if John Denver had experienced a similar dawn as I was experiencing at that very moment to inspire the words to this song. Boy, I wish I could ask him... nah, no more thinking along those lines, and my mind changed the subject.

I thought today I would get up early and put in some good hours harvesting. I made a mental list of the herbs and things that needed harvesting: stinging nettle, horsetail grass, yarrow, mullein flowers, elder flowers, raspberry leaves, strawberry leaves—all along the road and creek-bed.

And from the garden: all the mints—spearmint, peppermint, pineapple mint, chocolate mint (and another kind I couldn't recall the name of). The chamomile definitely needed harvesting. It was nearly taking over the herb garden. It needed thinning too. Not to mention the peas that were ready to pick. Also the yellow dock needed harvesting along the paths. It was at its prime to pick.

I decided it was time to stop thinking about it and start *doing* something about it. I slipped out of bed trying hard not to make a sound to disturb Jenny Pearl or Destiny Rose, who was also sleeping in the same bed on the other side of me. I walked quietly past the crib where Kelsey May was sleeping and out the bedroom door. Then I tiptoed past the boys bedroom where Jared, Jordan, Jonathan and Brendan were all asleep and on down the stairs.

I went into the bathroom and continued with my "moving morning meditation" as I slipped on my clothes from yesterday (a pair of flowered stretch shorts and a teal t-shirt). I then went into the living room and stretched myself out on the Native American motif rug. I did about 15 minutes of combined yoga and Pilates exercises. Then I tied on my jogging shoes, grabbed a large plastic garbage bag and scissors, and slipped quietly out the front door.

I started down our long driveway (two and a half miles to be exact) and before long I was joined by our two dogs, Shamu (our adolescent Rottweiler) and Fuchsia (a wonderful crossbreed we'd adopted from a friend). She was a great guardian dog for me and the kids, warding off wolves, bears, mountain lions and other such entities (physical and non-physical).

I jogged about a half mile down the driveway with Shamu and Fuchsia at my side taking in all the splendors of a perfect morning. The sun had just peaked across the mountains into our nestled valley haven, illuminating herbs and flowers along the embankment between the musical creek and roadside.

My heart sang praises to God for the beauty which surrounded me, and the love within my heart for Him was full to overflowing. I stopped at a junction in the road where a shaded woodland path led me to a stand of stinging nettle. I carefully approached it with gratitude and thanksgiving in my heart for the marvelous gifts of healing it provides. As I used the scissors to cut off the tops of several of them, I verbally thanked each plant for its sacrifice in sharing with my family and others its healing benefits. A few of them acknowledged me by brushing up against me giving me a warm, stinging sensation. But I was grateful that most of them were kind enough to acknowledge me in other ways through the spirit.

I returned to the driveway and walked slowly up the hill back home, feasting upon luscious blackberries all along the path. What a delightful breakfast I enjoyed!

About halfway home I noticed an Elder tree that had nearly turned all of its flowers into berries. I asked the tree if I could take the remaining clusters of flowers so that I could dry them for a special blend of Elder flower and peppermint tea. She agreed it would be all right.

As I was cutting the clusters of Elder flowers, I accidentally cut off one that had a beautiful, tan crab spider resting upon it. I apologized to the spider and carefully eased and encouraged it off and on to a clump of Elder flowers left on the tree.

I carried the clusters of Elder flowers in one hand and the bag full of stinging nettle in the other hand and walked up the road home singing another of John Denver's songs:

> Thank-you for this precious day
> These gifts you give to me
> My heart so full of love for you
> Sings praise for all I see

Oh sing for every mother's love
For every childhood tear
Oh, sing for all the stars above
The peace beyond all fear

(The next verse I changed a little bit to suit my own needs.)
This is for the pure in heart
Who long to build a home
Who gather here among the Saints
So they won't be alone
Are they not some dear mother's child
Are they not you and I
Are we the ones to turn away
And scorn their sacrifice

Or are they just like falling leaves
Who give themselves away
From dust to dust, from seed to shear
And to another day
If I could have one wish on earth
If all I can conceive
T'would be to see another spring
And bless the falling leaves

It's around 8:00 a.m. as I write this and even now I hear the stirring of children waking up. But before I go to begin my daily motherly duties, I thought I would share this short segment of my life with any and all who might read this, to let you know that life is *still* good and there are *still* places in the world that are havens and sanctuaries for the Holy Spirit to live and dwell. It is in each of us to become that safe haven, that temple of pure light.

It's 9:00 p.m. and I'm upstairs in bed but the spirit keeps insisting that I write down the rest of the day's events. So, being one who never resists the insistence of the spirit, I will write the happenings of the day after I finished my morning walk. (By the light of dusk.)

Breakfast was next on the menu, and I opted for scrambled eggs complete with turkey-bacon and cheese. I thought it would be nice to add some wild mushrooms to the mixture, so I sent Jordan out to where we hang laundry to pick a few mushrooms that I saw growing there the other day. I cleaned, chopped and sautéed them with onions, garlic powder and butter. (Some of the kids don't like mushrooms so I cooked them separately from the eggs.)

After the breakfast clean-up, I organized the kids for our "harvest party" assigning Ariel and Destiny the job of picking peas along with the little boys as back-up. I then tackled the herb garden with my handy pair of kitchen shears.

I trimmed and thinned all the patches of mint (spearmint, peppermint, chocolate mint, and pineapple mint) and then cleared out the chamomile and put it into a large plastic bag. The rest we put into smaller plastic grocery bags to carry to the house (including a bag full of yellow dock). There we laid it all out on the porch roof on a bed-sheet to dry in the sun.

After that, we loaded everyone into the white Subaru station-wagon to go blackberry picking. We traveled up the mountain to "Inspiration Point" and down the back-side picking the rich, dark blackberries that grew along the side of the road. This time I was careful not to leave Kelsey and the keys in the car at the same time, as I nearly lost her and the car over an embankment the other day when she decided it was time for a driving lesson. (Kelsey's only two years old but processes information very quickly for her age.) Two hours later we were back home again with three or so gallons to make blackberry jam.

We hurried and got lunch. (Actually, Ariel pitched in and did most of the work as usual.) After that, the older kids were off on their bikes to head for the mailbox where I had agreed to meet them with the truck for a ride back.

I had the little kids with me (five in all) piled in the front cab of the Subaru Brat as we inched our way down the two and a half mile drive to where the older kids had left their bikes and were swimming in the creek just below our neighbor's bridge. Wet and refreshed, they piled their bikes into the back of the truck and hopped in.

When we got home, the next phase of our harvest party began. I set Jared and Destiny to work shelling peas while Ariel made green drink. The following is the recipe for this high energy herbal concoction.

Green Drink

> Blend in blender with water the following and strain:
> Alfalfa
> Horsetail grass
> Stinging Nettle
> Mints (we use 4 or 5 types of mint
> including spearmint, peppermint,
> chocolate mint, pineapple mint and
> a wild mint that grows by the creek)

Comfrey
Yellow dock
Marshmallow
Shepherd's purse
Lamb's quarters
Dandelion
Clover (red and white)
Raspberry leaves
Strawberry leaves

A good size grocery bag of herbs makes 2 gallons of green drink. Add 1 quart pineapple juice to each gallon for added flavor, or 1/2 cup honey and 2 lemons can also be added as a lemonade sweetener.

Green drink is the best overall tonic and energizer. I have used it for over 15 years. It also tastes great and kids love it. It is our "family vitamin supplement," and is especially good in pregnancy for building iron.

As Ariel prepared the green drink from some of the herbs we'd gathered that day, I tackled making 24 pints of blackberry jam. (Low sugar, of course as there's a new pectin available for low sugar recipes.)

By the time we'd finished our jobs, it was time for dinner. I prepared creamed peas and potatoes from the garden that were absolutely delicious! (There's always an added "special" flavor from home-grown vegetables from your own garden.)

If Christy had been there, she would have baked some zucchini bread or corn bread, but since she and Kurt were gone on a business trip to Seattle, we had to settle for store-bought bread and butter. I realize more and more each day how valid the statement is that "many hands make light work," as I recognize how much Christy makes up the difference in so many ways. I give thanks to God for bringing her into our lives and family where we have grown so much in love, caring and sharing.

Perhaps if we continue to develop into community we could become totally self-sustaining with people to run a dairy, bakery, poultry, etc. It is just *too much work* for one family to do *alone*. Perhaps, the Lord willing, this also will happen as He is the designer of all good things.

The light from the window is fading now and is too dim to write anymore. Good night.

Saturday, Aug. 5, 1995 (A week or so later)

Today, Kurt, Christy and I woke up at 6:00 a.m. to go to the farmer's market and to do some yard sales. By the time we were packed and ready to go it was nearly 6:30 (I also needed to get Jenny Pearl ready to go) and we all crammed into the cab of the Subaru Brat to make our weekly trek into Missoula—40 or so miles away.

By the time we got into town, it was pushing 7:30 and too late to get a good spot at the farmer's market, so we decided to go to breakfast first at "Frontier Pies" and then get whatever spots were left to set up after that.

We all enjoyed a vegetarian omelet with hash browns and whole-wheat toast. (Jenny Pearl nursed during breakfast.) We then helped Kurt unload and set up at the farmer's market. (He was selling shirts, books, handmade boots, moccasins and sandals; and fire-starters this week. His main reason, I think, for going is to socialize and "make connections.")

After dropping Kurt off at the farmer's market, Christy and I took off towards the Rattlesnake area to do yard sales. As we were traveling down the road, we both discussed what we needed to find that week at yard sales. We made a list of things and then "sent it out," so to speak, into the spiritual realm.

We've had surprising success with this method—when we make a mental and verbal list like this. We've known many friends of ours that do the same thing with varied success. I guess you could call it an "affirmation of our needs list" or "prayer petition."

Kurt had given us $50 to spend (which was real generous of him), and Christy had $10 left in her purse from her trip to Seattle. So all together we had $60 to work with to fulfill our "needs list."

But as always we knew that the Lord would provide "sufficient for our needs" and our righteous desires. So we began to verbalize our needs which included:

1. School clothes for Deserae and Ariel (as they both desired to go to public school this year).
2. A computer for me to get my book typed into and also for Jared. (Who'd do homeschool if I could get him on a computer. But finding a computer at a yard sale was highly unlikely.)
3. A rug for the bathroom floor.
4. Jelly jars for bottling more blackberry jam. (We had over 5 gallons of picked blackberries waiting for us to jam.)
5. A cherry pitter (We picked up a box of cherries on our way back from Flathead Lake that needed bottling.)
6. Shoes for the little boys. (They were at a "hard-on-shoes" age at 3, 4, and 5.)

7. Birthday presents for Kelsey, Jordan, and Aubrey whose birthdays were August 16, 20 & 21.

Christy needed some new clothes for herself, and although she didn't express it verbally, I knew it was on her mind. And I, of course, was always open to finding something "new" (or should I say "interesting") to wear as it's always fun to recycle old clothes. I've been recycling for over 15 years now my clothes and I can't even remember the last time I bought something new for myself from a department store. (Although Kurt and Christy have bought me special dresses for special occasions.)

For the most part, I've always tried to buy everything we possibly can "second hand" because I believe there is enough wasted merchandise (and wasted money) generated by department store buying. I always tell everyone I know that even if I were wealthy and could afford the prices they were asking in the department stores, I'd still opt to do my shopping at rummage sales or second-hand stores. I guess there is always the thrill of finding that "perfect treasure" that someone else may consider "trash." It's the adventure of the unknown that draws me to yard sales each Saturday morning, realizing that the competition is stiff and the likelihood of finding "just what you need" is slim. (Especially in Missoula where everyone is impoverished and looking for a "good deal.")

So Christy and I set out on our yard sale quest up Rattlesnake Canyon, our hopes running high for a "good deal." (And a good parking place as the reverse gear in our Brat had gone out.)

The second yard sale we came to was in a driveway on the north side of the street. We pulled into a spot across the street next to someone's driveway so no one could park in front of us. It's barely 8:30 and already the "early birds" have arrived for the "catch of the day."

As we hurry in for our share of the action, the first thing I notice is a computer, complete with a monitor and disk drive. I casually look at it closer and notice it's an Apple III Computer and wondering if that's an "obsolete brand" having no knowledge of computers whatsoever. Then I look at the price—$12 for the entire outfit including a bunch of programs. I look at Christy and she looks at me and we both about keel over.

"It must not work," was Christy's first comment. "Either that or they must have left out a zero on the end of the price. It's got to be worth at least $120 if it works."

"I'll go ask," was my response as I headed over towards the person who looks to be the proprietor. I had Christy stay with the computer to make sure no one else grabbed it before I negotiated the deal.

After a bit of interrogation, I find out that the computer does indeed work, and it does only cost $12. The only problem was that they didn't have change for a $50 bill, and I told them to hold the computer while I went to find change at the next rummage sale. But just as we were leaving they were able to round up change from a "little brother" which saved us a trip going back and perhaps the chance of losing our "good deal." We loaded the computer on the back of the Brat and covered it with a sheet we purchased at our first yard sale. (We also found a bathroom rug for a nickel. All it needs is a blue color enhancement from RIT dye.)

We were still flying high when we came to the third yard sale. It was located in the well-to-do part of Rattlesnake area. This time we scored finding oodles of clothes that fit Deserae, Ariel, Christy and me—all with name-brand labels (you know like Bum, GAP, LA Gear, Paris Sports Club, etc.—the names you pay a fortune for in a store. Christy has to clue me in on the latest name-brands as I don't pay much attention to that kind of thing. I look for natural fibers and good wear when I go looking for clothing.)

At that same yard sale, we also picked up a wonderful children's plastic, put-together, nuts and bolts car set for Jordan's birthday. (He's great at taking everything apart bolt by bolt but hasn't quite learned to put things back together again.) Christy and I both thought this would be the "perfect" birthday gift for Jordan. We also picked up a peg board set for Kelsey's birthday and a memory game for Christy's pre-school. Not to mention a new Rummicube game for the kids.

The next yard sale we came to we found a cute, cotton-knit sundress that would fit both Christy and me, and also a nifty make-up kit for Aubrey's birthday.

Then there were a few that we struck out at, and we knew it was getting late into the morning when most of the "good stuff" would be gone. It was only around 10:30 and we still had an hour or so before we had to pick up Kurt, and so we persisted. We were nearing the end of our rummaging, finding a few odds and ends here and there, when we came to one sale where the gal said she would be taking offers on all her "stuff" just to get rid of it. She had a lot of "stuff" left, and when we looked at the high prices, we could tell why. But we decided to look anyway and maybe offer her the prices we were used to paying at yard sales.

We were going through some clothes on a table when, lo and behold, there were three or four jelly jars stuck in the midst of them. "That's funny. I wonder what jelly jars are doing amongst the clothes?" I said to Christy as I grabbed them up in my hands to go pay for them. "Perhaps she has more."

The gal in charge was busy so I decided to look around for more jelly jars. There was a large box with a bunch of stuff on top that caught my attention so I walked over to it and lo and behold, underneath all the stuff there were *my* jelly jars. I was delighted to say the least and when I carried them over to Christy to show her I was bubbling over with joy.

"See, I knew we'd find them!" I exclaimed. We packed the rest of the box with clothes for Christy and also found four pairs of good shoes to fit the little boys and some nice outfits Jordan's size for his birthday. We offered the gal $5 for the lot of it, and she took the offer minus a nice work-out outfit she wanted $5 alone for. She said it was just too nice to give away at that price and that she knew a friend of hers who would like it. Christy wasn't too disappointed as she knew she was getting a "good deal" for the rest of the stuff.

We decided to hit one more yard sale before we went to pick up Kurt. We didn't score there but had about 5 or 6 yard-salers oohing and aahing over little Jenny Pearl and how beautiful she is. That really helped make my day, too.

We decided to pick Kurt up first at the farmer's market because I wanted to buy some statice (flowers that dry really well) from the people we'd picked statice from last year. It was around 11:30 and the farmer's market closes at noon, so I thought we'd better hurry to get a good parking spot. We had to park a few blocks away to find one from which we wouldn't have to back up.

On our way walking towards the farmer's market, we spied one more "yard sale" sign. Could we resist? Of course not! We still had time for one more sale!

It was in someone's back yard and most of the stuff looked pretty picked over except for a cute little pedal car that the little boys would absolutely adore. Unfortunately, someone had beaten us to it and the lady said they were coming back for it after they went to the farmer's market. They had paid $7.50 for it. (Out of our price range as we only had $2 left.) I told the lady I had three birthdays coming up and was looking for birthday presents. She then said she had a cute little tricycle in her storage shed she'd be interested in "getting rid of." She unlocked the shed and pulled out one of those nice "metal trikes" that was still in good condition except for the paint. I asked her how much she wanted for it and she asked how much I'd be willing to pay. I told her I didn't want to insult her, but the only money I had left to spend was $2. Believe it or not, she took it! We left the trike there to come back for it later as we needed to get to the farmer's market before it closed.

We hurried along the rows of luscious produce and colorful flowers to where the statice people were getting ready to close up. Christy was stopped by a friend from Pinesdale who gave her two enormous cucumbers from his green house. They chatted for awhile while I headed for the statice.

The lady who sold statice had had her baby six months earlier and had wanted a home delivery but was afraid to do it because of her age. The spirit kept prompting me to get to know her so that I could maybe assist her at her delivery. But delivering babies is a very personal affair, and I don't usually push myself on people to attend their deliveries. Our potential friendship sort of came to an end when the statice season ended, and we'd picked all that they wanted us to pick. I had intended on keeping in touch with her during her pregnancy to see how she was doing and if she needed any help or advice. I gave her one of my books on natural child birth, but it's hard to keep in touch with people without a phone. Anyway, to make a long story short, she shared with me how she had to have an emergency C-section because she couldn't dilate completely. She thought it had something to do with her being "stressed-out" because she had buried her father that same day.

I felt bad that I hadn't followed my spiritual promptings to keep in touch with her because I felt that I perhaps could have helped her. There are so many techniques for relaxation I'd learned over the 17 years or so I'd been involved in childbirth, that I was almost certain that I could have helped her have the natural home birth she'd desired.

Again, I kicked myself for not following the spirit both for her sake and for mine and the wonderful relationship we could have formed. Sometimes my shyness gets the best of me as I don't want to tread on sacred ground. But she was so warm and friendly to me and even gave me a huge bunch of statice for free. I had really missed a golden opportunity to make a special friend. I vowed once more to *never* resist the promptings of the spirit.

Christy and I left my "friend with the statice" to go find Kurt in the glitz and clamor of the "dry goods" part of the farmer's market. Kurt looked extremely yummy with his newly acquired tan and bleached-out hair. He said he had a fair enough day selling a few shirts and a pair of hand-made sandals.

We told Kurt where we'd parked, and he asked us to get the car and bring it around to where he could load it up easier. He wanted to wait awhile longer for a lady who was coming back to pay him for a shirt.

Christy and I walked down the street past the "hippie revival counter-culture" market area and ran into Matthew, our neighbor, at Higher Ground. We chatted briefly about blackberries and babies, and then decided to swing by the yard sale to pick up the tricycle we'd purchased earlier.

As we were walking through an alley next to the yard sale, lo and behold, there in a big, black, garbage bag overflowing with junk were *four more good canning jars* to add to our collection.

I carried the bottles while Christy carried Jenny and the trike back to the Subaru. (I'm glad Christy's from good Wyoming stock. She has a muscular strength I'm lacking being a city girl.) We then picked up Kurt who was standing in the middle of the road waiting.

At home, Christy and I set about canning the five or more gallons of blackberries for jam. We got 38 pints out of them and while they were cooling, I was ready to tackle the job of canning cherries. Then I mentioned the fact that we'd gotten everything we asked for at the rummage sales except for a cherry-pitter.

Then Christy mentioned that she had noticed some canning tools inside the box of jars we'd found but didn't know if any of them was a cherry-pitter as she'd never seen one before. She rummaged through the box of jars until she found the tools and, lo and behold, one of them *was a cherry pitter!* Can you believe it! We laughed 'til we cried. God is so good to us. Praise His name.

In summary of this chapter on following the spirit, Lou Gold made a beautiful statement at the 1995 Windstar Symposium when he asked, "Why is it that we think that the things we make are better than the gifts that are given?"

Sometimes the gifts that are given are so rich and unexpected that we're not sure how to handle them. This was the case when I experienced my "oneness experience" with Patrick which literally "blew my mind." One of the most incredible "mind-blowing" spiritual experiences I shared with Patrick is included in my book, *Heartsong*. I've included it here to give you some background for the "Walk Your Talk Therapies" at the end of this chapter.

"Our spirits have had fun playing together. But now it is time to rest and relax. I have a wonderful tape I bought today with music depicting the four elements—earth, air, fire and water. I would like you to listen to it with me."

"And so how do you propose to do that, Patrick? Play it through the phone?"

"Oh, Little One," Patrick laughed. "You do still have much to learn."

With that he hung up the phone and I was left to wonder what in the world he was talking about. But Patrick was right. It was time for rest and relaxation. I undressed and slipped between the sheets. Almost immediately Patrick's spirit entered the room and asked permission to be one with me again. There was no hesitation in my acceptance, and as we joined in spiritual communion, pure ecstasy filled my soul again. After a few moments of awakening the *Kundalini* and experiencing a few spiritual orgasmic rushes opening all of my chakras, Patrick's spiritual energy or vibration began to change.

At first the energy became like that of the earth—firm and solid—

penetrating me as if a mountain were being thrust up through the Earth in volcano-like eruptions. It was powerful energy, breaking open each chakra with a penetrating orgasmic thrust. And wow, was it satisfying! I had never felt so firmly rocked with each powerful spiritual orgasm.

Then the energetic vibration changed and became like that of air, totally different, with breezy, finger-like currents of air caressing me, pulsating a beautiful windsong to my soul. I felt lovingly caressed, as if I were being stroked by Patrick's spiritual fingers. It was like the spirit of the wind inviting me to join in a oneness celebration of breezy ecstasy—and I did—feeling the orgasmic rushes move up and down my chakras.

Again the vibrations changed to that of fire. I felt the intense fire of the *Kundalini* energy, igniting me with flames of passionate, fiery orgasms. Ah... it was so explosively irrepressible...so warm, so alive! My soul was on fire with Patrick's fiery thrusts that I felt I would explode into flames!

Finally, the energy vibrations changed to that of water—cool and calming, with wave after wave of liquid passion filling my soul to over-flowing. Like the flow of the river to the sea...like the fountain of living waters being poured inside me. I felt the flood of Patrick's spiritual energies pulsing my chakras open. My spirit was overflowing with the love Patrick flowed inside me.

And though my energy centers were blown wide open, it was all I could do to contain all of it—the energies of earth, air, fire and water. My heart began singing praises to God for the gift of grace he'd given me...to experience making spiritual love with Patrick.

As for Patrick—all I could do as he brought me deeper and higher with each spiritual climax to a greater awakening was to express his name over and over again in spirit, telling him how much I loved him!

Scriptural References: Genesis 1:31: St. John 16:13; Acts 7:51, 17:24-31; Romans 8:1-4; 1Corinthians 6:19-20; 1Nephi 10:18, 19; 2Nephi 27:23; Ch.28; Alma 31:17,18; D&C 45:57,58, 93:23-36.

Walk Your Talk Therapies: Chapter Twelve
In Edmond Bordeaux Szekely's *The Essene Gospel of Peace,* he mentions the three "angels" which are given unto man for the cleansing of his temple:

The angels of air and of water and of sunlight are brethren. They were given to the Son of Man that they might serve him, and that he might go always from one to the other.

Holy, likewise, is their embrace. They are indivisible children of the Earthly Mother, so do not you put asunder those whom earth and heaven have made one. Let these three brother angels enfold you every day and let them abide with you through all your fasting.

For I tell you truly, the power of devils, all sins and uncleannesses shall depart in haste from that body which is embraced by these three angels. As thieves flee from a deserted house at the coming of the lord of the house, one by the door, one by the window, and the third by the roof, each where he is found, and whither he is able, even so shall flee from your bodies all devils of evil, all past sins and all uncleannesses and diseases which defiled the temple of your bodies…

In the following five therapies we will learn to connect with and celebrate the *oneness* that we share with all four elements—earth, water, air and fire—as we *realize that we are part of everything, and everything is a part of us.*

Therapy One: *Becoming One with the Earth*

Find a spot in nature where you can be completely alone and undisturbed for at least several hours. (An entire day would be the ideal.)

Now, take off *all* of your clothes so you are "buck naked"—the way you arrived here on this planet. Find a comfortable spot to sit on the bare Mother Earth. Pick a spot that you will be comfortable—out of the sun if it's a hot day or you might get sunburned. Just sit there and observe with all of your senses everything that is happening around you.

This process is similar to what the Native American's call "Vision Quest" in which they go to a sacred place after three or so days fasting and sit in the exact same place without food, water or sleep until they receive "vision." Since, we modern "Native Americans" aren't adapted to this type of endurance, you can start out slowly with perhaps an hour session at a time.

The purpose of the "Vision Quest" is to begin to feel the connection, that *oneness* with the "spirit-that-moves-in-all things" by becoming "like a rock." A "rock," as the Native Americans suggest is a "recording device" in which everything is recorded regarding the activities that surround it.

As you become *like a rock,* record inside yourself all the activities that are going on around you, taking in every little detail, utilizing all of your senses.

Smell the fragrance of the trees and flowers that surround you.

Feel the breeze on your face, or the bugs that crawl on or land on you. Feel the warmth or coolness of Mother Earth as you sit on her.

Listen to the birds or chipmunks chattering in the trees. Also listen for the still, small voice of the spirit in the wind.

Taste the air in your mouth as you breathe it in and out.

Sense the sunlight on your face and body, enlightening your very being with its penetrating rays.

Feel and sense it all as if you have been there a thousand years and as if you will be there a thousand years longer. Then record it in your every cell, in the depth of your very being. Feel the *oneness* you are with every other cell and being in existence. Become *one with the Earth* as you become "a rock."

Therapy Two: *Becoming One with the Water*

This therapy is one of my favorites and can be done alone or with someone you love. The very best place is at a secluded, natural, hot springs. (Our favorite is called "Gold Bug" in Idaho or Diamond Fork Hot Springs in Utah.) If you don't have a natural hot springs near you, find a nice Jacuzzi, (or a bathtub will do if you lack other options.)

As in the previous therapy, take off all your clothes so you're in your "birthday suit." (Don't attempt to do this at public hot springs or you might get kicked out or arrested for "indecent exposure.")

Now, as you immerse yourself naked into the warm water, imagine yourself becoming as fluid as the water. Swim and move with the motion and rhythm of the water as if you are *one with the water, and the water is one with you.* Make love to the water, realizing that about 75% of your body is made of this marvelous, fluid substance. Let the fluidity of this precious substance surround you with its life-giving warmth and energy.

Ultimately, as you are able to connect with the *spirit of the water*, you will feel the *oneness* with the life force which is in *water.* And you will honor and appreciate the water for what it represents to you and all beings on the planet—*life!* No longer will you take *it* for granted and abuse the privilege of drinking pure, unpolluted *water.*

I have a confession. While Kurt and I were experiencing this *oneness* experience with water at one of our favorite hot springs, we got so *into* it that it aroused us sexually to where we ended up making passionate love in the hot springs. This is when our beautiful Kelsey May was conceived and she, to this day, is so attracted and at *one* with water that we have a hard time keeping her away from it. She's our little "Aqua-Muchacha" (water baby).

Therapy Three: *Becoming One with the Air*

As in the first therapy of this series, find a spot in nature where you will be alone and undisturbed for an hour or so. Pick a day when the wind is blowing or right before a storm. I did this "therapy" once during a lightning storm on top of our own "Inspiration Peak." It was so incredible and passionate that Kurt and I ended up making love after that and conceiving our beautiful daughter, Jenny Pearl. So be careful if you do this with a partner—it may be sexually stimulating.

Take off all of your clothes and expose your entire body to the caresses of the *air*. Feel the *air* caressing your naked body as if it were "making love" to you, and you were "making love" to it. Move your body to the rhythm of the *wind* and dance to that rhythm as if you are *wind* itself. Or imagine yourself as a bird or a butterfly with your wings spread soaring and flying with the wind beneath your wings lifting you up, higher and higher into the heavens.

Breathe in the *spirit of the air* and feel it become a part of you—spirit to spirit. Feel the *oneness* you are with the *air* and the life-giving properties it gives you. Remember that you could not live or survive a moment without this life-giving substance—*air*. Honor this substance *air* by not polluting it unnecessarily. Work to bring clean air to all of life which lives and breathes on this beautiful planet. It is *the breath of life.*

Therapy Four: *Becoming One with Fire*

This therapy can be done alone or with friends and can be done clothed or naked.

Choose a safe place in nature away from trees or anything that is flammable. (Do it at a time of year when there is no fire danger.) Then build a *safe* campfire, preferably at night-time so you can better observe the properties of fire.

As you sit close to the flames of the campfire, (don't get so close that you could burn yourself, but do get close enough that you can be intent on watching the flames) observe them as they lick and flicker in a spiral motion and transmute the energy of the wood into pure light. As you watch and observe this transmutation process, become as you're able, a flame of spiraling energy. Feel the power of the *kundalini* transmute the substance of your body into pure light.

Keep doing this until you become *one* with the flames of the *fire* and they become one with you, warming your soul with the power and energy of the *kundalini..*

Once I observed a girl who came for a visit who really became *one with fire*. She would play with it in her hands allowing the flames to spiral through her fingertips. Then she would dance in and around the fire as if she herself was a flame of fire. It was so fascinating and beautiful to watch, and although I've never done this myself, I was in complete awe at her ability to truly connect and become *one with fire.*

Therapy Five: *Becoming One with the Four Elements—Earth, Water, Air and Fire*

There's nothing like the sacredness of a Native American "Sweat Lodge Ceremony" in order to experience the oneness you can become with all four elements—*earth, water, air* and *fire.*

If you can find someone in your area who performs "sweats," I strongly recommend participating in one especially if it's performed by someone who really knows what they're doing like an Indian "Shaman" (or holy man).

We've had limited success in performing our own "sweats" here at Higher Ground, and since I'm a mere novice at constructing a sweat lodge and performing the ceremony, I would recommend you research this out yourself by reading books on it or asking questions to those who have participated in one. One of the books I highly recommend on the subject of Native American Ceremony is one by Ed McGaa, Eagle Man called *Mother Earth Spirituality.*

Chapter Thirteen
The Merkabah

In my first Kundalini/Tantric Energy Awakening Class at Heartsong Healing Center in Holladay, Utah, one of my students loaned me a fascinating book, *The Secret of the Flower of Life* by Drunvalo Melchizedek. In the first chapter entitled "Remembering Our Ancient Past" was an interesting section on "The Mer-Ka-Ba."

The word Mer-Ka-Ba is made up of three smaller words, Mer, Ka and Ba, which, as we are using them, came from ancient Egyptian. It is seen in other cultures as *merkabah, merkaba* and *merkavah.* There are several pronunciations, but generally you pronounce it as if the three syllables are separate, with equal accents on each. *Mer* refers to a specific kind of light that was understood in Egypt only during the Eighteenth Dynasty. It was seen as two counterrotating fields of light spinning in the same space, which are generated by certain breathing patterns. *Ka* refers to the individual spirit and *Ba* refers to the spirit's interpretation of its particular reality. In *our* particular reality, *Ba* is usually defined as the body or physical reality. In other realities where spirits don't have bodies, it refers to their concepts or interpretation of the reality they bring with them.

When I googled "Merkabah" on the internet and searched for images, these are two of the images that came up (I've redesigned these for my book):

I was astonished to see how these two images correlated so well to my own model of Celestial Integrity. I then googled some more information on the internet and found this from Wikipedia, the free encyclopedia:

> The Hebrew word **Merkaba** ("chariot", derived from the consonantal root *r-k-b* with general meaning "to ride") is used in Ezekiel (1:4-26) to refer to the throne-chariot of God, the four-wheeled vehicle driven by four *"chayot"* (Hebrew: "living creatures"), each of which has four wings and the four faces of a man, lion, ox, and eagle.

When I was a young girl, I remember learning a song in grade school about Ezekiel's "chariot of fire." It went something like this:

Ezekiel saw a wheel
Way up in the middle of the air
Ezekiel saw a wheel
Way in the middle of the air

And the little wheel runs by faith
And the big wheel runs by the grace of God
'Tis a wheel in a wheel
Way in the middle of the air

I then looked up Ezekiel 1:4-26 in my handy Bible. I won't quote it as even a Bible scholar like me has a difficult time with certain Bible symbology. However, I did think the commentary about it in the Wikipedia was quite interesting.

> According to the verses in Ezekiel, the analogy of the Merkaba image consists of a chariot made of many angels being driven by the "Likeness of a Man." Four angels form the basic structure of the chariot. These

angels are called the "Chayot" (living creatures). The bodies of the "Chayot" are like that of a human being, but each of them has four faces, corresponding to the four directions the chariot can go (north, east, south, and west). The faces are that of a man, a lion, an ox (later changed to a child or cherub) and an eagle…

The four Chayot angels represent the basic archetypes that God used to create the current nature of the world. Ofannim, which means "ways", are the ways these archetypes combine to create actual entities that exist in the world. For instance, in the basic elements of the world, the lion represents fire, the ox/earth, the man/water, and the eagle/air. However, in practice, everything in the world is some combination of all four, and the particular combination of each element that exist in each thing are its particular Ofannim or ways. In another example, the four Chayot represent spring, summer, winter and fall. These four types of weather are the archetypal forms. The Ofannim would be the combination of weather that exists on a particular day, which may be a winter-like day within the summer or a summer-like day within the winter.

The Man on the throne represents God, who is controlling everything that goes on in the world, and how all of the archetypes He set up should interact. The Man on the throne, however, can only drive when the four angels connect their wings. This means that God will not be revealed to us by us looking at all four elements (for instance) as separate and independent entities. However, when one looks at the way that earth, wind, fire and water (for instance) which all oppose each other are able to work together and coexist in complete harmony in the world, this shows that here is really a higher power (God) telling these elements how to act.

This very lesson carries over to explain how the four basic groups of animals and the four basic archetypal philosophies and personalities reveal a higher, godly source when one is able to read between the lines and see how these opposing forces can and do interact in harmony. A person should strive to be like a Merkaba, that is to say, he should realize all the different qualities, talents and inclinations he has (his angels). They may seem to contradict, but when one directs his life to a higher goal such as doing God's will (the man on chair driving the chariot) he will see how they all can work together and even complement each other. Ultimately, we should strive to realize how all of the forces in the world, though they may seem to conflict can unite when one knows how to use them all to fulfill a higher purpose, namely to serve God.

This all seemed so familiar when I related it to my *Kundalini* experiences with Patrick, when he used all four elements—fire, earth, water, and air to spin all of my *chakras* (Sanskrit word for wheels) open. I wondered if the Merkabah had anything to do with Kundalini energy and chakra opening. When I read further on the Wikipedia site I found the following information very interesting:

> In medieval Judaism, the beginning of the book of Ezekiel was regarded as the most mystical passage in the Hebrew Bible, and its study was discouraged, except by mature individuals with an extensive grounding in the study of traditional Jewish texts.
>
> **Hekhalot** ("Palaces/Temples") writings are the literary artifacts of the Maasei Merkavah. The main interests of all Hekhalot writings are accounts of mystical ascents into heaven, divine visions, and the summoning and control of angels, usually for the purpose of gaining insight into Torah. The *locus classicus* for these practices is the biblical accounts of the Chariot vision of Ezekiel (Chap. 1) and the Temple vision of Isaiah (Chap. 6). It is from these, and from the many extra-canonical apocalyptic writings of heavenly visitations, that Hekhalot literature emerges. Still, it is distinctive from both Qumran literature and Apocalyptic writings for several reasons, chief among them being that Hekhalot literature is not at all interested in eschatology, largely ignores the unique status of priesthood, has little interest in fallen angles or demonology and it "democratized" the possibility of divine ascent. It may represent a rabinnization of these earlier priestly ideologies.
>
> The title, "Hekhalot" (palaces), derives from the divine abodes seen by the practitioner following a long periods of ritual purification, self-mortification, and ecstatic prayer and meditation. In their visions, these mystics would enter into the celestial realms and journey through the seven stages of mystical ascent: the Seven Heavens and seven throne rooms. Such a journey is fraught with great danger, and the adept must not only have made elaborate preparation, but must also know the proper incantations, seals and angelic names needed to get past the fierce angelic guards, as well as know how to navigate the various forces at work inside and outside the palaces.

Not only did this remind me of the signs and tokens revealed in the Mormon Temple ceremonies which I participated in years earlier, but it reminded me of the journey I take each time my Kundalini energy is opened up by God and I ascend through my seven chakras (throne rooms or heavens) to commune with God. This was all incredibly fascinating stuff to me and also another validation in my quest to discover the oneness within myself and the oneness without—which permeates all religions and spiritual thought-forms.

On another website created by the same author of the book, The Ancient Secret of the Power of Life, Drunvalo Melchizedek he goes onto to describe the Merkaba, it's function, and how to activate it:

One of the functions of the Mer-Ka-Ba is to act as the vehicle to take the spirit and the body into the next world. However, this function—and most of the other possibilities—is impossible to obtain until something changes within the person. The Mer-Ka-Ba is situated around the human body like a three dimensional geometric web that is dormant and nonfunctional, waiting for the right moment. When the spirit that inhabits the body remembers that it is there and begins to change certain aspects of itself, an incredible transformation begins to grow.

It was believed in ancient times, and even written about by the Hebrews, that the Merkavah could be turned on by certain principles in meditation. This involves breathing changes, and mind, heart, and body changes that alter the way a person perceives the Reality. From my perspective, it is the beginning of "Enlightenment."

And yet it is clear that the Mer-Ka_Ba can also be "activated" as the New Agers say, by other methods beside the male-style instructions using the breathing changes mentioned above. It can also become functional through methods that are purely female. Through the true living of qualities such as love, faith, trust, truth and compassion, the Mer-Ka-Ba can spontaneously become alive. In other words, very pure human character can translate into a living Mer-Ka-Ba field around the person, even if that person doesn't initially know it is there.

And yes, absolutely, the Mer-Ka-Ba is alive. It is a living field, not a purely mechanical field of energy. Because it is a living field, it responds to human thought and feeling, which is the way to connect to the field. So the "computer" that guides the Mer-Ka-Ba is the human mind and heart. The possibilities are endless.

Yes, the possibilities *are* endless once we create our own Merkabah or Celestial Integrity. Then we have the power to create as God creates—ad infinitum—which means endlessly. This is our eternal inheritance as children of God and co-creators *with* God. This is, in essence, our connection with God—or our journey toward God.

Chapter Fourteen
RETURNING TO ONENESS:
VISION OF RAINBOW LIGHT CENTERS

RAINBOW LIGHT CENTERS

MISSION STATEMENT: We are all free and loving beings on the path to personal sovereignty and oneness with others. When we heal ourselves of the illusions that keep us in separation, we will finally realize (real eyes) the truth that we are all one.

PURPOSE: The purpose of Rainbow Light Centers is to create facilities, which will facilitate personal healing and community healing. Through classes and experiential healing programs, we will identify and heal the illusions that keep us in a state of SIN (separation within). Through cooperative community living, we will identify and heal the illusions that keep us in a state of SHOUT (separation without). The Rainbow Light Center is a basic prototype for other communities everywhere.

PHILOSOPHY: The rainbow is white light diffused into six incremental spectrums of color, i.e. red, orange, yellow, green, blue, and violet. Each color, vibrationally, represents an energy center, or what is commonly known as a chakra. The facility is set up as a 6-sided hexagon with a biodome, representing white light, the seventh or crown chakra, in the center. The white light is diffused into six different color waves or branches. Each branch or section of the facility represents an energy center where different creative objectives are manifest. For example:

RED= GATHERING AND CONFERENCE—**THE POLITICAL CENTER**
ORANGE= SOCIAL AND SENSUAL—**THE THERAPY CENTER**
YELLOW= POWER AND ECONOMIC—**THE WORK-OUT/RETAIL CENTER**
GREEN= NURTURING AND HEART—**THE DINING CENTER**
BLUE= CREATIVE AND VOCAL—**THE ENTERTAINMENT CENTER**
VIOLET= SPIRITUAL AND INTELLECTUAL—**THE LIBRARY/ MEDITATION CENTER**

The awareness and balance of all colors or energies of the incremental light spectrum is the objective of the light center. Individual balance and then integration of all colors of the rainbow represents wholeness, health or holiness and can be explored in the Garden of Eden Biodome where white light is centralized. It is where we can become children of God (light) exploring our own innocence in a lush, green living environment where the fruits of all trees, including the tree of life, are available and can be partaken of freely—without sin.

QUOTES

In his last years on Earth, the great teacher, Paramhansa Yogananda repeatedly and urgently spoke of a plan that he said was destined to become a basic social pattern for the New Age: The formation of "world brotherhood colonies" as he called them would be formed. In almost every public lecture, no matter what his announced subject, he would digress to urge people to act upon his proposal.

"The day will come," he predicted, "when this idea will spread throughout the world like wildfire. Gather together, those of you who share high ideals. Pool your resources. Buy land in the country. A simple life will bring you inner freedom. Harmony with nature will give you happiness known to few city dwellers. In the company of other truth seekers it will be easier for you to meditate and to think of God."

Intentional Communities
J. Donald Walters

An "Eco-village" is a small village of people who strive for ecological and economical sustainability. But it goes far beyond this physical state of being. As a spiritual body of believers, we are not just a collection of people with diverse talents and ideologies. As we come to realize our potential in community, we begin to manifest the truth that the whole is much greater than the sum of its parts. We realize that no one is in charge, only a higher source and that source will assist us in bringing the higher vibration of light and love that will transcend us into the new age of enlightenment. (White Buffalo Woman)

There is nothing more powerful than an idea whose time has come. (Author unknown)

I say unto you, be one: and if ye are not one, ye are not mine. (Doctrine & Covenants 38:27)

When we understand the blueprint of the true Temple—the sacred, life-giving balance of male and female energies inherent in the cosmos itself and the symbolism that portrays the composite wisdom of antiquity—blessings will begin to flow like a gentle river into the parched lands of Earth. As found in the promise of Isaiah, the desert shall bloom. Universal peace and well-being can be restored when the blueprint for the Temple is embraced in our consciousness. The blueprint is:

The Woman with the Alabaster Jar
Margaret Starbird

It's about time we begin it
To turn the world around,
It's about time we start to live it
The dream we've always known,
It's about time we start to see it
The family of man,
It's about time
It's about changes
And it's about time...
It's about you and me together
And it's about time.
(words by John Denver)

His disciples said, "When will you appear to us and when shall we see you?"

Jesus said, "When you strip off your clothes without being ashamed, and you take your clothes and put them under your feet like little children and trample them, then (you) will see the son of the living one and you will not be afraid."

The Gospel of Thomas

God, in both Judaism and Islam, was One. God was a unity. God was everything. The forms of the phenomenal world, on the other hand, were numerous, manifold, multifarious and diverse. Such forms bore witness not to the divine unity, but to the fragmentation of the temporal world. If God was to be discerned in the creation at all, it was not in the multiplicity of forms but in the unifying principles running through those forms and underlying them. In other words, God was to be discerned in the principles of shape—determined ultimately by the degrees in an angle—and by number. It was through shape and number, not by representation of diverse forms that God's glory was held to be manifest. And it was in edifices based on shape and number rather than on representational embellishment, that the divine presence was to be housed.

The Temple and the Lodge
Michael Baigent and Richard Leigh

They are content with healthy food,
pleased with useful clothing,
satisfied in snug homes,
and protective of their way of life.

Toa Te Ching

LEVEL ONE—COMMON AREA

CHAKRA ONE—RED ENERGY
GATHERING AND CONFERENCE—POLITICAL CENTER

The political system of the center is foundational to advance any of the other energy centers. Without a secure political system the entire center has no structure. It is like the skeletal system of the body which forms the structure of the body. A secure political system includes the following elements:

1. Basic—it must be easily understood by all community members so it is not confusing.
2. Written format—a written copy must be easily attainable by all community members so it cannot be misquoted.
3. Voted on by all members—all members must have a right to vote on the structuring of the political system and all amendments.
4. Communication—frequent, extensive communication is required in order for full disclosures to take place regarding decisions made by the political system.
5. Members will have voting privileges according to the amount of investment they put into the center i.e. money, materials, credits, work hours, etc.
6. Decisions will be made by consensus (if possible) or by democracy (if impossible).
7. Each member is considered as an individual whether male or female, married or single, and has equal rights in all political decisions. Age of accountability will be determined by the community.

PRIMARY POLITICAL CONCERNS:

1. Location of center. Where should the center be located: urban, rural, wilderness? Consider the needs of all those who want to be initially involved.
2. Investment. How much do we want to invest in the center? Do we want to create a mortgage payment or do we want everything paid in cash, free and clear? Consider how many members want to be involved initially and how much they want to invest. Can we use indigenous or recycled materials to cut down costs?
3. Building design. Do we want to submit different building designs and then vote on them? Do we want to accept the Rainbow Light Center's building design?
4. Political structure. How much political structure do we want/ need to make it secure? Do we want rules/penalties or simply guidelines? Who enforces them?
5. What sort of security do we want the center to fall under? Trust, church, corporation, etc. Discuss the pros and cons of all the options.

6. What sort of organizational structure do we want? Hierarchy—President, vice-president, secretary or consensual committees? Or both?

7. How often should we meet to discuss community concerns?

8. How do we involve new members to the community? Do we screen them somehow? Have a probationary period to live with them to get acquainted?

9. What rent prices should be determined for private living quarters? What prices for membership dues?

10. To what extent do we want to interface with the extended community?

CHAKRA TWO—ORANGE ENERGY
SOCIAL AND SENSUAL—THERAPY CENTER

The therapy rooms of the center are designed to create healing for body, mind and spirit. When body, mind and spirit are healed and integrated, we can then create more sustainable relationships. This center is the sensual center and like the reproductive system of the body. It is also the pleasure center where we enjoy the pleasures of our own bodies or temples. Classes will be held for members and nonmembers of the community including: yoga, chakra therapy, tantra, massage, health and wellness, nutrition, etc. All community members are encouraged to attend and also teach whatever classes they feel qualified in. Therapy rooms are also available for hands-on therapy in bodywork, mindwork and spiritwork by qualified technicians. Self-help programs will be utilized along with personal instruction and equipment use.

Intimate relationships at the center will be encouraged and personal choice regarding sexual and expanded relationships will be respected. The laws of the current legal system will also be recognized with regards to age, marriage and family relationships.

Social gatherings such as dances, group massage, retreats, sacred ceremony will be encouraged on a regular basis. This helps to bond and keep the social structure healthy. All details concerning the social center will be determined by the social committee. The therapy rooms will also act as an income source.

CHAKRA THREE—YELLOW ENERGY
POWER AND ECONOMICS—WORK-OUT/RETAIL CENTER

There must be a way to be economically sustainable and this pertains to the power center. By creating a retail store and also a workout center, we can have a way in which to create income. Of course there are also ways of creating incomes in other areas such as therapy, theatre, consumer products, bookstore, produce, internet businesses, etc. But this center is specifically designed to create economic sustainability. It is like the digestive system of the body wherein products and services are utilized for the maintenance of the body.

The economic system, like the political system, must be basic and easy to understand. Here are a few ideas concerning the structure of the economic system.

1. Money is equal in value to credits.
2. Credits can be obtained by community work or material donation.
3. Credits for work is equal regardless of special titles. For example, a gardener is paid an equal wage as a therapist per hour in community service. One hour = 10 credits
4. Credits can be used to pay rent, obtain more voting privileges, bartered for services or cashed if necessary.
5. A bookkeeper will be hired for credits or wages to keep track of the economic system.
6. Outside economic ventures are encouraged to not only bring in needed capital but to interface with the extended community.

Community members will be encouraged to utilize the workout center to build healthy, strong bodies. Membership pricing will be determined by the economic committee. The retail store will include health and nutritional products and will also be a source of income.

CHAKRA FOUR—GREEN ENERGY
NURTURING AND HEART—THE DINING CENTER

The dining room area will exhibit a sense of nurturing, health and well-being. Whole foods will be prepared on a daily basis by community members and/or hired chefs depending upon availability and expense. A juice bar offering refreshments such as purified/ionized water, green drinks, smoothies, juice and goat's milk will be available on a daily basis. Organic foods will be grown on site in the organic gardens offering a full array of delectable delights. Organic meat and animal by-products such as eggs, milk, and cheese will also be produced and harvested by members of the center. This can also be utilized as an economic resource. This center represents the circulatory system of the body as the heart pumps the nourishing life-blood throughout the body. The heart also represents the electro-magnetic or "love" energy of the body.

CHAKRA FIVE—BLUE ENERGY
CREATIVE AND VOCAL—ENTERTAINMENT CENTER

The expression of creative energy is an exciting path to healing. The entertainment center offers a format for creative expression in the form of music, vocalization, theatre and drama. Members and non-members alike can enjoy the entertainment of professionals and non-professionals in the art of performing or performing arts. Orchestrated performances offered to the public can also be a great source of income for the center. Also, qualified teachers can create an income source by offering classes in music, drama, art, and crafts. This center represents the respiratory system of the body. Inspiration (as in respiration) is also the infusion of the Holy Spirit or "breath of life". It is this creative energy that enlivens our souls and makes us co-creators with God.

CHAKRA SIX—VIOLET ENERGY
SPIRITUAL AND INTELLECTUAL—
MEDITATION/LIBRARY CENTER

We can explore the spiritual and intellectual aspects of ourselves in the meditation and library center. This center represents the central nervous system or "brain" of the body. The quiet and serene environment of this center invites you to enjoy personal meditation in a designated area on comfortable meditation mats. Yoga, TM, Tai Chi, Ki Gong and other transcendental practices can also be accomplished here on certain hours of the day. Or you can simply enjoy relaxing on a cozy couch absorbed in an interesting book. The lending library is available for members of the center. A bookstore could be included as an income source and a way for members to purchase a new fascinating title at a discounted price.

Rainbow Light Center
Floor Plan

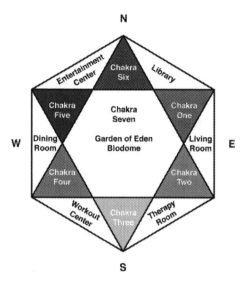

CHAKRA SEVEN—WHITE ENERGY
INTEGRATION—GARDEN OF EDEN BIODOME

The incremental spectrum of colors or energies when integrated becomes white light. This is represented in the Garden of Eden Biodome—a state-of-the-art passive solar greenhouse. Developed by Buckminster Fuller (who coined the phrase "Spaceship Earth") as a demonstration of how different climates—tropical, sub-tropical and temperate—can be obtained in one greenhouse facility. The truncated tetrahedron utilizes phi-harmonics, which is the basis for harmony in all living things. It is this mathematical principal which the pyramids of Giza were designed by and gave them their power of transcendence.

The biodome acts as a passive solar collector along with the hydrotherapy pools, which helps to heat and cool the entire facility for energy efficiency. The diverse temperatures ascending up the "Magic Mountain" in the center of the biodome allows growing of permaculture for each different climate. This means you could theoretically grow mangos, bananas, and oranges all year round inside your garden paradise.

Apart from being a unique ecologically and economically sustainable structure, the Garden of Eden biodome is just plain fun! It is a recreational, therapeutic, social, sensual, transcendental facility that involves all of the senses and sensibilities. Imagine yourself in a "clothing-optional" spa, exploring your environment free from the ravages of sin (separation within). It duplicates the Garden of Eden before the fall, or before we partook of judgment of the Tree of Good and Evil. When we've overcome the fall or "sin" (separation within) then we can all partake freely of the fruits of the Tree of Life—and live!

LEVEL TWO—PRIVATE AREA

The second level or level two is the private living space area, which will be divided into individual bedroom/bath suites. Each individual or couple can rent suites according to their own personal needs. This allows for personal "sacred space" and individual alone (all one) time for self-actualization. Suites can also be used for guests.

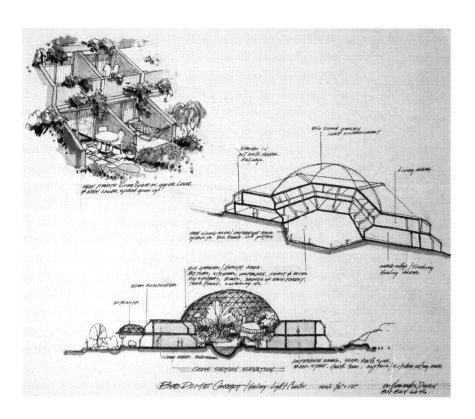

Afterward

At the completion of the first writing of this book in 1995 we had just five years left to prepare ourselves and our Mother Earth for the Millennium 2000. We have since passed that crucial point in man's and earth's history and are now looking toward the year 2012 as a critical year of cleansing, healing and awakening.

For there must needs be a cleansing and healing time for each and every one of us—including our Earth Mother—in order for us to move into the New Age of Enlightenment and enjoy the peace and beauty it offers. Right now, the Earth Mother is in great distress and disease (not easy) ready to begin her cleansing period. She will soon clear out the cancers of metropolitan malignancy, cleanse her arteries of the blockages and pollutions we've created in her waterways, heal her broken auric field of ozone, which we have inflicted upon her by our unchecked industrialism and lust for technology.

These diseases have not been caused by overpopulation as many believe. There is more than enough food and space on the Earth for our Mother to provide for Her children. It's just that some of us have become like the "gluttonous fat woman that fills her own fat belly without any thought of feeding her children or her children's children." (Lou Gold) This is the problem of blatant consumerism, and the problem must be resolved or we are going to kill ourselves and Mother Earth along with us!

"The most radical thing we can do to heal our planet is to stay at home… and begin to care for that sacred space that we can offer as an inheritance to our children's children seven generations in the future."

This is a quote from an enlightened man, Lou Gold, who was a presenter at the 1995 Windstar Symposium and has spent many long years of vigil in Vision Quest to save the wild places in the Pacific Northwest. (Thank you, Lou, for your clarity of vision and for sharing your life stories with us.)

It's about time that we took a very hard look at how our uncontrolled use of fossil fuel is killing our planet. We are mining our Mother Earth of Her essence—Her precious oil—and in the process it is killing us along with Her.

Our bodies consist of the same elements as our Earth Mother and if we consumed all of the oil and fat in our bodies—we would die! Not only that, but our fats and oils contain some of the worst toxins contained in our body, and when we burn our body fat for fuel, we also expel the toxins that are contained in these substances. That is why, when we burn fossil fuel as petroleum there are always toxic outgases which cause pollution. Also other petroleum products such as plastics, nylons, polyesters, synthetic chemicals, etc. cause toxic outgases in the environment when they break down. Isn't it about time we start looking beyond petroleum as a form of sustainable energy for our planet? It may be as simple as harnessing solar, wind or water energy in sustainable communities or "eco-villages" as a way of solving this energy crisis. Hunter and Amory Lovins have some valuable solutions included in Amory's book, *Soft Energy Paths: Towards a Durable Peace* which they have incorporated at their residence/institution called "The Rocky Mountain Institute" located in Snowmass, Colorado.

"There is more than enough food for all of us in this world—the problem we have is the political machinery we use to distribute it."

This is a quote from another Windstar Symposium presenter, Frances Moore Lappe, the well-known author of the revolutionary book, *Diet for a Small Planet*.

I completely agree with Frances Moore's insights on why the political and economical machinery prevents the "natural" distribution process of food to hungry people. One reason why people are starving even in America is the poor distribution of land among the people. Why people want to migrate to the "megatropolises" to "make a living" is a question beyond my grasp to answer. Isn't it interesting that one of the few times God intervened with man's natural process of "figuring it out" was at the time of the building of the tower of Babel? For some reason, mankind got the distorted notion that someway, somehow he could "build his highway to heaven" through his technological advances.

Well, God himself put a stop to *that one* by confounding all man's languages, so we were forced to live separately—*or at least in tribes!* That was God's answer to inner city violence and pollution...and man's technological pride. Yet, there are many of us who still wish to live in "Babylon" (babble on) and partake of her iniquities.

Overpopulation is a problem relative to where you live. Here in Montana the only "over-population problem" I experience is that of cattle which trespass and destroy some of our pristine wilderness beauty. Did you know that there are still "open-range" laws on the books of Montana that say you can "hang a man from the nearest tree" for cattle-rustling? We were told that if we even threatened the life of a cow caught trespassing on *our* land, we could get a prison sentence. Some laws are simply archaic and need to be changed!

As I travel the Midwest and into the Pacific Northwest, I am amazed at all the fertile tracts of land I see being wasted by inappropriate use of cattle ranching. "Do we really need red meat to survive into the 21st century?" It's a question we should seriously ask ourselves if we are to develop sustainable futures for all mankind.

Frankly, I haven't eaten a beef-steak for over ten years now, and I'm *not* suffering from any ill effects. In fact, "when we choose to eat lower on the food chain—we choose a healthier future for us and our planet." This is a quote from Ocean Robbins, son of John Robbins, author of the Pulitzer Prize nominated international bestseller *Diet for a New America—How Food Choices Affect Your Health, Happiness, and the Future of Life on Earth.* (Keep up the good work Ocean and John. You are both incredible!)

But let's get off the "band wagon" of diet and talk about the real issues here—individual and collective sovereignty to make choices that affect our future here on planet earth. The only *real* sovereignty we enjoy is when we are free from the systems that prevent us from truly following the path of the spirit. These systems *are indeed corrupt* and need to be dealt with before we can bring in the "New Age of Enlightenment."

Some of these systems which form what some believe are "conspiracies" are those governments, religions, businesses, and organizations which do not live up to their full integrity—governments which violate human rights, religions that work secret combinations and priest crafts, businesses that don't produce products with integrity, and organizations that claim that you must be a member to obtain their "corner on truth." These corrupt systems can choose either to "put their own houses in order" or God will put it in order Himself. (The first choice is much less painful than the second.)

I heard it said on a radio program that "if you want to get to the bottom of a conspiracy, just follow the money trail." I see that most systems have been corrupted because of profiteering or the "love of money." We must get this "love of money" out of "our system" before we can be effective vessels for God. Here's an example of how one of today's industries (the computer industry) is a "conspiracy to keep us in bondage to it."

As you already read in my book concerning my "yard sale adventures," I came across some computer equipment for my children to use in their home-school studies. I was delighted to find that the equipment worked perfectly—but then I came across one *big* problem. The computer companies no longer produce programs compatible for their older computer equipment. These perfectly good computers are now "obsolete" and have been replaced by "updated" computer equipment. (This is curious, I thought, since computers are "new" to my generation. Does this mean that I'm also "obsolete" and need to be replaced by "updated" equipment?) It's my opinion that these computer companies should be *made* to have integrity. If they are going to make computer equipment to last (which all industries should do—make products which last!), they should at least have the decency to provide the computer programs listed in their catalogues for those of us who intend to use the computer we purchased for a *very long time!*

The fact of the matter is this: we are all part of the "dark side conspiracy" whose only purpose in life is to test our integrity to see what we are made of. And it uses the well-known strategy of "divide and conquer" to see if we will come out a diamond…or a lump of coal. Any belief system, organization, or institution that keeps us trapped into believing that "we are separate from each other" and that "they hold all the answers to our sovereignty or enlightenment" is part of the conspiracy of the "dark side."

We all need to gain our own personal integrity whether at home, in the work place, or in our own religious organization—and then help those systems and organizations to gain the same. When we choose to no longer be a part of the *conspiracy* or "illusion of separation" by turning around (repenting) and accepting the at-one-ment, then we gain back our God-given inheritance as His children. Or, in other words, instead of walking backward into darkness—walk forward into the light. Then, and only then, can we journey forward to God and re-unite with Him/Her in *Celestial Integrity.*

In every person there is a vision or dream locked deep within the heart. In each and every one of us there is the power to unlock our hearts and let that vision or dream come out. It can take flight and "fly on wings of fire."

One of the visions or dreams I've had since I was a young child is a vision of a place on earth that was a piece of paradise or "heaven on earth." I guess it's that "longing for home" that's carried deep within each one of us.

Perhaps this is why I've always been attracted to those people who share that same vision and have been able to articulate it in song or verse. (Thank you, John, for sharing.)

Another one of my visions or dreams is to be able to share my story with others through writing and music. This has been one of the motivations to write this book—to share my life's vision with others.

I've also written and composed a few songs that I have, to a small degree, shared with a few close friends. Perhaps someday I will be able to share them with some "new-found friends" who may be reading this book and desire to hear me sing.

But for now, I'll share two of those songs, in verse, until I have the opportunity to sing them to you.

Crazy Lady

Some called the lady crazy
Got a dream caught in her eye
Some say she's full of fantasy
And they never could figure out why
And some who didn't know her
Say she's got the devil under her skin
But if they ever got close enough
Would know the heaven that dwelt within

She dreamed about a place somewhere
That she could call her home
She imagined a people
That she could call her own
She talked about a process
Of livin' in harmony
Where hate and envy disappear
And love flows gentle and fre

I see flowers bloomin' in sunlight
Rainbow dews from heaven above
Birds and butterflies wingin' in mid-flight
And the air is filled with love

I see you and me together
Livin' in perfect harmony
Let's imagine it all together
It's as simple as you and me

Perhaps the lady's crazy
But her dream is bound to come true
And if it's just a fantasy
I hope other folks have one too
And if she's full of the devil
Then he must be a pretty good guy
'Cause I know that lady's heart is true
I'm that lady 'til the day I die

I see flowers bloomin' in sunlight
Rainbow dews from heaven above

Birds and butterflies wingin' in mid-flight
And the air is filled with love

I see you and me together
Livin' in perfect harmony
Let's imagine it all together
It's as simple as you and me
You and me
One, two, three

There is Time

Even now as I sit
Feel the sun shine on my face
Even now as I walk
Smell the flowers fill the space
Even now as I listen
I can hear the river hum
Today we must begin
Or tomorrow will never come

Even now as I watch
See my children smile in play
Even now as I touch
Feel the earth I see the day
When all of this is memory
There's no father to tell a son
Today we must begin
Or tomorrow will never come

Let our eyes turn towards the heavens
To seek the guidance of His light
Let our hands reach down to Earth
To seek the goodness of Her might
Let our hearts feel for each other
With love and truth we can overcome
Each is our brother or our sister
We must learn to live as one
And there is time …
A little time…

So little time…
Let it be mine

Even now I feel the pain
My heart is broken in despair
Even now I see the tears
I cry for people to only care
Even now there still is hope
All the wrongs can be undone
If today we will begin
Then tomorrow
We'll live as one

Let our eyes turn towards the heavens
To seek the guidance of His light
Let our hands reach down to Earth
To seek the goodness of Her might
Let our hearts feel for each other
With love and truth we can overcome
Each is our brother or our sister
We must learn to live as one
And there is time …
A little time …
So little time…
Let it be mine
And there is time

For ye were sometimes darkness but now are ye light in the Lord; walk as children of light.

(Ephesians 5:8)

And I will give them one heart and I will put a new spirit within you: and I will take the stony heart out of their flesh, and will give them a heart of flesh:
That they may walk in my statutes, and keep mine ordinances, and do them: and they shall be my people, and I will be their God.

(Ezekiel 11:19, 20)

The Beginning